Henry Adams · Historical Essays

Anglistica & Americana

A Series of Reprints Selected by
Bernhard Fabian, Edgar Mertner,
Karl Schneider and Marvin Spevack

139

1973

GEORG OLMS VERLAG
HILDESHEIM · NEW YORK

Henry Adams

Historical Essays

(1891)

1973

GEORG OLMS VERLAG
HILDESHEIM · NEW YORK

O

Nachdruck der Ausgabe New York 1891
Printed in Germany
Herstellung: Strauß & Cramer GmbH, 6901 Leutershausen
ISBN 3 487 04645 8

HISTORY OF THE UNITED STATES.

BY

HENRY ADAMS.

HISTORICAL ESSAYS

BY

HENRY ADAMS

———•———

NEW YORK
CHARLES SCRIBNER'S SONS
1891

University Press:

JOHN WILSON AND SON, CAMBRIDGE.

CONTENTS.

———◆———

HISTORICAL ESSAYS.

———◆———

PRIMITIVE RIGHTS OF WOMEN.[1]

ACCORDING to the generally accepted opinion of writers on Primitive Institutions, the original position of the married woman was one of slavery, or akin to slavery. By this phrase is meant not merely subjection to superior force, but to legalized force. In all ages, the weak were the victims of the strong, and were often treated with severity not essentially different from the treatment of slaves; but the exercise of force by the strong over the weak did not constitute slavery, even in the most barbarous societies. Unless the law declared men or women to be slaves, they were, in the view of the law, free, notwithstanding their inability to obtain redress.

The common view of marriage as a primitive institution implies in the man more than arbitrary superiority, such as he exercised over the child, which still remained free. The woman's slavery was assumed

[1] Revision of a lecture delivered at the Lowell Institute, Dec. 9, 1876.

1

to be for life. As a child she was subject to the
absolute authority of the male parent, extending over
life and death. Her marriage originated, according
to the most recent scientific historians, either in purchase or in capture; and in either case the woman
was the property of the man. The wedding ring was
the symbol of marital power. The right of the husband to sell his wife still survives in the popular
traditions of England; the forms of capture are still
common in barbarous society, and may be seen even
in highly civilized countries; while the forms of purchase are thought to be well-nigh universal. · " While
wives were captured, if there was any sense of property at all, wives would be regarded as property.
When, at a later stage, they came to pass from the
houses of their birth into alien houses, by purchase,
they would still be property." [1] The recorded history of early society offers numberless illustrations of
the unbounded power which the husband exercised
over his wife, and the Roman law was especially
emphatic in extending over her the *patria potestas*,
in which the Romans blended their conceptions of
the family relation. " The family was based not
upon actual relationship, but upon power; and the
husband acquired over his wife the same despotic
power which the father had over his children." [2]

[1] McLennan's Studies in Ancient History, pp. 136, 137. Edition of 1886.

[2] The Early History of the Property of Married Women. A
Lecture delivered March 25, 1873, by Sir H. S. Maine. See the
Early History of Institutions, p. 312.

Starting from the assumption that the wife was in origin a slave, either by capture or by purchase, the commonly received theory of her escape from this degradation assumed a gradual rise in the moral standard of civilized society, and finally attributed the complete triumph of women to the influence of Christianity, with its high moral ideals and its passionate adoration of the Virgin Mother.

Such seems to be the doctrine of modern investigators. In theory they have carried back the origin of society to a stage anterior to the institution of marriage, — a stage of communism. The original community is believed to have had no idea, or only a rudimentary idea, of private property; and as men emerged from the condition of animals, they possibly held all things in common within their communal association. Theoretically, men and women, like all else, in the earliest stage of society were communal property. No tie connected individual men and women together. No man had the right to appropriate any one woman to himself, nor had any woman the right to appropriate to herself any one man. Such communities were large families and small States, with a strongly democratic organization and an elected chief or chiefs. All their members were equal, for all were brothers and sisters. Mothers there were, but fathers were unknown. Where no permanent tie existed between men and women there could be no conception of paternity and no notion of paternal authority. The mother alone was important

in the parental relation. The earliest family therefore, so far as it could exist at all, was a system
of relationship through women ; and the germ of
the future family organization was embodied in the
mother, not in the father.

Such pure communism, if it ever existed in real
life, ceased at a very early time. No such communal
society, — that is to say, no society in which communal marriage was practised, — has been found or
is recorded as existing in times past; nor is it essential to history that precisely such an institution as
communal marriage should ever have existed in the
strictness of its forms. A mass of evidence has been
collected, which leaves no reasonable doubt that the
first organized human society approximated more or
less nearly to this type. In all countries and through
all ages its traces have been found ; and in this respect the primitive tribes of Africa, of Asia, and of
America, both north and south, unite in telling a
common tale. In its day this social organization was
a step in the progress of the race. Under the shelter of communal society man found such protection
against the dangers that beset his first steps as to
cause its development over the world. If primitive
communism had not been beneficent in its results, it
could never have attained such development. Wild
as man was, and disgusting as the more degraded
tribes and communities were, the best of them, and
all those from which further advance came, were
marked by good qualities, or they could never have

risen to a higher stage. Many communities were doubtless mild in manners and not unhappy in their modest range of interests. Where the conditions of life were favorable and wilder hordes remote, these communities cultivated their common fields from year to year, from century to century, from era to era, and did no conscious wrong. They had wars, and these were no doubt cruel; they had superstitions, which were no doubt both cruel and gross; their range of thought was narrow and their mode of life low; their relations with the world beyond their tribal connection were those of war; but within the bounds of their own society they succeeded in constructing a social fabric that compared with any that succeeded to it for successful adaptation of means to ends. After it had long passed away the world still looked back to it with regret, and not a few of the prettiest and tenderest verses of the classical poets recalled that idealized golden age when men lived together as brothers, when peace and content reigned on earth, when mankind was not devoured by the thirst for gold, when all were of one family, and all the products of the earth or of industry were held by brothers in common.

Assuming that any typical form of primitive communal society ever existed, no long time can have elapsed before some communities must have begun to depart from the normal type; and in some cases this departure must have taken that direction which the strongest human instincts pointed out. Of these

instincts few if any are more energetic than the instinct of property. Man loves most that which is
his own; and that which he most loves he is most
anxious to have for his own. Here and there in the
rudest human society passions must have developed
which are recognized even in animals. Probably this
development went on simultaneously in many centres,
and worked in many different lines. In this respect
the characteristics of all the great races were already
sharply marked at their first appearance in recorded
history. We cannot know what special influences
caused some to throw off more completely than
others the old habits of communism, to substitute
the practices of private property; but enough remains to show that the distinctions between races
were to no small degree founded upon this difference
of policy.

Probably the institution of marriage had its origin
in love of property. Both men and women were
united in this, — that whatever they loved best, they
wished to possess. The usual theory holds that the
communal system would not permit the gratification
of this desire at the expense of communal rights,
and that therefore men were driven to gratify their
passion by purchasing or by capturing women from
neighboring and hostile tribes. In support of this
doctrine the extraordinary frequency of the forms
of purchase and capture is relied upon as conclusive
evidence; but if so, the position of the purchased or
captured wife must have been regulated by laws very

different from those that controlled the disposition of other purchased or captured property.

American students of primitive history have one great advantage. To them archaic communistic society is not, or at least need not be, a mere historical theory. The entire race of American Indians from Behring's Straits to the Straits of Magellan were, and to a certain extent still are, in the stage of communism. The American Indian is the best representative of the social system to which he belonged. Communism in Europe and Asia has been disturbed or affected by subsequent complicated developments; in America it was subjected to no such strain. If it be assumed, as is becoming inevitable, that the American Indian was a branch from a primitive stock, from which it became separated at a very early day, and thenceforth pursued a course of development little influenced from without, institutions common to American Indians must have been inherited from that primitive ancestry which belonged to them and to Asia alike. This is the more probable, because the communism of the North American Indian and the general character of his institutions were but one or two steps more primitive than those of the Germans when the Germans first came into the light of history.

Every Indian tribe was subdivided into clans, and the first remarkable characteristic of the clan was that it simulated the supposed form of the primitive commune. The men were classed as brothers, the women as sisters; but what was most suggestive, marriage between them was prohibited as incestuous, and, unlike many of the prohibitions of archaic law, the rule was rigidly enforced. Men and women married only into other clans than their own.

Marriage was the rule of Indian customary law, and every form of primitive marriage common elsewhere was common among the Indians; but the apparent historical relation between these forms was not what European writers have adopted in explanation of their so-called marriages by capture, purchase, and other modes, implying slavery or absolute property in the woman.

The formal Indian marriage, and probably the oldest of all legal forms, was " marriage by legal appointment;" that is, the selection and allotment, by the elders of the clans, of some woman belonging to one clan, to live with some man belonging to another.[1]

This form of marriage often took the appearance of purchase. The parents of the woman received gifts from the suitor, according to the advantages of the match.[2] In some tribes the practice grew into an abuse, as private property became more common; girls were sold, and custom authorized the sale;[3] but in its origin the so-called purchase was only a detail of the primitive formal marriage, as appears from its

[1] Annual Report of the Bureau of Ethnology, 1881–1882, lix.

[2] Dorsey's Omaha Sociology; Report of Ethnological Bureau 1881–1882, p. 258.

[3] Clark's Indian Sign-Language, pp. 243–246.

legal consequences. A true sale would have deprived
the woman of her position in the clan; but in law
the Indian woman remained after such a marriage
as before a member of her family and tribe, entitled
to her rights and proper protection, like any other
woman or any man. Nothing but her own misconduct could deprive the woman of her position in the
tribe, and even her misconduct rather affected her
social position than her legal rights. She could assert her rights as long as she had friends. Indians
have been known to sell their wives; but such an
abuse, like similar abuses among other races, left the
woman still free, with her customary rights intact,
and by no means trifling in extent.

Marriage by legal appointment, with gifts, was the
formal customary Indian marriage; but primitive
law, after recognizing the rigor of custom, commonly
provided for legalizing violations of the strict code.
Equitable processes existed by the side of formal
processes for most acts that required the sanction
of the clan, whether in America, Asia, or Europe.
Several irregular forms of marriage were recognized
and sanctioned by Indian custom.

1. Elopement, which was evidently in some degree a protest against constraint of the woman's
choice. Any runaway couple, escaping to the forest,
living there until the next regular day of limitation,
might then return to their clans, and their marriage
was held to be valid. Every tribe usually fixed a day
of limitation for such offences against strict forms, at

least one in each year, when pursuit or punishment of offenders must cease.

2. Capture, not as an act of war or from another tribe, but always from a clan of the same tribe. If the attempt at capture was successfully resisted, it could not be repeated in the particular case. If it succeeded, the man kept the woman, the marriage was valid, and no punishment was allowed.

Such a form of capture affected in no respect the rights of the captured woman in the Indian community. She became neither a slave nor property, but remained as before, in most cases, a member of her own family and clan; her children followed her line of descent, and the husband belonged to her as much as she belonged to her husband. In some tribes the husband seemed to belong to the wife even more than the wife to the husband.

3. Capture in war. So little had the form of capture to do with creating in the captor a right of property in the woman captured, that when women of enemy tribes were taken in war, they were necessarily adopted into some clan before they could be appropriated as wives. Captives could live only as brothers or sisters of some group. They became, by the act of adoption and marriage, members of clans, with the rights of other members. Slavery was unknown to the great families of Indians between the Atlantic and the Rocky Mountains, and no such social institution was recognized in their customary law. Captives were either killed or adopted.

4. Another more curious form of irregular marriage was by duel. Under certain conditions, not precisely explained, a young man without a wife might challenge a man to whom more than one wife had been assigned; and if he succeeded in the combat, he had an admitted right to the woman.

All these forms of marriage had the same legal effect. In certain respects the woman came under the power of her husband; in other respects she retained rights of no little importance. She had the right of divorce, and might return to her own family, or dismiss her husband. She could, if she preferred, claim the protection of her own family against her husband; and her claim was effective, if she had relations strong enough to enforce her rights. Her murder was atoned for or avenged, like that of any other member of the tribe. In most cases she was the head of the family; her husband usually came to live with her, not she with him, and her children belonged to her clan, not to their father's.

The line of inheritance and descent was commonly through females; titles descended through females. The property of the husband and wife was usually kept distinct during marriage, and held in separate ownership; in case of separation each took his or her effects. A striking illustration of the position of the Indian women was offered by the well-known custom that when an Iroquois sachem died, and a council was held to elect his successor, this council consisted of all the adult male and female members of the tribe ; and among the latter the mother of the deceased ruler exercised a decisive influence.

The marriage relation was of a very shifting kind, but the wife, as such, was neither a slave captured in war nor purchased property, nor property of any kind in the strict sense; she was a free member of her own tribe and clan. The rule among the Indian race was that the family meant the mother's family ; but as if to show that even in the extreme antiquity of society all the great lines of development had already been seen and marked out, according to Mr. Morgan there were tribes in Central America, and those naturally the most advanced, which had adopted the conception of relationship through the father, and founded their polity on this principle.

From the American Indians turn to the oldest records of European and Asiatic society. To Egypt of course we look first for light; and though the field of Egyptian history has been as yet barely touched, the most superficial examination shows evidence sufficient for the present purposes. No one can enter an Egyptian Museum without seeing the weakness of any theory which assigns to Egyptian women, even in extreme antiquity, the position of slaves. On the contrary, the further one's inquiries are carried into the remotest regions of Egyptian history, — even into that age of the pyramid-builders, so remote that Egyptologists hesitate to fix for it a date within a possible error of some thousands of years, — the evidence which proves the social position of women to have been highest in the ages most distant becomes more convincing. The female line of descent was followed regularly if not invariably among Egyptians, as among American Indians. The queen sat on the throne with her husband ; her statue rests in the tomb by his side. At all periods the sister and the wife were held in the highest respect, and a trace of the old communal society remained in the well-known Egyptian custom by which the sister frequently if not habitually became the wife. " The Egyptian woman," says Mariette Bey, " occupied a large place in the family. The rights which were hers by birth were not absorbed in those of her husband, and she transmitted them intact to her children. At certain epochs the family tables often name the mother to the exclusion of the father. In the most ancient inscriptions the love between husband and wife is sometimes expressed in delicate and touching language."

The position taken by woman in the Egyptian philosophy and religion is more curious and still more decisive. Among the commonest Egyptian monuments are the famous triads or trinity of deities. This trinity represents a man, a woman, and a child. The male deity, most widely known under the name of Osiris, appears to have represented the creative power, the principle of light struggling with darkness, and overcome by it only to be brought again to life through the aid of the woman. Osiris was

the generator, — the fructifying force of Nature; the
sun with its mysterious energy which called life into
being. By his side sat the woman, Isis, the sister,
the wife, — that mysterious power which according
to the physiological ideas of that day gave only shelter and protection to the germ of being, resembling
the earth teeming with life under the beams of the
sun. The third member of the Egyptian trinity was
the child, Horus or Ra, who completed the mysterious circle, returning again to the father, never
designated as the son, but represented as the father
self-engendered; for in the Egyptian trinity, as in
the Christian, the father and the son were one, — the
insoluble mystery of generation, insoluble then as
now, ever returned upon itself.

In so elevated and philosophic a system of theology where shall we look for the degradation of
the woman? Not surely in the mere fact that the
place assigned to the mother was of secondary importance, inasmuch as the father and not the mother
was considered as author of the child's existence.
The mother was as essential to the trinity as the
father or the son. Isis stood on the same plane as
Osiris. Never from the beginning to the end of that
marvellous history whose records still remain the
most astonishing monuments of human development,
can we find reason to suppose that the family sprang
from the exercise of force, and that the wife was a
slave or the descendant of slaves. The Christian
philosophers of a later period, probably influenced

by their close connection with Alexandria, adopted the trinity, and in adopting it, dethroned the woman from her place. Yet even then, notwithstanding this degradation, the irresistible spread of Mariolatry, the worship of the Virgin Mother, proved how strongly human nature revolted against the change.

The races of Western Europe showed tendencies more strongly marked. In all branches of what is commonly known as the Aryan stock, — Celt, Roman, Greek, German, and Scandinavian, — are indications that at some period antecedent to recorded history, a social rebellion against the old communal system had been felt. The institution of marriage, the law of descent in the male line, the importance of the family and the authority of the father, are characteristics so distinct in the whole Aryan group as to countenance the idea that this was in fact the real origin of the race, and that the primitive Aryan stock broke away from the original communal society with no other distinctive principle. Perhaps the institution of the family was the means of their extraordinary success, and of the domination which they established wherever they set their feet. Historically, the family is but an example of the energetic realization of those natural affections and that passion of property which lie deepest of all passions in humanity. The race which followed this path with the most vigor must have been the strongest race and the best fitted to conquer. Such a race had a natural instinct for law ; its taste for the acquisition of private property re-

quired development of legal principles ; its faculty
of adopting reforms in society proves its intellectual
versatility ; and what are all these but the same characteristics which appear again ages afterward, in the
greatest of all the works of their descendants, — in
the civil law of Rome, and in the common law of
England ?

Turning to the Greeks and to their literature, un-
mistakable traces prove the existence at no very remote time of the same class of institutions as those
of the American Indians. Descent and inheritance
through women to the exclusion of men ; subjection of the persons of women to obligations which
seem to have had their origin in the old communal
ties ; even distinct efforts to force them back under
the burden of those obligations after they had once
freed themselves, — all these are recorded, and all
point in one direction. Yet it may be doubted
whether these were any part of pure Greek civilization. Probably they belonged to the races which
the Greek overran and ruled ; and if traces of the
old communistic system are found in Greek literature or history, they crept in, as afterward the corruption of the East crept into the society of Rome.
Fortunately something is known of the heroic age of
the Greeks. The Homeric poems are a monument
of early Greek society ; and the peculiarity of the
Homeric poems which causes them to stand in sharp
contrast with later Greek literature is, that they invariably treated women and the marriage contract

with respect which subsequent literature of no country or age can show. If marriage were really the child of force, if the wife were a captured or a purchased slave, we should find a trace of it here; but no such trace exists.

Ulysses in one of his accounts of his origin said, —

> " It is my boast that I am of the race
> Who dwell in spacious Crete, — a rich man's son,
> Within whose palace many other sons
> Were born and reared, the offspring of his wife;
> But me a purchased mother whom he made
> His concubine brought forth to him.
> And yet Castor Hylacides from whom I sprang
> Held me in equal favor with the rest."

The wife, in contrast with the purchased mother, was always a free woman, with rights which her husband could not disregard. The whole story both of the Iliad and the Odyssey is little more than a running commentary on the Greek law of marriage. I will not stop to discuss the legal status of Helen of Troy, although her position offers some remarkable illustrations of law; but the Odyssey offers little else. This poem opens with an account of the state of affairs at Ithaca after Ulysses had been absent twenty years. The neighboring chiefs, assuming Ulysses to be dead, made common cause to compel his widow Penelope to choose a second husband. They came in a body to the abode of Ulysses, and there seated themselves with the formal intention of eating Penelope and her son Telemachus out of house and home if she did not accede to their wish. In this

2

case what was the legal status of Penelope, the assumed widow? Was she a slave? Was she under the authority of her husband's family, or of her own son? Or had she fallen back under the authority of her own family? What were her legal rights, if she had any? How did the suitors show their sense of her inferiority as a woman to their dignity as men? How did they expect to compel her to carry out their wishes?

It was not the beauty of Penelope which brought the suitors to her house with a system of wooing so energetic. Homer represents Penelope as still handsome, but she could hardly have been less than forty years old, and most if not all her suitors were young enough to have been her sons. Distinct evidence is given that not merely her youth and beauty caused her to be so ardently sought; she possessed attractions independent of these, and more potent to fix the affections of the Achaian suitors. Penelope was the widow of the chosen chieftain of all the Ithacans; she was wealthy in her own right; she carried with her to her future husband a certain claim to the coveted position of chieftain which her husband had held, and this too in face of the claim by inheritance which belonged to her son Telemachus.

Telemachus was the heir to his father's wealth; he was the owner of the house in which his mother lived; he was head of the family in his father's absence; but his property was encumbered by his mother's claims, and he could not pay off these claims without reducing himself to the position of a comparatively poor man. He would have been well pleased had his mother settled the difficulty by accepting and marrying one of the suitors, even on the chance of his father's return. He would have been still better pleased had his mother consented to go back to her own father, and so relieve him and his estate; but he did not dare to send her back, since such an act on his part would have been an infraction of the terms of the marriage contract between Ulysses and Penelope, and would have subjected Telemachus to the claims of his mother's family for large damages on her behalf, — claims that would certainly have been enforced. Penelope was mistress to decide what to do, and she preferred to make no decision. We are left to surmise her motives. What hindered her from at once dismissing the suitors and insisting upon maintaining her widowhood? Possibly she feared their resentment; but probably the Greek custom, which amounted to law, required that the widow should marry again, if not too old. At all events she did not decide, and the suitors, to the disgust of Telemachus, went on eating day by day the flocks and herds which were the bulk of his wealth. Between his mother and the suitors Telemachus was in despair; and the second book of the Odyssey shows him calling a public council to force a solution of the difficulty. The story continues, in the words of Mr. Bryant's translation : —

" He took the seat
Of his great father, and the aged men
Made way for him.   And then Ægyptius spake:

'Hear, men of Ithaca, what I shall say.
No council, no assembly have we held
Since great Ulysses in his roomy ships
Departed from our isle.   Who now is he
That summons us ?'

As thus he spake, Ulysses' son rejoiced
In his auspicious words, nor longer kept
His seat, but yielding to an inward force
Rose midst them all to speak, while in his hand
Pisenor, the sagacious counsellor
And herald, placed the sceptre.   Then he turned
To the old man Ægyptius, speaking thus:

'O aged man, not far from thee is he
Who called this council, as thou soon shalt know.
Mine chiefly is the trouble; I have brought
No news of an approaching foe, . . .
Nor urge I other matters which concern
The public weal ; my own necessity,
The evil which has fallen on my house,
Constrains me.   It is twofold: first, that I
Have lost an excellent father, who was king
Among you, and ruled o'er you with a sway
As gentle as a father's.   Greater yet
Is the next evil, and will soon o'erthrow
My house and waste my substance utterly.
Suitors, the sons of those who in our isle
Hold the chief rank, importunately press
Round my unwilling mother.   They disdain
To ask her of Icarius, that the king
Her father may endow her, and bestow
His daughter on the man who best may gain
His favor ; but with every day they come
Into our palace, sacrificing here
Oxen and sheep and fatling goats, and hold

High festival, and drink the purple wine
Unstinted, with unbounded waste; for here
Is no man like Ulysses to repel
The mischief from my house.   Not such are we
As he was to resist the wrong.   We pass
For weaklings, immature in valor; yet
If I had but the power assuredly
I would resist, for by these men are done
Insufferable things, nor does my house
Perish with honor.' " . . .

To this speech Antinous, one of the suitors, made
the following significant answer : —

"Telemachus, thou youth of braggart speech
And boundless in abuse, what hast thou said
To our dishonor ?   Thou wouldst fix on us
A brand of shame.   The blame is not with us,
The Achaian suitors; 'tis thy mother's fault,
Skilled as she is in crafty shifts. . . .

            . . . Now let the suitors make
Their answer to thy words, that thou mayst know
Our purpose fully, and the Achaians all
May know it likewise.   Send thy mother hence,
Requiring that she wed the suitor whom
Her father chooses and herself prefers.
But if she still go on to treat the sons
Of Greece with such despite, too confident
In gifts which Pallas has bestowed on her
So richly, . . . so long will we consume
Thy substance and estate as she shall hold
Her present mood. . . . She to herself
Gains great renown, but surely brings on thee
Loss of much goods.   And now we go not hence
To our affairs nor elsewhere till she wed
Whichever of the Greeks shall please her most.'
   And then rejoined discreet Telemachus :

> ' Antinous, grievous wrong were it to send
> Unwilling from this palace her who bore
> And nursed me. . . .
> And should I of my own accord and will
> Dismiss my mother, I must make perforce
> Icarius large amends, and that were hard.
>   . . . Think not I
> Will ever speak that word.' "

The conference broke up, and a temporary suspension of hostilities was effected. Telemachus on the one hand was determined to drive out the suitors, and even to kill them if he could ; while the suitors were well disposed to forestall him by putting him to death at once, and sharing his estate among themselves, while the succession to the throne should be decided by the choice which Penelope should make of a husband. In their deliberations, the suitors expressed their intentions with frankness, especially Antinous, their most active leader : —

> " Let us be first to strike
> And slay him in the fields or on the way,
> And taking his possessions to ourselves,
> Share equally his wealth.   Then may we give
> This palace to his mother and the man
> Whom she may wed, whoever he may be."

The father and the brothers of Penelope counselled her to wed Eurymachus, the wealthiest and the least objectionable of the suitors, and it was understood that she would carry to him the rank which Ulysses had held. The widow's choice would in this respect decide the election ; and Telemachus distinctly admitted that this solution would be satisfactory to him if it relieved his estate quickly from the impending ruin.

In the face of all this, Penelope paid no attention to the opinions or wishes of any one. She regarded the desperation of her son with as little sympathy as she did the cool advice of her father and brothers and the too marked attentions of her suitors. Her action was contrary to the advice and wishes of her relatives and connections on both sides. She was perfectly independent. She relied on her legal rights, which until the death of her husband was formally ascertained were sufficient to protect her; and according to the poem these rights were respected. Neither the suitors nor Telemachus, nor any of the family of Ulysses, nor her own family, ventured to restrain her independence of action.

This is but one example from many which Homer offers of the position of women in the earliest Greek society. Turning next from Greece to Rome, the inquiry is checked by the difficulty that Romans were not a very poetic or a romantic people. No great monument of their primitive condition, like the Homeric poems, is extant; probably none ever existed. Hardly a vestige of their early history has survived in an authentic form. The most primitive of their extant laws belongs to a period of development far in advance of that now in question. Moreover, the Romans threw themselves into the reaction against primitive communism with a degree of energy, not to say of violence, which went far beyond anything known in other branches of the Aryan stock. The Roman family not only exaggerated the characteristics of the wide-spread hostility to old communistic ideas, and asserted in the strongest manner the principle of relationship through males, but it went even to the extravagance of annihilating relationship through females ; not only did it make the father the head of the family, it absorbed the family in the father ; not only did it raise the authority of the husband over the wife, it asserted the astounding principle that the wife was the daughter of her husband. Alone among Aryan races the Romans, with their extravagant logical sequence, inferred from the premise of paternal headship the conclusion that that headship carried with it the rights of absolute property ; and if of absolute property over the chattels of the family, why not also over the children ; and if over the children, then since the father, in giving his daughter in marriage, conveyed with her to her husband all the rights which he himself enjoyed, it necessarily followed that the wife stood toward her husband in the position of a daughter, and that his power over her was unlimited.

This was already the theory of the law when the law first becomes known ; but this theory was limited and controlled in practice by influences which were also peculiar to the Romans. In no country has the family been so serious and so sacred a thing as among the Romans at the time when this theory of their law prevailed. The sanctity with which it was invested, elevated and dignified the position of wife and child in spite of the perverted letter of the law. No complaint comes from Roman history of the abuse of the enormous power thus vested in the father. Nowhere has the family been so intimate and so united a fabric as in Rome. Almost from the first the Romans seem to have felt that their family law was not defensible in practice, and was inconsistent with the theory of the State. During a long series of years the Roman jurists continued to devise new expedients for evading the consequences of their own legal doctrines. Step by step they emancipated the wife; they emancipated the son; they tried to explain or to smooth away the extravagances of their own creation, until at last they did it so successfully that not only was the husband's authority over the wife destroyed, but the whole family organization was shaken to pieces.

In any case the authority conferred upon the husband by the Roman law did not prove the degradation of women. Whatever that authority was, it was exercised over the wife, not because she was a woman, but because she was a daughter. To the paternal power the man as well as the woman was subject; and no matter what age the man had attained, he was, during the lifetime of his father, under the same domestic rule as his sister or his mother.

There remain to be considered the institutions of the great German race from which we more directly claim descent. Like the other branches of the Indo-European stock, the German founded his society firmly on the family, with its masculine peculiarities ; but the German family was still, as compared with the Roman, a loose and flexible structure, and more than one suggestion is to be found in the early German law pointing to that communal society so evidently the starting place of human institutions.

Like the Greeks, some of the German tribes had strong romantic tendencies and poetic instincts. Little of the pure German poetry which has survived illustrates the subject now under discussion, but the rudest and least Romanized branch of the German race left some extraordinary literary monuments; and among the northern barbarians who struggled most desperately against the civilizing and centralizing influences of their day were portions of the Scandinavians, who, when their power was at last finally broken, and their country lay helpless at the feet of their conqueror, still refused to accept the fate of war, and abandoning their homes, betook themselves to the sea, with the resolution to accept life only on the condition of preserving undiminished those rights which consisted principally in recognizing no one as master, and in waging private war on their private enemies. One considerable mass of these men, carrying their families with them, crossed the ocean, and a thousand years ago found the absolute freedom which they sought in a spot where they were little likely to be disturbed. They established a commonwealth in Iceland ; and there they lived, and after their own manner flourished for many years in the complete enjoyment of all their archaic liberties. Their society was in many respects remarkable, but in none more so than in that of its literature. Iceland alone among western countries has left an heroic poem, which, for historical interest if not for artistic merit, can stand by the side of the Odyssey. The " Njalsaga," as it is called, is a piece of pure, or nearly pure, and authentic primitive history, and offers an invaluable picture of Scandinavian society, at a period of development not very unlike that described in the Odyssey.

The Njalsaga, like the poems of Homer, turns on the character of a woman, and I will use the language of Mr. Dasent's translation in order not to lose the vivacity and quaintness of the original. Hallgerda was her name. She was fair-haired, and had so much of it that she could hide herself in it; but she was lavish and hard-hearted. A suitor named Thorwald asked her of her father in marriage. The father warned his future son-in-law of her temper; but his answer was : " Lay down the terms of the match, for I will not, let her temper stand in the way of our bargain." Then they talked over the terms of the bargain; and Hauskuld, the father, never asked his daughter what she thought of it, for his heart was set on giving her away, and so they came to an understanding as to the terms of the match. Hauskuld then told Hallgerda of the bargain he had made, and she said : " Now that has been put to the proof which I have all along been afraid of, that thou lovest me not so much as thou art always saying, when thou hast not thought it worth while to tell me a word of all this matter.　Besides, I do not think this match so good a one as thou hast always promised me."

Hauskuld's reply indicates the power which the father in almost every period exercised over his daughter's choice of a husband.　" I do not set so much store by thy pride as to let it stand in the way of my bargains ; and my will, not thine, shall carry the day if we fall out on any point."

Hallgerda gave way, and the marriage took place. But she revenged herself upon her husband by her intolerable temper, until one day within the first year of their marriage her husband was stung by an insult to such anger that he gave her a blow on the face that drew blood.　That same day she caused him to be murdered, and then she rode home to her father. He was obliged to pay the legal atonement for the life of his son-in-law to the family of the murdered man, while Hallgerda took up her residence again in her father's house, and her property accumulated till it had reached a great sum.

After a time another suitor appeared.　His name was Glum.　This time the father was better advised than to dispose of his daughter without consulting her. They sent for Hallgerda and she came thither, and two women with her.　She had on a cloak of rich blue wool, and under it a scarlet kirtle, and a silver girdle round her waist ; but her hair came down on both sides of her bosom, and she had turned the locks

up under her girdle. She sat down; greeted them
all with kind words and spoke well and boldly, and
asked what was the news. After that she ceased
speaking.

Then Glum said: " There has been some talk between thy father and my brother and myself about a
bargain. It was that I might get thee, Hallgerda, if
it be thy will as it is theirs; and now, if thou art a
brave woman, thou wilt say right out whether the
match is at all to thy mind; but if thou hast anything
in thy heart against this bargain with us, then we will
not say anything more about it."

Hallgerda said: " I know well that you are men of
worth and might, ye brothers; I know too that now I
shall be much better wedded than I was before; but
what I want to know is, what you have said already
about the match, and how far you have given your
words in the matter. But so far as I now see of thee,
I think I might love thee well, if we can but hit it off
as to temper."

So Glum himself told her all about the bargain and
left nothing out, and then he asked Hauskuld and
Hrut whether he had told it right. Hauskuld said he
had, and then Hallgerda said: " Ye have dealt with
me so well in this matter, my father and Hrut, that I
will do what ye advise, and this bargain shall be
struck as ye have settled it."

After that Hallgerda's goods were valued, and Glum
was to lay down as much against them, and they were
to go shares, half and half, in the whole. The mar-

riage took place, and Hallgerda kept her word. She
lived happily with her husbånd for a time; but her
want of heart was again the cause of her second husband's murder by the same hand which had slain the
first.   Hallgerda went back again to her father's
house, and was there in the course of time married to
a third husband, one of the heroes of the story.   He
was a wise and high-minded man.   His wife made
his life miserable, and developed the utmost ingenuity
in the effort to embroil him with his friends and
neighbors in quarrels of every sort; but he succeeded
for the most part in keeping his temper and in ward-
ing off the dangers caused by her conduct.   Even
toward her his patience seemed inexhaustible, until
one day he detected her in a peculiarly base theft;
and in his wrath at the disgrace she had brought
upon him, he slapped her face.   She said she would
bear that slap in mind, and repay it if she could.   As
usual she was as good as her word.   Gunnar, her
husband, was at last attacked in his house one night,
and was hard pressed by the attacking party.   He
wounded eight men and killed two, but his enemies
succeeded in cutting his bowstring, and he could not
hope to hold them at bay unless he could procure
another string.

Then Gunnar said to Hallgerda: " Give me two
locks of thy hair; and ye two, thy mother and thou,
twist them together into a bowstring for me."

" Does aught lie on it?" said she.

" My life lies on it," he said; " for they will never

come to close quarters with me if I can keep them off with my bow."

"Well," she said, "now I will call to thy mind that slap on the face which thou gavest me ; and I care never a whit whether thou holdest out a long while or a short."

She sat by, all that night, and saw her husband slowly exhausted by one wound after another, until at last his enemies could come near enough to kill him ; but he did not turn his hand against her, and Hallgerda lived to enjoy the wealth acquired from her three murdered husbands, and to bring more misery and death on her friends.

Surely a woman of this stamp was no slave, no descendant of slaves, no possible connection of slaves. All the fierce and untamable instincts of infinite generations of free, wild animals were embodied in her. Nor were her legal rights those of a dependant. No Norse pirate, no Danish jarl, enjoyed more completely than she the legal rights of a free citizen. Marriage is described as a sale, and this passage might be quoted to prove that the father sold his daughter to her first husband without her consent ; but what sort of a sale was that which carried with it no rights of property over the thing sold ? The father conveyed to the husband no more than the father himself had, and the *patria potestas* was no part of Scandinavian or German law. The father conveyed to the husband simply the rights of guardianship, not rights of property, — the right to act as her representative, with the corresponding duties; the right to the control and charge of her property while she remained his wife, and certain rights of inheritance in case of her death, though these apparently depended in each case on the terms of the contract. In that stage of society the rights of the husband over the wife were less extensive than they now are. Her position was more independent; her ability to hold property was quite as complete; her protection against ill-treatment, if anything, was more effective than· it is now.

One final resource the wife always had. The Scandinavians were not yet much advanced beyond the Indians of America in their view of marriage as a voluntary association, which might be terminated at the will of either party. Another passage of the Njalsaga throws light on the Scandinavian law of divorce. Unna, wife of Hrut, was dissatisfied with her husband and wished to leave him. She took counsel with her father, who on hearing her reasons was satisfied with their force, and being the best lawyer in Iceland advised her as to the proper way of securing her divorce without risk of opposition or of personal constraint. She was to throw her husband off his guard by appearing happy and good-tempered, and then when he was absent from home in the summer on necessary business, and when all the men of the district had ridden away to the annual meeting of the Thing, or popular assembly and court of law, she must summon her own people to ride with her to the Thing; and when she was ready to start she must, in the presence and with the witness of the men who were to bear her company, go before her marriage bed and declare herself separated from her husband by such separation as would hold good before the laws of the land and the judgment of the great Thing. At the door of the house she must take the same witness. After this she must make her way as safely as she could to her father at the Thing.

All this she did, and successfully joined her father at the Thing. Then she went to the hill of laws and declared herself separated from Hrut, her husband; and this proceeding constituted a full and valid divorce according to Scandinavian law. Her husband came home, and on learning what had happened, knit his brows and held his peace. He saw that the divorce was accomplished, and that he could do nothing to invalidate it. The affair did not end there. Unna had carried a marriage portion to her husband, of which he during the marriage had the possession and management. Naturally Hrut was not disposed to be generous in a case where he had been so ungenerously treated, and he therefore took no steps to return the property. His wife's father consequently brought a suit against him to compel surrender. Hrut met and defeated the suit by challenging the father to the wager of battle, — a challenge which the father's age and inferior strength made it folly to accept. This broke off the suit so far as the father was concerned. Unna, however, the divorced wife, was still the rightful owner of the property, and could recover possession whenever she could find a representative whose physical strength and legal knowledge were sufficient to overcome Hrut. This she ultimately did, and the affair ended in the recovery of the property and the maintenance of the divorce.

The sole legal inferiority of women to men consisted in their subjection to guardianship. This limitation of their legal capacity seems to have been due to their physical inability to perform the public duties of men. A woman could not go to war. She could not act as her own champion in the inevitable wager of battle. She had to act through her next of kin, or through some person whom she appointed as her legal representative; but one of the most firmly established principles of society obliged her family to protect her in such cases, and until such a protector or representative was found, her rights simply lay dormant.

This is not the place to enter into any elaborate examination of the other codes of northern law to find light on this subject. The same principles will be found to underlie the whole fabric of northern society. That women as a weaker class suffered from violent deprivation of their rights, and that in many cases, perhaps habitually, they were treated without much regard to them, may be true; so doubtless were children; but violation of law never was law. One must look back beyond the records of history for any condition of pure force among the races from which modern institutions and theories are derived. Among these races can be found no evidence of a lawless stage of society. If one may judge from the faint indications that remain, their faculty for instituting progressive laws gave them their superiority over rival races.

A favorite theory has insisted upon regarding the wedding ring as a badge of servitude or a symbol of purchase. This idea cannot be maintained. The wedding ring appears in its origin to have been merely the earnest money which bound the contract of marriage between the father and the husband, and was not the only symbol of the kind in early custom, although no other survives in modern use. The ring proved, not that marriage was a sale, but that marriage was a civil contract executed according to the strict formalities of contracts in the primitive law ; it proved, not that women were deprived of rights, but that their rights were secured to them in marriage by the most careful provisions known to early society.

On a world made up of the two great elements of Roman society, with its ruined family system and its debauched morality on the one side, and Germany, with barbarism resting on a strong family organization, on the other, the Christian church began its work of creating a new unity and a new morality for mankind. For more than a thousand years the Church profoundly affected and even controlled the conditions of social existence and the ethical tendencies of law. On no branch of law did it exercise a more marked influence than on the law of marriage. Historians, aware of this influence, have naturally assumed that the elevation of women from what was supposed to have been their previous condition of degradation and servitude was due to the humanitarian influence of the Church. In truth, the share of the Church in the elevation of women was for the most part restricted to a partial restoration of rights which the Church herself had a principal share in taking away from them. The Church was a Roman church; it rose to power under the intense moral reaction against the corruptions of the Empire; and of all the corruptions of the Empire none had been more scandalous and more fatal than the corruption of the women. For sufficient cause the women of the later Empire found little favor in the eyes of the Church. In the early days the ascetic principle was strong in religion, and women as such, even the best of women, were not sought by men whose present existence was as nothing in their eyes, and to whom the price of eternal happiness lay in the avoidance even of temptation to worldly life. Next to the purification of morals, and indeed as one principal means toward it, the Church felt with most intensity the necessity of discipline and obedience in society, and taught that lesson with only too much earnestness and success. The rise of Christianity marked the diminution of women's social and legal rights both in the old imperial world and in the new Germanic race, which flung itself with all the ardor of its fresh enthusiasm into the ideas of the new religion. A long time elapsed before the pure humanitarian influences of Christianity got the upper hand, and began to struggle with the manifest injustice toward women which the Church had either stimulated or permitted.

In the mean time church doctrines were more frequently calculated to inculcate the duties than the rights of women. The moral aspect of marriage and its religious meaning were pressed with emphasis, which did not often stop to weigh the immediate importance of the legal and temporal contract. The Church regarded as of greater consequence to the happiness of mankind, here and hereafter, that women should be obedient to their bishops and their husbands than that they should be encouraged to protect themselves. Perhaps anything that tended to depress the legal status and the civil rights of women, tended at the same time to make them more and more dependent on the Church, and to turn their minds more passionately toward the one channel through which consolation and protection came.

The Church ultimately made persistent and partly successful efforts to protect women from the inevitable results of its own policy, but these efforts could never have gone to the point of restoring them to the independent position they held either under the Roman or the German law. The Church, for example, frowned upon divorce and sternly forbade it; yet

which was likely to suffer most under an enforced yoke, the man or the woman, — and why was the law not as competent then to make a contract that should protect the woman, as the Church was to intervene by a purely ecclesiastical principle ? The Church felt with reason that society should be taught to obey ; and of all classes of society, the women who were least in need of learning that lesson were obliged to learn it most thoroughly. The Church established a new ideal of feminine character. Thenceforward not the proud, self-confident, vindictive woman of German tradition received the admiration and commanded the service of law and society ; not the Hallgerdas, the Brunhildas, the Fredegundas, were the women whose acts were chronicled and whose will was obeyed. Such women were the horror and the shame of the Church, unless, like the great Countess Matilda of Tuscany, they paid to the Church that obedience which they refused to their husbands. In reprobation of these the Church raised up, with the willing co-operation of the men, the modern type of Griselda, — the meek and patient, the silent and tender sufferer, the pale reflection of the Mater Dolorosa, submissive to every torture that her husband could invent, but more submissive to the Church than to her husband. For her and such as her was the kingdom of heaven reserved, while a fate of a very different kind was in store for the defiant heroine of the heroic age.

These mediæval conceptions belonged to a time when the most pressing necessity of society was con-

centration, and when discipline was the chief lesson to
be learned.   The process by which the free and democratic German world had to be trained was long and
painful.   The wretchedness of feudal tyranny was
succeeded only by the sharper inflictions of concentrated power.   For centuries the most intelligent
part of society set its heart on building up a social
fabric which should rest not on human but on divine
authority.   The principle of authority was essential;
and authority, when not resting on the will of society,
could find no other logical support than the divine
will.   The conditions of their existence precluded the
Church, the arbitrary monarch, the feudal noble, and
the husband of that day from resting the claim of
authority on the consent of society.   Thus the family,
like the State, took on the character of a petty absolutism; and to justify in theory the sacrifice of rights
thus surrendered by the wife and children, whether
in the form of the harsh provisions of the law toward
women or the even harsher rules of primogeniture,
men fell back on what they called the patriarchal
theory, and derived the principles they required from
a curious conglomeration of Old Testament history
and pure hypothesis.

England was the country which carried these theories to the most extreme conclusions in her law; but
England was also the country which resisted their
application most successfully.   Luther led the way
by overthrowing in northern Germany the divine
authority of the Roman church.   England struck the

first blow at the whole system in her rebellion against
the theory of divine right in the State. Luther and
Cromwell were conservatives in a wider sense than
they imagined. They represented more than the protest against religious or political absolutism. The
movement which they led could not come to a legitimate end without effecting a readjustment of the
whole social balance, which the exigencies of a pressing immediate necessity had for a thousand years
thrown from its natural equilibrium.

Future history can hardly produce any new experience which has not its prototype in the past. If
modern society is destined to move at all, it can only
move on the same lines which have already and repeatedly been followed out to their conclusions. If
it carries the tendency toward the independence of
women to its logical extreme, it will find that Rome
has already travelled that path. If it reacts toward
a re-establishment of the family in sterner aspect,
it will find that this reaction has again and again
told its whole story. If it seeks a moral from which
to draw all the light that history can throw on its
true interests, this moral is obvious and trite. All
new discoveries in the record of human development
point to the familiar facts that the most powerful instincts in man are his affections and his love of property ; that on these the family is built; that no other
institution can be raised on the same or on equally
strong foundations ; that for this reason the family is
the strongest and healthiest of all human fabrics ;

that it always has and probably always will trample every rival system under its feet; and finally, that just in the measure that society has on the one side carried the theory of the family to an exaggeration, or has allowed it to fall into contempt, has been the violence of the reaction.

CAPTAINE JOHN SMITH.[1]

SOMETIME GOVERNOUR IN VIRGINIA, AND ADMIRALL OF NEW ENGLAND.

CAPTAIN JOHN SMITH belonged to the extraordinary school of adventurers who gave so much lustre to the reign of Elizabeth, and whose most brilliant leader King James brought to the Tower and the block. Like Raleigh, though on a much lower level, Smith sustained many different characters. He was a soldier or a sailor indifferently, a statesman when circumstances gave him power, and an author when occasion required. Born in Lincolnshire in 1579, of what is supposed to have been a good Lancashire family, at a very early age he became a soldier of fortune in the Low Countries, and drifted into the Austrian service, where he took part in the campaign of 1600 against the Turks. Afterward he reappeared as a soldier of the Prince of Transylvania, who gave him a coat-of-arms, which was registered at the Herald's College in London. His extraordinary adventures during the three or four years of his life in Eastern Europe were related in his Autobiography,

[1] Originally printed in the North American Review for January, 1867.

or "True Travels," a work published in London in 1630, near the close of his life. Dr. Palfrey's History of New England contains the earliest critical examination of this portion of Smith's story from an historical and geographical point of view, with a result not on the whole unfavorable to Smith.[1]

In 1604 Smith was again in England, where he soon began to interest himself in the enterprise of colonizing America.

On the 10th of April, 1606, King James conferred a charter upon certain persons in England, who took the title of the Virginia Company, and who proceeded to fit out an expedition of three small vessels, containing, in addition to their crews, one hundred and five colonists, headed by a Council, of which Edward Maria Wingfield was chosen President, and Captains Bartholomew Gosnold, John Smith, John Ratcliffe, John Martin, and George Kendall were the other members. After various delays this expedition dropped down the Thames December 20 of the same year, but was kept six weeks in sight of England by unfavorable winds. After a long and difficult voyage, and a further delay of three weeks among the West India Islands, the headlands of Chesapeake Bay were passed April 26, 1607. On the 14th of May following, the colonists formally founded Jamestown.

In the mean while trouble had risen between Smith and his colleagues. Smith's story was told in the "Generall Historie" as follows : —

[1] Palfrey's History of New England, i. pp. 89–92, note.

" Now, Captain Smith, who all this time from their departure from the Canaries was restrained as a prisoner upon the scandalous suggestions of some of the chiefe, (envying his repute), who fained he intended to usurpe the Government, murther the Councell, and make himselfe King ; that his confederats were dispersed in all the three ships, and that divers of his confederats that revealed it would affirm it. For this he was committed as a prisoner. Thirteen weeks he remained thus suspected, and by that time the ships should returne, they pretended out of their commisserations to refer him to the Councell in England to receive a check, rather then by particulating his designes make him so odious to the world, as to touch his life, or utterly overthrow his reputation."

Captain Newport, who was about to return to England, exerted his influence so strongly in favor of harmony that Smith was allowed to resume his seat among the Council ; but he was not liked by the persons in control of the expedition, and some little light on the causes of their dislike or suspicion may be found in a passage of Wingfield's " Discourse," which said of Smith that " it was proved to his face that he begged in Ireland, like a rogue without a lycence," — and he adds, " To such I would not my name should be a companyon." If Smith was accused of conspiring to obtain power, the dark events and questionable expedients of his varied and troubled career might well be flung in his face, and produce a considerable influence on the minds of his judges. Harmony was a blessing little known among the unhappy colonists, and before the close of the year, Captain

George Kendall, another of the members of the Council, was accused of the same crime with which Smith had been charged, and was tried, convicted, and actually executed.

Newport, who had great influence over the colonists, sailed for England June 22, leaving three months' supplies behind him, and promising to return in seven months with a new company of settlers. His departure was followed by disasters and troubles of every description. The mortality was frightful. More than forty deaths took place before September, some caused by fevers and sickness, some by the Indians, but the larger number by famine. The kindness of the Indians alone, according to the express statement of Percy, who was among the survivors, preserved the remaining colonists from the fate of the lost Roanoke settlement of 1585.

Even this condition of the colony, though during five months together not five able-bodied men could mount the defences, had no effect in quieting the jealousies and dissensions of the leaders. Captain Gosnold died, leaving only Wingfield, Ratcliffe, Smith, and Martin in the Council. The last three combined to depose Wingfield; and this revolution took place September 10, without resistance. Ratcliffe, as the next in order, was chosen President.

" As at this time," said Smith, " were most of our chiefest men either sicke or discontented, the rest being in such dispaire as they would rather starve and rot with idleness then be perswaded to do anything for their owne reliefe without constraint, — our victualles being now within eighteene dayes spent, and the Indians' trade decreasing, I was sent to the mouth of ye river to trade for Corne, and try the River for Fish; but our fishing we could not effect by reason of the stormy weather." Fortunately the Indians were found willing to trade for corn, and by means of their supplies the lives of the settlers were saved. On the 9th of November, Smith made a longer excursion, partially exploring the Chickahominy, and was received with much kindness by the Indians, who supplied him with corn enough to have "laded a ship." Elated by his success and encouraged by the friendly attitude of the savages, — or, according to his own account, eager "to discharge the imputation of malicious tungs, that halfe suspected I durst not, for so long delaying," — he determined to carry on his exploration of the Chickahominy to its source. On the 10th of December he started in the pinnace, which he left at a place he called Apocant, forty miles above the mouth of the Chickahominy, and continued his journey in a barge. Finally, rather than endanger the barge, he hired a canoe and two Indians to row it, and with two of his own company, named Robinson and Emry, went twenty miles higher. " Though some wise men may condemn this too bould attempt of too much indiscretion, yet if they well consider the friendship of the Indians in conducting me, the desolatenes of the country, the propabilitie of [discovering] some lacke, and the malicious judges of my actions at home, as also to have some matters of worth to incourage our adventurers in England, might well have caused any honest minde to have done the like, as wel for his own discharge as for the publike good."

At length they landed to prepare their dinner, and Smith with one Indian walked on along the course of the river, while Robinson and Emry with the other Indian remained to guard the canoe. Within a quarter of an hour he heard a hallooing of Indians and a loud cry, and fearing treachery, he seized his guide, whose arm he bound fast to his own hand, while he prepared his pistol for immediate use. As they " went discoursing," an arrow struck him on the right thigh, but without harm. He soon found himself attacked by some two hundred savages, against whose arrows he used his guide as a shield, discharging his pistol three or four times. The Indian chief, Opechankanough, then called upon him to surrender, and the savages laid their bows on the ground, ceasing to shoot.

" My hinde treated betwixt them and me of conditions of peace; he discovered me to be the Captaine. My request was to retire to ye boate; they demaunded my armes; the rest they saide were slaine, only me they would reserve; the Indian importuned me not to shoot. In retiring, being in the midst of a low quagmire, and minding them more then my steps, I stept fast into the quagmire, and also the Indian in drawing me forth. Thus surprised, I resolved to trie their mercies; my armes I caste from me, till which none durst approach me. Being ceazed on me, they drew me out and led me to the King."

Thus far, to avoid confusion, the account has followed the "True Relation," written by Smith, and published in London in 1608, the year after the events described.[1] In 1624 Smith published in London his "Generall Historie," which contained a version of the story varying essentially from that of the "True Relation." In continuing the account of his captivity, the two narratives will be placed side by side, for convenience of comparison, and the principal variations will be printed in Italics.

After describing the circumstances of his capture, which took place far up the Chickahominy River, Smith continued in his double narrative : —

A TRUE RELATION.	THE GENERALL HISTORIE.
1608.	1624.
"They drew me out and led me to the King. I presented him with a compasse diall. . . . With kinde speeches and bread he requited me, conducting me where the Canow lay, and John Robinson slaine, with 20 or 30 arrowes in him. Emry I saw not. I perceived by the aboundance of fires all over the woods, *at each place I expected when they*	"Then according to their composition they drew him forth and led him to the fire where his men were slaine. Diligently they chafed his benumbed limbs. He demanding for their Captaine they showed him Opechankanough king of Pamaunkee, to whom he gave a round ivory double-compass Dyall. Much they marvailed

---

[1] *A True Relation of Virginia.* By CAPTAIN JOHN SMITH. With an Introduction and Notes, by CHARLES DEANE. Boston. 1866.

A TRUE RELATION
(*Continued*).

would execute me, yet they used me with what kindnes they could. Approaching their Towne, which was within 6 miles.where I was taken, . . . the Captaine conducting me to his lodging, a quarter of venison and some ten pound of bread I had for supper; what I left was reserved for me, and sent with me to my lodging. Each morning 3 women presented me three great platters of fine bread; *more venison than ten men could devour I had;* my gowne, points and garters, my compas and a tablet they gave me again; though 8 ordinarily guarded me, I wanted not what they could devise to content me; and still our longer acquaintance increased our better affection. . . . I desired he [the King] would send a messenger to Paspahegh [Jamestown] with a letter I would write, by which they shold understand how kindly they used me, and that I was well, least they should revenge my death; this he granted, and sent three men, in such weather as in reason were unpossible by any naked to be endured. . . . The next day after my letter came a salvage to my lodging with his sword to have slaine me. . . . This was the father of him I had slayne, whose fury to prevent,

THE GENERALL HISTORIE
(*Continued*).

at the playing of the Fly and Needle. . . . *Notwithstanding, within an houre after they tied him to a tree, and as many as could stand about him prepared to shoot him,* but the King holding up the Compass in his hand, they all laid down their bowes and arrowes, and in a triumphant manner led him to Orapaks, where he was after their manner kindly feasted and well used. . . . Smith they conducted to a long house where *thirtie or fortie tall fellowes did guard him,* and ere long *more bread and venison was brought him than would have served twentie men.* I think his stomach at that time was not very good; what he left they put in baskets and tyed over his head; about midnight they set the meat again before him. All this time not one of them would eat a bit with him, till the next morning they brought him as much more, and then did they eate all the olde, and reserved the newe as they had done the other; which made him think they would fat him to eate him. Yet in this desperate estate to defend him from the cold, one Maocassater brought him his gowne in requitall of some beads and toyes Smith had given him at his first arrival in Virginia.

4

the King presently conducted me to another Kingdome, upon the top of the next northerly river, called Youghtanan. Having feasted me, he further led me to another branch of the river called Mattapament; to two other hunting townes they led me, and to each of these countries a house of the great Emperor of Pewhakan, whom as yet I supposed to bee at the Fals; *to him I told him I must goe, and so returne to Paspahegh.* After this foure or five dayes march, we returned to Rasawrack, the first towne they brought me too, where binding the Mats in bundles, they marched two dayes journey and crossed the river of Youghtanan where it was as broad as Thames ; so conducting me to a place called Menapacute in Pamaunke, where yᵉ King inhabited. . . .

"From hence this kind King conducted mee to a place called Topahanocke, a kingdome upon another River northward. The cause of this was, that the yeare before, a shippe had beene in the River of Pamaunke, who having been kindly entertained by Powhatan their Emperour, they returned thence, and discovered the River of Topahanocke, where being received with like kind-

"Two dayes after, a man would have slaine him (but that the guard prevented it) for the death of his sonne, to whom they conducted him to recover the poore man then breathing his last. . . . In part of a Table booke he writ his minde to them at the Fort, and . . . the messengers . . . according to his request went to Jamestowne in as bitter weather as could be of frost and snow, and within three dayes returned with an answer.

"Then they led him to the Youthtanunds, the Mattaponients, the Payankatanks, the Nantaughtacunds, and Omawmanients upon the rivers of Rapahannock and *Patawomeck, over all those rivers* and back againe by divers other severall nations to the King's habitation at Pamaunkee, where they entertained him with most strange and fearfull Conjurations. . . .

"At last they brought him to Meronocomoco, where was Powhatan their Emperor. Here more than two hundred of those grim Courtiers stood wondering at him, as he had been a monster; till Powhatan and his trayne had put themselves in their greatest braveries. . . . At his entrance before the King, all the people gave a great shout. The Queene of Appa-

nesse, yet he slue the King and tooke of his people; and they supposed I were hee, but the people reported him a great man that was Captaine, and using mee kindly, the next day we departed. . . .

" The next night I lodged at a hunting town of Powhatams, and the next day arrived at Waranacomoco upon the river of Pamauncke, where the great king is resident. . . .

" Arriving at Weramocomoco, their Emperour . . . kindly welcomed me with good wordes and great Platters of sundrie Victuals, *assuring mee his friendship, and my libertie within foure dayes.* . . . Hee desired mee to forsake Paspahegh, and to live with him upon his River, — a Countrie called Capa Howasicke; hee promised to give me Corne, Venison, or what I wanted to feede us; Hatchets and Copper wee should make him, and none should disturbe us. This request I promised to performe; and thus having with all the kindnes hee could devise, sought to content me, hee sent me home *with 4 men,* one that usually carried my Gowne and Knapsacke after me, two other loded with bread, and one to accompanie me. . . .

" From Weramocomoco is but

matuck was appointed to bring him water to wash his hands, and another brought him a bunch of feathers, instead of a Towell to dry them. *Having feasted him after their best barbarous manner they could, a long consultation was held; but the conclusion was, two great stones were brought before Powhatan; then as many as could lay their hands on him dragged him to them, and thereon laid his head; and being ready with their clubs to beate out his braines, Pocahontas the King's dearest daughter, when no intreaty could prevaile, got his head in her armes, and laid her owne upon his to save him from death; whereat the Emperour was contented he should live to make him hatchets, and her bells, beads, and copper.* . . .

" Two dayes after, Powhatan having disguised himselfe in the most fearfullest manner he could . . . more like a devil than a man, with some two hundred more as blacke as himselfe, came unto him and told him now they were friends, and presently he should goe to Jamestowne, to send him two great gunnes and a gryndstone, for which he would give him the Country of Capahowosick, and for ever esteeme him as his sonne Nantaquoud. So to Jamestowne

A TRUE RELATION
(Continued).

12 miles, yet the Indians trifled away that day, and would not goe to our Forte by any perswasions; but in certaine olde hunting houses of Paspahegh we lodged all night. The next morning ere Sunne rise, we set forward for our Fort, where we arrived within an houre, where each man with truest signes of joy they could expresse welcomed mee, except M. Archer, and some 2 or 3 of his, who was then in my absence sworne Counsellour, though not with the consent of Captaine Martin. Great blame and imputation was laide upon mee by them for the losse of our two men which the Indian slew; insomuch that they purposed to depose me; but *in the midst of my miseries it pleased God to send Captaine Nuport, who arriving there the same night so tripled our joy as for a while these plots against me were deferred*, though with much malice against me, which Captain Newport in a short time did plainly see."

THE GENERALL HISTORIE
(Continued).

with 12 *guides* Powhatan sent him, *he still expecting (as he had done all this long time of his imprisonment) every houre to be put to one death or other, for all their feasting.* But almightie God (by his divine providence) had mollified the hearts of those sterne Barbarians with compassion. The next morning betimes they came to the Forte. . . .

" *Now in Jamestowne they were all in combustion, the strongest preparing once more to run away with the Pinnace ; which with the hazzard of his life, with Sabre, falcon, and musket shot, Smith forced now the third time to stay or sinke.* Some, no better than they should be, had' plotted with the President the next day to have put him to death by the Leviticall law, for the lives of Robinson and Emry, pretending the fault was his that had led them to their ends: but *he quickly tooke such order with such lawyers, that he layd them by the heeles till he sent some of them prisoners for England.* . . .

"Newport got in and arrived at James Towne not long after the redemption of Captaine Smith. . . .

"Written by Thomas Studley, the first Cape Merchant in Virginia, Robert Fenton, Edward Harrington, and J. S."

Comparison of the two narratives thus for the first time placed side by side, betrays a tone of exaggeration in the later story. Eight guards, which had been sufficient in 1608, were multiplied into thirty or forty tall fellows in 1624. What was enough for ten men at the earlier time would feed twenty according to the later version. In 1608 four guides were an ample escort to conduct Smith to Jamestown, but they were reinforced to the number of twelve sixteen years afterward. With the best disposition toward Smith, one cannot forget that he belonged to the time when Falstaff and his misbegotten knaves in Kendal Green appeared upon the stage. The execution wrought upon the lawyers who wished to try Smith for his life on his return to Jamestown was prompt and decisive according to the story of 1624, but in 1608 " in the midst of my miseries it pleased God to send " Captain Newport to defer the plots of Smith's enemies. With sabre, falcon, and musket-shot he forced the mutinous crew of the pinnace to stay or sink, according to the " Generall Historie," while the " True Relation " was silent as to any feat of arms, but simply said that Captain Newport arrived the same evening.

The same exaggeration marked the account of Smith's treatment among the savages. According to the story written a few months after the event, a people was described, savage, but neither cruel nor bloodthirsty ; reckless perhaps of life in battle, but kind and even magnanimous toward their captive. The " True Relation " implied that no demonstration

was made against Smith's life, such as he described
in 1624 as occurring within an hour after his capture.   Only a few days after he was taken prisoner,
he directed Opechankanough to take him to Powhatan, and even then he knew that he was to be
allowed to return to Jamestown.   "To him I told
him I must go, and so return to Paspahegh."   Powhatan received him with cordiality, and having sought
to content him with all the kindness he could devise,
sent him with a guard of honor back to his friends.
In the "True Relation," the behavior of the Indians toward Smith was more humane than he would
have received at the hands of civilized peoples.   He
found no cause to fear for his life, except from a
savage whose son he had killed, and from whom
Opechankanough protected him.   One line indeed
alluded to a fear that they fed him so fat as to
make him much doubt they meant to sacrifice him;
but this evidence of the kindness of the Indians
implied that he believed himself to have been mistaken in having entertained the suspicion.   Yet
in 1624, throughout his long imprisonment, he was
still expecting every hour to be put to one death or
another.

These variations would not concern the ordinary
reader of colonial history, if they stopped at trifling
inconsistencies.   They would merely prove the earlier
narrative to be the safer authority for historians to
follow, which is an established law of historical criticism.   The serious divergence occurred in Smith's

account of his visit to Powhatan, which in 1608 was
free from the suspicion of danger to his life, but in
1624 introduced Pocahontas as his savior from a cruel
execution. The absence of Pocahontas, and of any
allusion to her interference, or of reference to the
occasion on which she interfered, makes the chief
characteristic of the earlier story, and if the law of
evidence is sound, requires the rejection of the latter
version as spurious.

Smith's silence in 1608 about his intended execution and his preservation by Pocahontas was the more
remarkable, because the "True Relation" elsewhere
mentioned Pocahontas, with every appearance of
telling the whole share she had in Smith's affairs.
Smith's captivity occurred in December. In the
following month of May, Smith imprisoned at Jamestown some Indians whom he suspected of treachery.
The "True Relation" continued : —

"Powhatan, understanding we detained certaine Sal-
vages, sent his daughter, a child of tenne yeares old,
which not only for feature, countenance, and proportion
much exceedeth any of the rest of his people, but for
wit and spirit the only Nonpareil of his Country : this
he sent by his most trustie messenger, called Rawhunt,
as much exceeding in deformitie of person, but of a
subtill wit and crafty understanding. He with a long
circumstance told me how well Powhatan loved and
respected mee, and in that I should not doubt any way
of his kindnesse he had sent his child, which he most
esteemed, to see me : . . . his little daughter he had
taught this lesson also."

Smith regarded Pocahontas as a person so much worth winning to his interests that he surrendered the prisoners to her.

" We guarded them as before to the Church, and after prayer gave them to Pocahontas, the King's Daughter, in regard of her father's kindnesse in sending her. . . . Pocahontas also we requited, with such trifles as contented her, to tel that we had used the Paspaheyans very kindly in so releasing them."

Had Pocahontas saved Smith's life four months before, Smith would have been likely to surrender the prisoners out of gratitude to her, rather than " in regard of her father's kindnesse in sending" his favorite child to ask a return for his own hospitality.

No American needs to learn that Pocahontas is the most romantic character in the history of his country. Her name and story are familiar to every schoolboy, and families of the highest claim to merit trace their descent from the Emperor's daughter that saved the life of Captain John Smith. In the general enthusiasm, language and perhaps common-sense have been strained to describe her attributes. Her beauty and wild grace, her compassion and disinterestedness, her Christian life and pure character, have been dwelt upon with warmth the more natural as the childhood of the nation furnished little latitude to imagination. One after another, American historians have contented themselves with repeating the words of the " Generall Historie," heaping praises which no critics were cynical enough to gainsay, now on the virtues of Pocahontas, and now on the courage and constancy of Smith.

The exclusive share of the later narrative in shaping popular impressions was well shown by the standard authority for American history. In the early editions of Bancroft's " History of the United States," the following version of Smith's adventure was given : —

" The gentle feelings of humanity are the same in every race, and in every period of life ; they bloom, though unconsciously, even in the bosom of a child. Smith had easily won the confiding fondness of the Indian maiden ; and now, the impulse of mercy awakened within her breast, she clung firmly to his neck, as his head was bowed to receive the strokes of the tomahawk. Did the childlike superstition of her kindred reverence her interference as a token from a superior power? Her fearlessness and her entreaties persuaded the council to spare the agreeable stranger, who might make hatchets for her father, and rattles and strings of beads for herself, the favorite child. The barbarians, whose decision had long been held in suspense by the mysterious awe which Smith had inspired, now resolved to receive him as a friend, and to make him a partner of their councils. They tempted him to join their bands, and lend assistance in an attack upon the white men at Jamestown ; and when his decision of character succeeded in changing the current of their thoughts, they dismissed him with mutual promises of friendship and benevolence."

In a note appended to these paragraphs the author quoted : —

" Smith, I. 158–162, and II. 29–33. The account is
fully contained in the oldest book printed on Virginia,
in our Cambridge library. It is a thin quarto, in black-
letter, by John Smith, printed in 1608, — A True
Relation, etc."

The story, in passing through the medium of Mr.
Bancroft's mind, gained something which did not
belong to the original, or belonged to it only in a
modified degree. The spirit of Smith infused itself
into the modern historian, as it had already infused
itself into the works of his predecessors. The lights
were intensified ; the shadows deepened ; the grada-
tions softened. The copy surpassed its model. This
tendency went so far that the author quoted the
" True Relation " as the full authority for what was to
be found only in the " Generall Historie," if indeed it
was all to be found even there. When Mr. Bancroft
collated his version of the story with the black-letter
pamphlet in the Cambridge library, the popular reputation of Smith had already created an illusion in his
mind resembling the optical effect of refracted light.
He saw something which did not exist, — the exaggerated image of a figure beyond.

The labors of Charles Deane have made necessary
a thorough examination into the evidence bearing on
Smith's story ; and Deane's notes make such an inquiry less laborious than the mass of material seemed
to threaten. With that aid, an analysis of the evidence can be brought within narrow compass.

The first President of the colony was Edward

Maria Wingfield, who in September, 1607, was deprived of his office, and placed in confinement by Smith and the other members of the Council. When Newport — who with a new company of settlers arrived at Jamestown Jan. 8, 1608, immediately after Smith's release — began his second return voyage to London, he took the deposed President Wingfield with him, and they arrived safely at Blackwall on the 21st of May. Wingfield kept a diary during his stay in Virginia, and after his return he wrote with its assistance a defence of himself and his administration, privately circulated in manuscript, and at a later period used by Purchas, but afterward forgotten and hidden in the dust of the Lambeth Library. From this obscurity it was drawn by Mr. Deane, who published it with notes in the fourth volume of the Archæologia Americana in 1860.[1] Excepting a few papers of little consequence, this is the earliest known writing which came directly from the colony. The manuscript of Smith's " True Relation," its only possible rival, could not have reached England before the month of July, while Wingfield's manuscript was intended for immediate circulation in May or June. Wingfield's work, which was called " A Discourse of Virginia," is therefore new authority on the early history of the colony, and has peculiar value as a test for

[1] *A Discourse of Virginia.* By EDWARD MARIA WINGFIELD, the First President of the Colony. Edited by CHARLES DEANE, Member of the American Antiquarian Society, and of the Massachusetts Historical Society. Boston: Privately printed. 1860.

the correctness of the " True Relation." Its account
of Smith's captivity could only have been gained from
his own mouth, or from those to whom he told the
story, and its accuracy can be tested by the degree
of its coincidence with the " True Relation."

A number of passages in this short pamphlet
would be worth extracting; but the inquiry had
best be narrowed to the evidence in regard to
Pocahontas. The passage from Wingfield, telling
of Smith's adventures among the Indians, ran as
follows : —

" *Dec*. The 10th of December Mr. Smith went up
the ryver of the Chechohomynies to trade for corne. He
was desirous to see the heade of that river ; and when
it was not passible with the shallop, he hired a cannow
and an Indian to carry him up further. The river the
higher grew worse and worse. Then he went on shoare
with his guide, and left Robinson and Emmery, twoe of our
men in the cannow, which were presently slaine by the
Indians, Pamaonke's men, and he himself taken prysoner ;
and by the means of his guide his lief was saved. And
Pamaonché haveing him prisoner, carryed him to his
neybors wyroances to see if any of them knewe him for
one of those which had bene, some two or three yeres
before us, in a river amongst them Northward, and taken
awaie some Indians from them by force. At last he
brought him to the great Powaton (of whome before wee
had no knowledg), who sent him home to our towne the
viii^th of January. . . .

" Mr. Archer sought how to call Mr. Smith's lief in
question, and had indited him upon a chapter in Leviticus

for the death of his twoe men. He had had his tryall the same daie of his retorne, and I believe his hanging the same or the next daie, so speedie is our law there ; but it pleased God to send Captn. Newport unto us the same evening to our unspeakable comfort, whose arrivall saved Mr. Smyth's life and mine."

Deane, in editing Wingfield in 1860, furnished a note upon this passage, in which for the first time a doubt was thrown upon the story of Pocahontas's intervention. Yet the discovery of Wingfield's narrative added little to the evidence contained in the " True Relation," — always a well-known work. The " Discourse " supplied precise dates, fixing Smith's departure on the 10th of December, and his return on the 8th of January, his absence being exactly four weeks in length ; it said that Smith's guide saved his life, which might be a variation from the story of the " True Relation ;" it dwelt on the danger Smith ran, from the enmity of Archer, which might be only the result of Wingfield's dislike of that person. In general, this new evidence, though clearly independent of the " True Relation," confirmed it in essentials, and especially in the omission of reference to Pocahontas. So remarkable an incident as her protection of Smith, if known to Wingfield, would scarcely have been omitted in this narrative, which must have contained the version of Smith's adventures current among the colonists after his return to Jamestown.

These two works are the only contemporaneous authority for the first year of the colonial history. A wide gap intervenes between them and the next work; and the strength of Deane's case rests so largely on the negative evidence offered by the " True Relation " and the " Discourse," that for his purpose further search was useless. Every one, whether believing or disbelieving the " Generall Historie," must agree that Pocahontas was not mentioned, either by name or by implication, as the preserver of Smith's life either by Smith in the " True Relation " or by Wingfield in his " Discourse." The inquiry might stop here, and each reader might be left to form his own opinion as to the relative value of the conflicting narratives; but the growth of a legend is as interesting as the question of its truth.

Newport returned to England April 10, 1608, carrying Wingfield with him, and leaving Ratcliffe President of the Colony, with Martin, Smith, and Archer in the Council, together with a new member, Matthew Scrivener, who had arrived with Newport. Smith in June explored successfully a part of Chesapeake Bay, and returning July 21, found, according to the " Generall Historie," the colonists in a miserable condition, unable to do anything but complain of Ratcliffe, whose principal offence appears to have been his obliging the colonists to build him " an unnecessary building for his pleasure in the woods." Ratcliffe, whose real name was Sicklemore, was a poor creature, if the evidence in regard to him can be believed. He was deposed, and Scrivener, Smith's " deare friend," though then exceedingly ill, succeeded him as President. This revolution was rapidly effected; for three days later, July 24, Smith again set out with twelve men, to finish his explorations, and made a complete tour round the bay, which supplied his materials for the map published at Oxford in 1612. He did not return to Jamestown till the 7th of September, and on the 10th he assumed the Presidency, " by the Election of the Councell and request of the Company." Scrivener appears merely to have held the office during Smith's pleasure, and voluntarily resigned it into his hands.

The history of Smith's administration of the colony from Sept. 10, 1608, till the end of September, 1609, is given in the " Generall Historie," and may be studied with advantage as an example of Smith's style. Whatever may have been the merits of his government, he had no better success than his predecessors, and he not only failed to command obedience, but was left almost or quite without a friend. He was ultimately deposed and sent to England under articles of complaint. The precise tenor of these articles is unknown; but Mr. Deane has found in the Colonial Office a letter of Ratcliffe, alias Sicklemore, dated Oct. 4, 1609, in which he announced to the Lord Treasurer that " this man [Smith] is sent home to answere some misdemeanors whereof I perswade me he can scarcely clear himselfe from great imputation of blame." Beyond a doubt the difficulties of the situation were very great, and the men Smith had to control were originally poor material, and were made desperate by their trials; but certainly his career in Virginia terminated disastrously, both for himself and for the settlement. The Virginia Company, notwithstanding his applications, never employed him again.

The colony went from bad to worse. George Percy, a brother of the Earl of Northumberland, succeeded Smith in the Presidency. The condition of the colonists between Smith's departure in October, 1609, and the arrival of Sir Thomas Gates in May, 1610, was terrible. Percy was so "sicke hee could neither goe nor stand." Ratcliffe, with a number of others, was killed by Indians. The remainder fed on roots, acorns, fish, and actually on the savages whom they killed, and on each other, — one man murdering his wife and eating her. Out of the whole number, said to have been five hundred, not more than sixty were living when Gates arrived; and he immediately took them on board ship, and abandoning Jamestown, set sail for England. Only by accident they met a new expedition under Lord Delaware, at the mouth of the river, which brought a year's provisions, and restored the fortunes of the settlement. In spite of the discouragement produced in England by these disasters, the Company renewed its efforts, and again sent out Sir Thomas Gates with six vessels and three hundred men, who arrived in August, 1611. The government was then in the hands of Sir Thomas Dale, who assumed it in May, 1611, and retained it till 1616. If the ultimate success of the colony was due to any single man, the merit appears to belong to Dale; for his severe and despotic rule crushed the insubordination that had been the curse of the State, compelled the idle to work, and maintained order between the colonists and the Indians.

In the mean while Smith, who had taken final leave of the colony, appears to have led a quiet life in London during several years. Lost from sight during the years 1610 and 1611, he appeared again in 1612 busied in the same direction as before. In that year he published at Oxford a short work called " A Map of Virginia. With a Description of the Countrey, the Commodities, People, Government, and Religion. Written by Captaine Smith, sometimes Governour of the Countrey. Whereunto is annexed the proceedings of those Colonies, &c., by W. S." The latter part of the publication, which purported to be drawn from the writings of certain colonists, was afterward reprinted, with alterations, as the Third Book of the " Generall Historie," from the title of which it appears that " W. S." stood for the initials of William Simons, Doctor of Divinity.

In this tract only one passage bore upon Smith's story of Pocahontas. Among the customs described as peculiar to the Indians was the form of execution practised against criminals. Their heads, Smith said, were placed upon an altar, or sacrificing-stone, while " one with clubbes beates out their braines." During his captivity Smith added, not indeed that he had actually seen this mode of execution, but that an

Indian had been beaten in his presence till he fell senseless, without a cry or complaint. The passage is remarkable for more than one reason. In the first place, the mode of execution there described was uncommon, if not unknown, among the Indians of the sea-coast; in the second place, the passage contained the germ of Smith's later story. Practised lawyers may decide whether, under the ordinary rules of evidence, this passage implies that Smith had himself not been placed in the position described, and future students may explain why Smith should have suppressed his own story, supposing it to have been true. The inference is strong that if anything of the sort had occurred, it would have been mentioned here; and this argument is strengthened by a short narration of his imprisonment given in the second part of the pamphlet, for which Dr. Simons was the nominal authority. This version ran as follows: —

"A month those barbarians kept him prisoner. Many strange triumphs and conjurations they made of him; yet he so demeened himself amongst them as he not only diverted them from surprising the fort, but procured his own liberty, and got himself and his company such estimation among them that those savages admired him as a Demi God. So returning safe to the Fort, once more stayed the pinnace her flight for England."

This work was, as above mentioned, afterward reprinted, under the author's name, as the Third Book of the "Generall Historie." The passage just quoted was there reproduced with the evidently intentional substitution of "six or seven weekes" for "a month," as in the original. In the "Generall Historie" the concluding paragraph was omitted, and in its place stood, "The manner how they used and delivered him is as followeth." Then, breaking abruptly into the middle of the old narrative, the story which has been quoted was interpolated.

The narrative in the second part of the "Map of Virginia," of which the above extract forms a part, was signed by the name of Thomas Studley alone, while in the "Generall Historie" the enlarged account bore also the signatures of Edward Harrington, Robert Fenton, and Smith himself. A question may arise as to the extent to which these persons should be considered as dividing with Smith the responsibility for the story. Thomas Studley died on the 28th of August, 1607. Both he and Edward Harrington had lain four months in their graves before Smith ever heard of Powhatan or Pocahontas. The date of Robert Fenton's death is not so clear, but there is no reason to suppose that he had any share in the narration of events which Smith alone witnessed.

The argument so far as the Oxford tract is concerned would be strong enough, if it went no further; but it becomes irresistible when this tract not only mentions Pocahontas, but introduces her as the savior of Smith's life, although it says no word of her most famous act in this character. The allusion occurred

toward the end of the pamphlet, where the assumed
writer took occasion to defend 'Smith against certain
charges, one of them being an alleged scheme on his
part of marrying Powhatan's daughter Pocahontas in
order to acquire a claim to the throne. The writer
denied the charge, and added : —

  " It is true she was the very nonparell of his kingdome, and at most not past 13 or 14 yeares of age. Very
often shee came to our fort with what shee could get for
Captaine Smith, that ever loved and used all the countrie
well, but her especially he ever much respected ; and she
so well requited it that when her father intended to have
surprised him, shee, by stealth in the darke night, came
through the wild woods and told him of it."

  The Oxford tract of 1612 may be considered decisive that down to that date the story of Pocahontas
had not been made public. Here we take leave of
Smith as an authority for a period of some ten years,
during which he published but one work, not relating to the present subject. An entirely new class of
colonists had in 1610–1611 taken the place of the
first settlers, almost exterminated by the disasters of
1609–1610. Among the new-comers in the train of
Lord Delaware, in 1610, was William Strachey, who
held the office of Secretary of the Colony. Little is
known of Strachey, except that after his return to
England he compiled a work called the " Historie of
Travaile into Virginia," never completed in its original plan, but still extant in two neatly written manuscripts, printed by the Hakluyt Society in 1849. The

date of its composition was probably about the year 1615. It consisted largely of extracts from Smith's previous works, though without acknowledgment of their origin ; it also contained original matter, and especially some curious references to Pocahontas,[1] but no reference, direct or indirect, to her agency in saving Smith's life, and no trace of the high esteem which such an act would have won for her.

Next in order after Strachey's manuscript comes a work which is quite original, and gives perhaps the best account of the colony ever made public by an eye-witness. This is a small volume in quarto, printed in London in 1615, and called " A True Discourse of the Present Estate of Virginia . . . till the 18th of June, 1614, together with . . . the Christening of Powhatan's daughter and her Marriage with an Englishman. Written by Raphe Hamor, late Secretarie in the Colonie." It contains a minute and graphic story how " Pocahuntas, King Powhatan's daughter, whose fame has spread even to England, under the name of Non Parella," while staying with some tribe, subject to her father, on the Potomac, was seized and carried away by Captain Argol, who had sailed up that river on a trading expedition. Her imprisonment as a hostage at Jamestown, her visit to her father's residence with Sir Thomas Dale and a strong force of English, Powhatan's failure to redeem her, and her subsequent marriage to John Rolfe April 5, 1613, are all circumstantially nar-

[1] See Deane's edition of the True Relation, p. 72.

rated; and finally an extremely interesting account
is given of a visit which Hamor made to Powhatan,
and of the conversation he had with that extraordinary savage. Besides this work of Hamor, the volume also contains several letters from persons in
Virginia, one of which is by John Rolfe, written with
the object of justifying his marriage. Afterward,
when the arrival of Pocahontas in England had excited an interest throughout Europe in her story,
Hamor's book was translated and published in
Germany.

Although repeated allusions to Pocahontas occur in
the works already mentioned, in Hamor she makes,
for the first time, her appearance as a person of
political importance. In the " True Relation " Smith
represented her as a pretty and clever child ten years
old, once sent with a trusted messenger by Powhatan to the fort to entreat the liberation of some
Indians whom Smith had seized. The Oxford tract
mentioned her as a friend of Smith, but a mere
child. Strachey gave a curious description of her intimate relations with the colony during his residence
there : —

" Pocahuntas, a well featured but wanton yong girle,
Powhatan's daughter, sometymes resorting to our fort,
of the age then of eleven or twelve yeares, would get the
boyes forth with her into the markett place, and make
them wheele, falling on their hands, turning up their
heeles upwards, whome she would followe and wheele
so her self, naked as she was, all the fort over."

Pocahontas was then apparently considered as a child like any other; but from the time when Argol treacherously seized her she took an important position, — in the first place, as the guaranty of a peace which Powhatan promised, and preserved during the remainder of her life and of his own; in the second place, as a person calculated to excite interest in England in behalf of the colony; and finally, as an eminent convert to the English Church, through whom a religious influence might be exercised among her father's subjects. Hamor's book was filled with her history, and Rolfe's letter showed much anxiety to prove the propriety of his course in marrying her. Both writers were interested in exciting as much sympathy for her as could be roused. Yet neither the one nor the other alluded to the act which has since become her first claim to praise, and which has almost thrown the rest of her story out of sight. There is no reason to suppose that in Virginia in 1614 the persons best informed were yet aware that Pocahontas had saved Smith's life.

In the month of June, 1616, Sir Thomas Dale arrived at Plymouth on his return home, bringing with him among his suite the baptized Pocahontas, then called Rebecca Rolfe, who with her husband and child came at the charge of the Company to visit England, and to prove to the world the success of the colony. She became at once the object of extraordinary attention, and in the following winter she was the most distinguished person in society. Her portrait taken at that time still exists, and shows a somewhat hard-featured figure, with a tall hat and ruff, appearing ill at ease in the stiff and ungraceful fashions of the day. Gentlemen of the court sent the engraving, as the curiosity of the season, in their letters to correspondents abroad. The Church received her with great honor, and the Bishop of London gave her an entertainment, celebrated in enthusiastic terms by Purchas. At the court masque in January, 1617, Pocahontas was among the most conspicuous guests. The King and Queen received her in special audiences ; and to crown all, tradition reports, with reasonable foundation, that King James, in his zeal for the high principles of divine right and the sacred character of royalty, expressed his serious displeasure that Rolfe, who was at best a simple gentleman, should have ventured so far beyond his position as to ally himself with one who was of imperial blood.

Just at that time, when the influence of London society had set its stamp of fashion on the name of the Indian girl, and when King James had adopted her as rightfully belonging within the pale of the divinity that hedges a king, Samuel Purchas, " Parson of St. Martin's by Ludgate," published the third edition of his " Pilgrimage." Purchas, although not himself an explorer, was an enthusiast on the subject of travels and adventures ; and in compiling the collection now so eagerly sought and so highly valued by collectors of books, he had, so far as related to Virginia, the direct assistance of personal witnesses, and also of manuscripts now unhappily lost except for his extracts. He was well acquainted with Smith, who "gently communicated" his notes to him, and who was in London, and visited Pocahontas at Brentford. Purchas himself saw Pocahontas. He was present when "my Honble. and Revd. Patron the Lord Bishop of London, Dr. King, entertained her with festivall state and pompe beyond what I have seen in his great hospitalitie afforded to other ladies," in his "hopefull zeale by her to advance Christianitie." He knew Tomocomo, an Indian of Powhatan's tribe, who came with her to England. "With this savage I have often conversed at my good friend's Master Doctor Goldstone, where he was a frequent guest; and where I have both seen him sing and dance his diabolicall measures, and heard him discourse of his countrey and religion, Sir Thomas Dale's man being the interpretour." He knew Rolfe also, who lent him his manuscript Discourse on Virginia. Yet Purchas's book contained no allusion to the heroic intervention on behalf of Smith, the story of whose captivity is simply copied from Simons's quarto of 1612; the diffuse comments on men and manners in Virginia contain no trace of what would have been correctly regarded as the most extraordinary incident in colonial history.

Silence in a single instance, as in Wingfield or in Strachey, might be accounted for, or at all events might be overlooked; but silence during a long period of years and under the most improbable circumstances, cannot be ignored. Wingfield, Smith himself, Simons, Strachey, Hamor, Rolfe, and Purchas, all the authorities without exception known to exist, are equally dumb when questioned as to a circumstance which since 1624 has become the most famous part of colonial history. The field is exhausted. No other sources exist from which to draw authentic information. Nothing remains but to return to Smith, and to inquire when it was that this extraordinary story first made its appearance, and how it obtained authority.

The blaze of fashionable success that surrounded Pocahontas in London lighted the closing scene of her life. She was obliged, against her will as was believed, to set out on her return to Virginia, but she never actually left the shores of England. Detained in the Thames by several weeks of contrary winds, her failing strength altogether gave way; and in March, 1617, in the word-play of Purchas, " she came at Gravesend to her end and grave." Her father, Powhatan, survived her less than a year.

Smith in the mean while was busied with projects in regard to New England and the fisheries. His efforts to form a colony there and to create a regular system of trade had little success ; but to spread a knowledge of the new country among the people of England, he printed, in 1616, a small quarto, called " A Description of New England," and in 1620 he published another pamphlet, entitled " New England's Trials," a second and enlarged edition of which appeared in 1622. There at last, in 1622, the long-sought allusion to his captivity occurred in the following words : —

"For wronging a soldier but the value of, a penny I have caused Powhatan send his own men to Jamestowne to receive their punishment at my discretion. It is true in our greatest extremitie they shot me, slue three of my men, and by the folly of them that fled took me prisoner ; yet God made Pocahontas the King's daughter the means to deliver me ; and thereby taught me to know their treacheries to preserve the rest."

The first appearance of this famous story can therefore be fixed within five years, — between 1617 and 1622, — although the complete account is only to be found in the "Generall Historie," printed in 1624, from which copious extracts have already been quoted. Only one point of difficulty still requires attention.

Smith there said (pp. 121–123) that when Pocahontas came to England he wrote for her a sort of letter of introduction to the Queen, or, in his own words, " a little booke to this effect to the Queen, an abstract whereof followeth."

" Some ten yeeres agoe, being in Virginia and taken prisoner by the power of Powhatan their chiefe King, . . . I cannot say I felt the least occasion of want that was in the power of those my mortall foes to prevent, notwithstanding al their threats. After some six weeks fatting amongst those Salvage Courtiers, at the minute of my execution, she hazarded the beating out of her owne braines to save mine, and not onely that, but so prevailed with her father that I was safely conducted to Jamestowne."

This letter rests on the authority of the " Generall Historie," and has neither more nor less weight than that work gives it. Smith's " abstract of the effect " of the little book was as liable to interpolations as the text of the " Generall Historie " elsewhere. At the time it was published, in 1624, not only had Pocahontas long been dead, but Queen Anne herself had in 1619 followed her to the grave, and Smith remained alone to vouch for his own accuracy. The Virginia Company had no interest in denying the truth of a story so well calculated to draw popular sympathy toward the colony.

Smith's character was always a matter of doubt. Thomas Fuller, one of Smith's contemporaries, published the " Worthies of England " some thirty years after Smith's death, when the civil wars had intervened to obliterate the recollection of personal jealousies, and when Smith must have been little remembered. Fuller devoted a page to Smith's history in the following vein : —

" From the Turks in Europe he passed to the Pagans in America, where, towards the latter end of the reign of Queen Elizabeth, such his perils, preservations, dangers, deliverances, they seem to most men above belief, to some beyond truth. Yet have we two witnesses to attest them, the prose and the pictures, both in his own book ; and it soundeth much to the diminution of his deeds that he alone is the herald to publish and proclaim them."

The essential evidence on each side of this curious question has now been exhausted, although it would be easy to argue indefinitely in regard to Smith's general character. This must be done by the first historian who attempts again to deal with the history of the Virginia Colony. The argument may be left for future and final judgment, but some reasonable theory is still required to explain the existence of the story assumed to be false. Deane, like Palfrey, hints that Smith in the latter part of his life fell into the hands of hack-writers, who adapted his story for popular effect. Perhaps the truth may be somewhat as follows.

The examination of Smith's works has shown that his final narrative was the result of gradual additions. The influence exercised by Pocahontas on the affairs of the colony, according to the account given in 1608, was slight. In 1612 she first appeared in her heroic character. Her capture and her marriage to Rolfe gave her importance. Her visit to England made her the most conspicuous figure in Virginia, and romantic incidents in her life were likely to be created, if they did not already exist, by the exercise of the popular imagination, attracted by a wild and vigorous picture of savage life.

The history of the emperor's daughter became, as Smith implied, a subject for the stage. Nothing was more natural or more probable. It is not even necessary to assume that Smith invented the additions to his own story. He may have merely accepted them after they had obtained a hold on the minds of his contemporaries.

In the mean while Smith's own career had failed, and his ventures ended disastrously, while in most cases he did not obtain the employment which he continued to seek with unrelaxed energy. In 1622 a disaster occurred in Virginia which roused the greatest interest and sympathy in England, and gave occasion for renewed efforts in behalf of the colony. The Indians rose against the English, and in the month of May a massacre took place around Jamestown. The opportunity was one not to be lost by a man who like Smith, while burning to act, was still smarting under what he considered undeserved neglect, and he hastened to offer his services to the Company, with a plan for restoring peace; but his plan and his offer of services were again declined. Still, the resource which he had frequently used remained, and by publishing the " Generall Historie " he made a more ambitious appeal to the public than any he had yet attempted. In this work he embodied everything that could tend to the increase of his own reputation, and drew material from every source that could illustrate the history of English colonization. Pocahontas was made to appear in it on every possible occasion, and his own share in the affairs of the colony was magnified at the expense of his companions. None of those whose reputations he treated with harshness appeared to vindicate their own characters, far less to assert their knowledge in regard to Pocahontas. The effort indeed failed of its object, for he remained unemployed and without mark of distinction.

" He led his old age in London, where his having a Prince's mind imprisoned in a poor man's purse rendered him to the contempt of such who were not ingenuous. Yet he efforted his spirits with the remembrance and relation of what formerly he had been and what he had done." So Fuller wrote, who might have known him in his later years. Smith died quietly in his bed, in London, in June, 1631. His will has been published by Deane, but furnishes little new information. In the absence of criticism, his book survived to become the standard authority on Virginian history. The readiness with which it was received is scarcely so remarkable as the credulity which has left it unquestioned almost to the present day.

HARVARD COLLEGE. 1786–1787.[1]

For the large and increasing class of instructors, or persons interested in the improvement of instruction in this country, few more entertaining and suggestive books could be written than a history of instruction at Harvard College, — an account, not of the numbers of students, or the gifts of donors, but of the processes tried, the experiments that failed, the discipline enforced, the customs observed, and, above all, the improvement in scholarship. One wishes to know with what standard the college started, and to what extent the standard has been raised or lowered. Since its foundation the college has greatly altered its character, and will continue to experiment with new methods and in new directions as rapidly as is safe. Its history is of no small importance to illustrate the growth of American society. Both as a social and as an educational question, the matter has interest.

Such a story to be well told should come directly from first sources, — and, with the exception of the college records, first sources are not easily reached.

[1] From the " North American Review " for January, 1872.

The college records have the disadvantage of telling a formal tale of boys' experiences and discipline, without entering into boys' feelings. One wishes to know what the student thought of himself, of his studies, and of his instructors ; what his studies and his habits were ; how much he knew and how thoroughly ; with what spirit he met his work, and what amount of active aid and sympathy he received from his instructors in his work or his amusements. The past left traditions of solid learning and careful training in the branches of study it assumed to deal with. One would like to know whether the present generation, in making what it calls its progress, has sacrificed anything once useful to its predecessors, aside from the further question whether such a sacrifice, if ever made, was a matter of necessity.

Unfortunately the means are wanting ; but this is not all. Attempts without number have been made to use college life as a groundwork for fiction, and the result has commonly been failure, for the reason that the field of interest is too narrow, and the attempt to enlarge it by introducing forced situations is more fatal to success than the narrowness of the field. The same difficulty would be found in a practical treatment of the subject. The details are numerous and fatiguing, the possible combinations few and simple. The treatment must make atonement for the want of incident; and such treatment could come only from a critic who could employ his labor to more effect in matters of wider and deeper interest. The student must remain content to have no history of education written from his stand-point.

Yet the family records of more than one household in New England contain papers that might be of service in following out this path of inquiry. One such manuscript record at least offers a curious and characteristic picture of the education given at Cambridge toward the close of the last century. The record is a student's diary for fifteen months in the years 1786-1787,[1] — years of great depression in America, immediately following the peace with Great Britain, but preceding the establishment of a responsible national government. The winter was famous for the outbreak and forcible repression of Shays's rebellion, which was the principal subject of interest in Massachusetts, and threatened for a time to affect the college. The student in question was a young man in his nineteenth year, who came late to the University, and joined the junior class March 15, 1786. He had a fair share of youthful crudities, but was as free from extreme prejudices as could be expected from a young man of his age, while his manner of looking at things occasionally betrayed a mind which had come into closer contact with grown and educated men than with people of his own age.

The student applied for admission to the junior class, in the third term of the junior year, when more than half the year's work was done. His

[1] The diary of John Quincy Adams.

examination showed the minimum required by the college after about three years of college education. The examination itself was a formal proceeding, and although the proportion of absolute rejections was small, yet admission was far from a matter of course. In this instance the applicant had a special examination, as he applied for admission at a time when no one else wished to enter.

March 15, 1786. Between 9 and 10 in the morning I went to the President's, and was there admitted before the President, the four tutors, three professors, and Librarian. The first book was Horace, where Mr. James, the Latin tutor, told me to turn to the Carmen sæculare, where I construed three stanzas and parsed the word *sylvarum*, but called *potens* a substantive. Mr. Jennison, the Greek tutor, then put me to the beginning of the fourth book of Homer. I construed —— lines, but parsed wrong ἀλλήλους. I had then παραβλήδεν given me. I was then asked a few questions in Watts's Logic by Mr. Hale, and a considerable number in Locke on the Understanding, very few of which I was able to answer. The next thing was geography, where Mr. Read asked me what was the figure of the earth, and several other questions, some of which I answered, and others not. Mr. Williams asked me if I had studied Euclid and arithmetic, after which the President conducted me to another room and gave me the following piece of English to turn into Latin, from the World: "There cannot certainly be an higher ridicule than to give an air of importance to amusements, if they are in themselves contemptible and void of taste; but if they are the object and care of the judicious and polite, and really deserve that distinction, the conduct of them is certainly of consequence." I made it thus : " Nihil profecto risu dignior quam magni æstimare delectamenta, si per se despicienda sunt atque sine sapore. At si res oblatæ atque cura sunt sagacibus et artibus excultis et revera hanc distinctionem merent, administratio eorum haud dubie utilitatis est." I take it from memory only, as no scholar is suffered to take a copy of the Latin he made at his examination. The President then took it, was gone about ¼ of an hour, returned and said, " You are admitted ; " and gave me a paper to carry to the steward.

The examination was not difficult, and the candidate, according to his own account, made no brilliant figure at it. Setting aside Watts and Locke, no longer so important a part of the liberal education as they formerly were, a candidate for the freshman class of to-day would think himself happy to escape with no more severe an examination than this. Yet this examination, so far as concerned the classics, represented not the minimum but the maximum of requirements, not for the junior year, but for the entire college course. Homer, Horace, Terence, and Cæsar were all that the student attempted to study. With the junior year, instruction in the classics ended. The following entry shows the condition of classical studies in the University : —

July 5, 1786. Mr. James gave us a piece of Latin to make, — the first the class have had since I have been here. This is the last week that we attend the Latin tutor, and last week we closed with Mr. Jennison (Greek).

In the senior year there are no languages studied in college. It is very popular here to dislike the study of Greek and Latin.

All that the student could do in college, in the direction of classical acquirements, was limited within a narrow margin represented by the examination described above. Another extract shows the student's opinion of his classical instruction.

May 10, 1786. We finished the Andria of Terence this morning. The class began it last February. I went through it at Haverhill in three evenings. However, it must be said that they study it only one week in four, and that week only four mornings; but even in that way it has taken thirteen lessons to go through this one play. We recite afternoons the Latin week in Cæsar, but I have had nothing to say this week. The class is so numerous that he (the tutor) cannot hear more than one half of them recite at once, and so he takes turns.

Students dropped the classics at Cambridge in the last century where they begin it in the present one. Homer and Horace, or Terence and a sentence in Latin composition, represented all the classical knowledge that Harvard gave; and beyond the simple construing of the text and the application of elementary rules of grammar, nothing was attempted.

In regard to mathematics, the same rule held. Euclid and arithmetic are no further advanced as mathematics than Homer and Horace as classics, if indeed they are so far; but mathematics were continued through the senior year, and apparently with comparative energy. Any other requirement, with the exception of logic and metaphysics, seems to have been unknown, unless geography were something more than the form which the single question repeated in the diary implies.

So far, then, as the standard of knowledge was concerned, it was low; and to judge from the account of the student, his success in satisfying even this low standard was not brilliant. Yet the best acquirements of the highest scholars in his class were no greater. Among the fifty graduates of his year, no one of sufficient superiority appeared to prevent him from carrying away an English oration at his Commencement, — a prize commonly given only to the best scholars.

The examination being over, the new student was fairly a member of the college. He did not appear at the college exercises until a week after his admission, when he went to the President.

March 22. Immediately after prayers I went to the President, who said, "You may live with Sir Ware, a Bachelor of Arts." I made a most respectful bow, and retired.

To persons who have forgotten this use of the title *Sir*, another extract may be of interest : —

July 19. *Commencement Day*. The new Sirs got quite high in the evening, at Derby's chamber, and made considerable of a noise.

Recitations then began. For one week the class recited in Euclid. The following week it recited in

Homer and the Greek Testament; the third week, in
Locke; the fourth, in Terence and Cæsar. This was
the round of studies; and when the four weeks were
passed, the process began again. The weeks were
classed as mathematical, metaphysical, Greek, and
Latin weeks, and no two of these subjects were ever
recited at the same time.

Six recitations in these branches occurred every
week. On Mondays and Wednesdays, both morning
and afternoon; on Tuesdays and Thursdays, only in
the morning. Friday was a leisure day for the whole
college, so far as regarded recitations. Saturdays
brought one early recitation in Doddridge's Divinity.
These were all the recitations. In addition frequent
lectures were given, both philosophical and doctrinal,
which the students of all classes attended; and literary exercises, as well as a regular exercise in decla-
mation, took place.

May 3, 1786. Wednesday and Monday are our two
busiest days in the week. This morning (Wednesday)
at 6 we went in to prayers, after which we immediately
recited (Homer). This took us till $7\frac{1}{4}$. At $7\frac{1}{2}$ we break-
fasted. At ten we had a lecture on Divinity from Mr.
Wigglesworth; it was upon the wisdom of all God's
actions, and justifying those parts of Scripture which
some have reproached as contrary to justice. At 11 we
had a philosophical lecture from Mr. Williams upon the
mechanical powers, and particularly the lever and the
pulley. At $12\frac{1}{2}$, dinner. At 3, an astronomical public
lecture upon the planet Mercury, a very circumstantial account of all its transits over the sun's disk. At 4 again

we recited (Greek Testament), and at 5 attended prayers
again, after which there are no more exercises for this
day, but we are obliged in the evening to prepare our
recitation for to-morrow morning. This I think is quite
sufficient employment for one day, but the three last days
in the week we have very little to do, — Thursdays and
Saturdays reciting only in the morning, and Fridays a
philosophical lecture.

A modern student would not think this work severe, for except the two recitations nothing required
preparation. Perhaps the most curious part of the
old arrangement was the subordinate place filled by
recitations, and it is certainly interesting to hear a
student in 1786, who had but seven recitations a
week, finding fault with the system: —

September 4, 1786. As we have no metaphysical tutor
here at present, we supposed that for the ensuing fortnight we should have no reciting. But the government
have determined that we shall continue to attend Mr.
Read. This is not an agreeable circumstance. A person
who does not belong to the University and hears only
the word " reciting," naturally concludes that the scholars are an idle set of fellows, because they are always
averse to recitations. Now the fact is just the contrary.
A person fond of study regards the time spent in reciting as absolutely lost. He has studied the book before
he recites ; and the tutors here are so averse to giving
ideas different from those of the author whom they are
supposed to explain, that they always speak in his own
words and never pretend to add anything of their own.
Reciting is indeed of some service to idle fellows, because it brings the matter immediately before them and

obliges them at least for a short time to attend to something. But a hard student will always dislike it, because it takes time from him which he supposes might have been employed to greater advantage.

A change in the recitations occurred in the senior year. Greek and Latin were dropped, and during the first quarter the seniors recited in mathematics alone, because the tutor in metaphysics had resigned, and his place had not been filled. Only on the 3d of October did the new tutor make his appearance and begin upon Burlamaqui's Natural Law, after which the two studies alternated during the rest of the year. The lectures were continued, and a new course, "very dry," was added, upon language. The principal professor did not satisfy the more zealous students : —

April 5, 1787. At 11 this forenoon Mr. Williams gave us the second philosophical lecture. It was upon the incidental properties of matter, and excepting very few deviations, was expressed in the same terms with that we had last year upon the same subject. Indeed, whether the professor's time is taken up by other studies, or whether he is too indolent to make any improvements in his lectures, it is said he gives every year the same course, without adding or erasing a line.

April 7. Mr. Williams gave us this forenoon a lecture upon motion, the same which we heard a twelvemonth past upon that subject.

Except for reading Burlamaqui and writing a large number of literary disquisitions, of a stereotyped and academic class, for college societies and public occasions, the best students had little employment. After the winter vacation, ending in the middle of February, afternoon recitations were dropped in the senior year, and the class had but five recitations a week for nine weeks, when recitations ceased.

This analysis of the college studies leads to the conclusion, enforced by every word of the diary, that for the ordinary enjoyments of University life, the last century was the golden age of the college. The most modest capacity could maintain itself upon such a level. This impression prevailed among the students, for the writer of the diary, speaking of a classmate in his twenty-fifth year, said : —

" He was, as he says himself, too old when he entered the University. From fourteen to eighteen I should suppose the best age for entering. The studies which are pursued here are just calculated for the tender minds of youth."

One cannot detect a sign of coercion on the part of the college government. An examination of any kind was strange to the college career. Rank was apparently unknown, except so far as it was vaguely intimated in the assignment of parts at exhibitions. These parts, if President Willard was to be believed, were the only incentive to study : —

April 11, 1787. I went down this morning to the President to know the determination of the corporation with respect to a private Commencement, and was told that the petition of the class was rejected, because they supposed that if public Commencements were lain aside, there would be no stimulus to study among the scholars, and they are afraid that by granting our petition they might establish a precedent which the following classes would take advantage of, and claim as a right what we only request as a favor. Another reason which Mr. Willard said had weight, although the gentlemen did not choose to avow it publicly, was the fear of offending the future Governor by depriving him of that opportunity to show himself in splendor and magnificence.

Another extract indicated patriarchal simplicity. On the student's first day in college, —

March 23, 1786. I did not hear the bell ring this morning, and was tardy at prayers. Every time a student is tardy at prayers he is punished a penny, and there is no eluding that law ; so that a student must prefer not attending prayers at all to being half a minute too late.

The instructors trusted only their general impressions in awarding distinctions. Misdemeanors, absences, and other shortcomings were punished by fines. The recitations were ordinary school-lessons :

June 13, 1786. This reciting in Locke is the most ridiculous of all. When the tutor inquires what is contained in such a section, many of the scholars repeat the two first lines in it, which are very frequently nothing to the purpose, and leave the rest for the tutor to explain, which he commonly does by saying over again the words of the author.

In regard to vacations and permissions of absence, the college law was not rigorous. In April the stu-

dents had two weeks holiday by law, but in practice
at least three. The summer vacation began July
13, and closed by law August 16, lasting five weeks,
but recitations were only resumed on the 21st. Two
weeks more were given in October, with the same
liberal margin. In the middle of December, 1786,
the supply of fire-wood fell short, and as none could
be obtained from the country, the students were sent
home and enjoyed a vacation of eight weeks, till February 7. Recitations began on the 12th. On the
23d " about half the class " had arrived. Thus in
the course of the year the college had seventeen weeks
of vacation, and twenty-one weeks of freedom from
required exercises. Add to this a liberal interpretation of the rule of attendance, and an equally liberal practice in regard to leaves of absence, and the
working terms of the college were by no means un-
reasonably long or severe. When the exercises were
most regular, many interruptions occurred, and the
amount of work accomplished, from a modern point
of view, was small.

A few extracts will illustrate the college practice :

April 26, 1786.   Put my name in at the buttery.
At the end of each vacation every scholar must go in
person and give his name to the butler. Any scholar
who stays away after the expiration of the vacancy,
unless he gives good reasons for it, forfeits 1*s.* 6*d.*
every night.

April 27.   No reciting this day, nor indeed this week.
The scholars that live near Cambridge commonly come

and enter their names in the buttery, and then go home again and stay the remainder of the week.

April 28. About half the college are now here. The bill at prayers is not kept till the Friday after the vacation ends.

May 1. We recite this week, etc.

August 17. The scholars are coming in very fast.

August 19. Almost all the college have got here now, and the new monitors, who must always belong to the junior class, took their seats yesterday.

August 21. We recite this week, etc.

December 12. The government this morning determined that if more than half the students should be destitute of wood, the college should be dismissed. The President went to Boston to consult the corporation upon the subject, and he informed Little this evening that the students would be permitted to disperse to-morrow morning.

December 13. This morning, immediately after prayers, the President informed us that the vacation would begin at present, and be for eight weeks, and hinted that the spring vacation might on that account be omitted.

The spring vacation was not in the least shortened by the hint.

With these eight weeks the student had a right to do what he pleased; yet since the exertions which were evidently not made in term-time may have fallen on the vacation, the inquiry how the most distinguished students of the oldest standing occupied their two months of winter vacation is not impertinent. The writer of the diary remained in college rooms to devote his time to his work, with less interruption than was otherwise possible.

"As I thought I should be able to study much more conveniently here than anywhere else, I obtained leave to remain in town. Bridge proposes staying likewise, and we shall live together. Bridge engaged for us both to board at Professor Wigglesworth's."

Other young men remained, no doubt for the same purpose, since their names occurred afterward on the list of parts at Commencement, attached to English orations and other honors. They were not without other society : —

December 18, 1786.   The young ladies at Mr. Wigglesworth's dined at Judge Dana's. I went down there with Bridge to tea, and passed the evening very sociably. The conversation turned upon divers topics, and among the rest upon love, which is almost always the case when there are ladies present.

Love was not mentioned as one of the college studies ; but if it was always discussed when ladies were present, these young gentlemen during this vacation devoted more attention to it than they had paid to Locke or Euclid.

The next day a slight improvement in tone was apparent : —

December 19.   Several of the class still remain, and until they are gone it will be impossible for us to study much. As they expect to go every day, they are rather dissipated, and more or less make us so.

December 20.   I have been rather more attentive today, and have written considerably.

After this spark of energy came a relapse. Descriptions of young ladies recurred with frequency, while, except for a single reference to Montesquieu, no evidence of absorbing mental application was recorded : —

December 22. Miss ——— is but eighteen, rather giddy and inexperienced. She has a very fair complexion and good eyes, of which she is sensible. Her face is rather capricious than beautiful, and some of her features are not handsome. Of this she is not so well apprised. Her shape is not inelegant, but her limbs are rather large. She is susceptible of the tender sentiments, but the passion rather than the lover is the object of her affection.

December 26. Mason finally took his leave and left us to ourselves, so that we shall henceforth be able to study with much less interruption than we have hitherto done.

December 27. In the evening we went down with Mr. Ware and Freeman to Judge Dana's. We conversed and played whist and sung till 10 o'clock. The ladies seem to have settled that we are to be in love ; but ideas of this kind are very common with the ladies, who think it impossible to live without love.

January 17, 1787. After tea we went down to Mr. Dana's. Miss E. was there, and Miss J. with her. Bridge accompanied this lady home, and after they were gone I had a deal of chat with Miss E., who has a larger share of sense than commonly falls to an individual of her sex. We conversed upon diverse subjects, but I can never give anything but general accounts of conversations, for I cannot always keep this book under lock and key, and some people have a vast deal of curiosity.

January 22. Almy has a larger share of sense than commonly falls to the lot of her sex, and that sense is cultivated and improved, — a circumstance still more uncommon.

March 2. I went to take tea at Mr. Pearson's. I got seated between Miss E. and Miss H., but could not enjoy the pleasures of conversation, because the music was introduced. Music is a great enemy to sociability, and however agreeable it may be sometimes, there are occasions when I should wish it might be dispensed with.

By that time the vacation had expired, and the student returned to the labors of five recitations a week. Besides the " Spirit of Laws," he had read, so far as can be gathered from his diary, Watson's " Chemical Essays," Sheridan's " Lectures on Elocution," a volume of the " Idler," and some algebra, in two months. He had also developed an uncommonly strong fancy for the study of female character, — a study not embraced in the official college curriculum, either then or afterward.

The 7th of February began the new term. On the 12th recitations began, one every day, except Friday. On the 15th a ball was given, at which Miss E. headed the list of ladies. The young gentlemen, among whom were most of the first scholars, retired to bed " at about four o'clock," and " rose just before the commons bell rang for dinner, quite refreshed, and not more fatigued than I commonly am." The dances became nearly as frequent as the recitations. On the 23d, " about one half the class are here." On the 27th, " almost all our class have arrived." Among other lectures, March 5 " Professor Pearson gave a lecture with which he concluded his observations upon the article. I did not hear many of them ;" but the same evening there was a meeting of the *Φ B K* at Cranch's chamber, at which a dissertation was read, of which the text is preserved, on the erudite question, " Whether love or fortune ought to be the chief inducement to marriage." This essay was done with much reflection and knowledge of the human heart, but was not a college exercise. March 7 he went to Haverhill, and returned on the 10th. On the 12th the parts were distributed for the next exhibition, and he received an English " Conference," with Freeman and Little, upon the Comparative Utility of Law, Physic, and Divinity.

March 14, 1787. Was employed almost all day in thinking upon the subject of my Conference. Wrote a few lines with much difficulty. Did not like the subject. Wished the Conference to the Devil.

Little and Freeman were of the same mind. After a week's labor the Conference was written, and the next week was devoted to the voluntary work of calculating the elements for a solar eclipse for May 15, 1836. This was also for an exhibition.

March 30. I have been somewhat idle for several days, and expect to continue so till the exhibition is over, for so long as that is before me I can pay very little at-

tention to anything else. I found this to be the case last
fall, and do now still more so; but thank fortune I have
only one more trial, at the worst, of this kind to go
through, which will be at Commencement, unless we
should obtain a private one. Distinctions of this kind
are not, I think, very desirable; for besides the trouble
and anxiety which they unavoidably create, they seldom
fail of raising the envy of other students. I have often-
times witnessed this with respect to others, and I am
much deceived if I have not lately perceived it with respect
to myself.

April 9. This is the last week on which our class
attend recitations.

If such were the duties of the most distinguished
scholars, those students who were not remarkable for
scholarship could not have been overworked; but on
that point no certain information was given, beyond allusions to gunning, fishing, and an occasional
" high-go."

Meanwhile a difficulty occurred.

August 26, 1786. Immediately after prayers we had
a class-meeting for the purpose of choosing a Valedictory
Orator and Collectors of Theses. When the votes were
collected it was found that there was no choice. A second attempt was made, equally fruitless. It was then
resolved that the choice of an Orator should be deferred,
and that the class should proceed to that of the choice of
Collectors. The one for Technology, Grammar, and Rhetoric was first balloted. Abbot 2d was chosen. The second Collector, for Logic, Metaphysics, Ethics, Theology,
and Politics, was then chosen. Fiske was the person.
The Mathematical part fell to Adams, and the Physical to

Johnstone. The meeting at about seven o'clock was adjourned till Monday evening, when we shall proceed to the choice of an Orator.

August 28. After prayers the class met by adjournment. The second ballot was between Freeman, Little, and Waldo. The third was between Freeman and Little, who finally carried it by a considerable majority. The class then all went to his chamber, but did not stay there more than an hour.

August 31. We had a class-meeting immediately after prayers. The committee of the class that was appointed to inform the President of the choice for an Orator, etc., reported that the President had not given his consent to have the Oration in English, because he thought it would show a neglect of classical learning. I motioned that the vote for having it in English should be reconsidered, but there was a considerable majority against it. It was then voted that the President should be informed that the class had determined to have an English Oration or none at all. The former committee all declined going again. Johnstone, Fiske, and Welch were chosen, but declined. It was much like Æsop's fable of the mice, who determined to have a bell tied round the cat's neck ; they were all desirous that it should be done, but no one was willing to undertake the performance of it. The meeting was finally adjourned till Monday next.

September 12. We had a class-meeting after prayers for determining the matter concerning a Valedictory Oration. By dint of obstinate impudence, vociferation, and noise, the minority so wearied out those on the other side that several of them went out; after which a vote was passed ratifying the proceedings of the last meeting.

Johnson, Sever, and Chandler 3d were then chosen as a committee to inform the President of the proceedings in the class.

September 18. We had a class-meeting after breakfast. The committee that was sent to inform the President of the proceedings of the class, informed that he had said he feared he should be obliged to direct the class to have the Oration in Latin. Notwithstanding this, it was voted by a majority of two that the class should still persist.

The President carried his point so far that there was no Class Day. In consequence of this, the members of the class began to leave Cambridge before the 21st of June, the usual day for separation. The parts for Commencement were distributed May 17.

May 24, 1787. Our class having no college exercises to attend to, and many of them having now finished their parts for Commencement, are generally very indolent. Riding and playing and eating and drinking employ the chief part of their time.

Long before Class Day the graduating students were scattered in every direction, only to return on the 18th of July to Commencement. Thus, as the result of the half-year since the 13th of December, the students who were to take their degrees had attended recitations at the rate of five per week, for nine weeks, and had further prepared exercises for one exhibition and Commencement. They had listened to one course of lectures, which they had for the most part already heard, and another on " the parts of speech," which the best of them thought a waste of time. They dispersed in May, without conception that there could be such a thing in the student world as an examination for degrees.

One or two more extracts, to illustrate the stringency of rules during term-time, must be admitted : —

May 4, 1786.   No reciting this morning on account of last night's class-meeting.   This is a privilege that all the classes enjoy, and I am told there have been in our class fellows so lazy and so foolish as to call a class-meeting merely for that purpose.

Naturally, class-meetings were frequent.

April 10, 1786.   No reciting this day because the government met to examine the reasons of those scholars that are absent, or have been within the last two quarters.

September 22.   Mr. Read sent for me this morning ; informed me that the exhibition was to come on next Thursday, and offered to excuse me from recitations till then, in case I was not prepared, as the time that had been given for getting ready was so short.   But, as it happened, I was not in need of more time.

October 9.   No reciting.   Mr. Burr is engaged to preach several Sundays at Hingham, and does not return early enough for the next morning recitation.

The rules were not more rigidly applied in regard to required exercises than in other respects, and neither instructors nor students considered themselves to be under any inflexible law.

Students who lived under so mild a government should have had no just cause of complaint, unless

that the means of the college did not satisfy the requirements of a liberal education. They might urge
that Euclid and Burlamaqui were dry nutriment to
satisfy the hunger of a whole year, but they could
scarcely maintain that a stepmother's hand, when
they cried for bread, threw them husks. Under a
system so nearly voluntary, a thorough accord should
have existed between the instructors and their best
scholars.

The President, Joseph Willard, was a graduate of
the year 1765, still a comparatively young man.
Many instructive hints as to his character were scattered through this diary : —

" It is against the laws of the college to call any undergraduate by any but his sir-name, and I am told the
President, who is remarkably strict on all those matters,
reproved a gentleman at his table for calling a student
Mr. while he was present."

Again : —

March 24, 1786.   After prayers I declaimed, as it is
termed ; two students every evening speak from memory
any piece they choose, if it be approved by the President.
It was this evening my turn, and I spoke from " As you
like it," — " All the world's a stage," etc.   When I came
to the description of the Justice, in fair, round belly, with
good capon lined, tutors and scholars all laughed, as I
myself truly represented the character.   But the President did not move a feature of his face.   And indeed I
believe it is no small matter that shall extort a smile from
him when he is before the college.

September 10, 1786.   Cranch and myself dined at the

President's. He is stiff and formal, attached to every custom and trifling form, as much as to what is of consequence. However, he was quite sociable; much more so, indeed, than I should have expected.

A portrait of the President in the pulpit was included : —

February 18, 1787. The President preached in the afternoon, when we were improved by a very laborious encomium upon Moses. Whatever the President's literary talents may be, he is certainly not an elegant composuist nor a graceful orator.

June 21, 1786. *Class Day.* This day the seniors leave college. There is no recitation in the morning, and prayers are deferred till 10 o'clock. The class then went down in procession two by two with the Poet at their head, and escorted the President to the chapel. The President made a very long prayer, in which, in addition to what he commonly says, he prayed a great deal for the seniors ; but I think he ought to get his occasional prayers by heart before he delivers them. He bungled always when he endeavored to go out of the beaten track, and he has no talent at extempore composition.

April 6, 1786. *Fast Day.* The President preached two sermons ; that in the afternoon especially I thought excellent, — no flowers of rhetoric, no eloquence, but plain common-sense, and upon a liberal plan. But the President has by no means a pleasing delivery. He appears to labor and struggle very much, and sometimes strains very hard, and making faces, which do not render his harsh countenance more agreeable.

The description indicated no ill-feeling toward the President; but a man cast in such a mould was not likely to throw life or novelty into the system over which he presided. He was an excellent representative of the old New England school, but he had little immediate connection with the undergraduates. The burden of labor fell on the four tutors, although the tutors were not obliged to perform so much work as would alarm the most lightly burdened tutor of the present day. Six or seven hours a week in the recitation-room, and the simplest instruction in the letter of the text-book represented the full extent of their duties, beyond the charge of the college discipline. A considerable opportunity for usefulness was open to the four tutors, and at least one or two of them might be supposed to impress the students with sympathetic activity. The relations between students and tutors were the subject of frequent comments in the diary : —

May 1, 1786. The Greek tutor is a young man ; indeed much too young (A. B. of 1782), as are all the tutors, for the place he occupies. Before he took his second degree, which was last Commencement, he was chosen a tutor of mathematics, in which he betrayed his ignorance often. Last fall he changed departments, and took up the Greek. His own class, the freshmen, were the first that laughed at him in that. He has improved since that, but still makes frequent mistakes. It is certainly wrong that the tutors should so often be changed, and be so young as they are. It would be better to choose a person immediately after he has taken his degree, than as they do ; because when a youth leaves college he is obliged to turn his attention to other studies, and forgets a great deal of what he studied at college, whereas when he has lately graduated he has all fresh in his mind. The Doctor affects a great deal of popularity in his class, and with the help of the late disagreement between the classes, he has pretty well succeeded; but he does not seem to care what the other classes think of him.

May 2. Our tutor gave us this morning a most extraordinary construction of a passage in Homer. Abbot 1st was beginning to construe the 181st line of the 6th book.

Πρόσθε λέων, ὄπιθεν δὲ δράκων, μέσση δὲ χίμαιρα,

he said, — "a lion before;" but the Doctor corrected him by saying it meant "superior to a lion." Abbot immediately took the hint and made it, "superior to a lion, inferior to a dragon, and equal to a wild boar."

An account of the metaphysical tutor was still less flattering: —

May 15, 1786. We recite this week to Mr. Hale in Locke. This is, upon the whole, the most unpopular tutor in college. He is hated even by his own class. He is reputed to be very ill-natured and severe in his punishments. He proposes leaving college at Commencement, and I believe there is not an individual among the students who is not very well pleased with it. One of my classmates said the other day, "I do not believe it yet; it is too good news to be true." Such are the sentiments of all the students with respect to him.

The writer felt no regard for the mathematical tutor: —

May 22, 1786.   We recite this week to our own tutor, in Gravesande's Experimental Philosophy.   This gentleman is not much more popular than the rest of the tutors. He is said to be very prejudiced and very vindictive.   He is liked in general by the class, however, and this may be a reason why I have not heard as much said against him as against the others.

He closed the list with a blast of indignation against the Latin tutor : —

May 8.   We recite this week in Terence and Cæsar to Mr. James.   This is the tutor of the oldest standing in the college ; he is very well acquainted with the branch he has undertaken, and persons that are not students say that he is much of a gentleman.   But it seems almost to be a maxim among the governors of the college to treat the students pretty much like brute beasts.   There is an important air and a haughty look that every person belonging to the government (Mr. [Professor] Williams excepted) assumes, which indeed it is hard for me to submit to.   But it may be of use to me, as it mortifies my vanity ; and if anything in the world can teach me humility, it will be to see myself subjected to the commands of a person that I must despise.   Mr. James is also accused of having many partialities and carrying them to very great length ; and moreover that those partialities do not arise from any superior talents or virtues in the students, but from closer and more interested motives. There are some in our class with whom he has been particularly severe, and some he has shown more favor than any tutor ought to show to a student.   I wish not his favor, as he may prize it too high ; and I fear not his severity, which he can never display if I do my duty.

The " interested motives " were more than a figure
of speech : —

May 3, 1786. We had after prayers a class-meeting
about making a present to our tutor. It is customary at
the end of the freshman year to make a present to the
tutor of the class ; but it has been delayed by ours to the
present time, and many would still delay it and lay it
wholly aside. The custom, I think, is a bad one, because
it creates partialities in a tutor, because it increases the
distinction between the wealthy and the poor scholars,
because it makes the tutor in some measure dependent
upon his class, and because to many that subscribe it is a
considerable expense ; but the salaries of the tutors being
so low, and it having been for many years an universal
custom, I am sorry to see our class so behindhand, and
several who could well afford it and have really subscribed meanly endeavoring to put off the matter from
quarter to quarter till they leave college.

A year later the writer became aware that the
question had two sides. Speaking of one of his
classmates, he said : —

" His spirit he discovers by relating how many times
he has insulted the President and the tutors, particularly
Mr. Read (the class tutor). He damns Mr. Read for being partial towards those who have always treated him
with respect, and against those who have always made it
a practice to insult him."

The relations between instructors and scholars were
far from satisfactory. Thoroughly cordial these relations never could be so long as college discipline remained in the hands of the instructors. The duty of

giving instruction, and the duty of judging offences
and inflicting punishment, could never be intrusted to
the same hands without injury to the usefulness of
the instructor. This evil was conspicuous in the last
century. Gentle as the rein was, and mild as were
the punishments, hostility between students and instructors was a traditional custom of the college,
and the one which created most annoyance to both
divisions of the University, — the teachers as well as
the taught. The system was wrong. While perhaps
more liberal in its forms than any that succeeded it,
the assumption of social superiority galled every one
subjected to it. The assumption created opposition,
and the records of the college showed persistent attempts, on the part of the students, to break down the
social barrier. Generation after generation followed
the same course. Rebellion after rebellion broke out
among the undergraduates. Only in proportion as
the college government began to act upon the principle that the student was the social equal of the
instructor, entitled to every courtesy due to equals,
did these disorders begin gradually to subside. Even
then the question of discipline remained a source of
incessant uneasiness, and the instructor known as a
strict disciplinarian, who attempted to combine his
duties as police-officer, judge, jury, and executioner
with his duties of instruction, sacrificed no inconsid-
erable share of his usefulness as instructor.

That the spirit of insubordination so persistently
exhibited was not due to distinctions of age, or hos-

tility to the instructing body as such, was proved by conflicts with others than the instructors. Another series of extracts illustrated this point : —

August 21, 1786. This afternoon, after prayers, the customs were read to the freshmen in the chapel. They are read three Mondays running in the beginning of every year, by the three first in the sophimore class, who are ordered to see them put in execution.

March 27, 1786. After prayers the senior class had a class-meeting, in order to check the freshmen, who, they suppose, have taken of late too great liberties. By the laws of the college all freshmen are obliged to walk in the yard with their heads uncovered, unless in stormy weather, and to go on any errand that any other scholar chooses to send them, at a mile distance. But the present freshmen have been indulged very much with respect to those laws, and it is said they have presumed further than they ought to have done.

March 28, 1786. After prayers, Bancroft, one of the sophimore class, read the customs to the freshmen, one of whom (McNeal) stood with his hat on all the time. He with three others were immediately *hoisted* (as the term is) before a tutor, and punished. There was immediately after a class-meeting of the freshmen, who, it is said, determined they would hoist any scholar of the other classes who should be seen with his hat on in the yard, when any of the government are there.

June 14, 1786. The freshmen, by their high spirit of liberty, have again involved themselves in difficulties. The sophimores consider themselves as insulted by them, and in a class-meeting, last evening, determined to oblige all the freshmen to take off their hats in the yard, and to

send them.   There has been a great deal of business between them to-day.   Mr. Hale has had several of them
before him.

June 15, 1786.   The struggle between the freshmen
and sophimores still continues.   They have been mutually
hoisting one another all day.

July 12, 1786.   The freshmen carry their enmity
against the sophimores a great deal too far.   They injure themselves both in the eyes of the other class and
in those of the government.   This afternoon, while Cabot
was declaiming, they kept up a continual groaning and
shuffling and hissing, as almost prevented him from
going through.

The freshmen ultimately carried their point, and
established their right to social equality ; but they
were obliged to struggle both against the college
system and against their immediate masters.   Their
disorders were but a repetition, against a different
authority, of still greater disorders on the part of
older classes, in the attempt to establish social rights
against college government.

The habits and manners of the time were not
rigorously correct : —

March 22, 1786.   As we passed by Milton Hall, we
saw the ruins of the windows.   On the 21st of March
the junior sophister class cease reciting at 11 in the
forenoon.   They generally in the evening have a frolic.
Yesterday they had it at Milton Hall, and as they are not
by any means at such time remarkable for their discretion, we saw many fractures in the windows of the hall
they were in.

March 15, 1786. The sophimore class had what is called in college a high-go. They assembled all together in the chamber of one of the class, where some of them got drunk, then sallied out and broke a number of windows for three of the tutors, and after this sublime manœuvre staggered to their chambers. Such are the great achievements of many of the sons of Harvard! Such the delights of many of the students here!

The manners indicated by these extracts were certainly free; but such offences were not considered heinous by the college government or by public opinion. The severity of discipline in the college was by no means such as to explain the ill-will between the students and the government. Although students considered such discipline annoying at the time, they learned afterward to accept, without a murmur, punishments which in the last century would have been thought monstrous; and this submission was due to the subsidence of the old antipathy to college government. In 1786 punishments, so far from being severe, were remarkably light, notwithstanding loud complaints against them.

As mentioned above, certain members of the college, on the night of March 15, 1786, indulged themselves in a drunken disturbance in the college grounds: —

March 23, 1786. After prayers the President read a paper to this effect: That on the evening of the 15th it appeared the sophimores had assembled at the chambers of one of the class and had behaved in a tumultuous, noisy

manner ; that at length they sallied out and were very
riotous, to the disturbance and *dishonor* of the University.
But as their conduct till then had been such as deserved
approbation, and was submissive, and as they early shew
a proper repentance for their fault, having presented an
humble petition to be forgiven, — therefore it had been
voted that no further notice should be taken of it ; but it
was hoped the students would not abuse the lenity of the
government, but rather show that they were deserving
of it. The freshmen, who are always as a class at variance with the sophimores, thought the government had
been partial ; and the consequence was that Mr. ———— ,
the tutor of the sophimore class, and who was supposed
to have favored them, and to have been the means of
saving them from severe punishment, had four squares
of glass broken in his windows. Such was the effect of
the lenity which was to induce the students to do their
duty.

A more curious case was the following : —

May 23, 1786. This morning a number of the seniors
were sent for by the President to go to his house at
8 o'clock. They went, and the parts were distributed
thus : Thompson, English Oration, A. M. ; Champlin,
Latin Oration, A. M. ; Fowle and Gardner 2d, each a
Poem ; Blake, English, and Andrews 1st, Latin Orations,
P. M. ; Harris, Dwight, Hubbard, and Parker, a Conference ; Bigelow and Crosby, Lowell and Taylor, Loring
and Sullivan, Forensics ; Lincoln and Warland, a Greek
Dialogue ; Bradford, Norton, Simpkins, and Wyeth, re-
spondents in Syllogistics, and all the rest opponents to
the same. These Syllogistics are very much despised by
the scholars, and no attention seems to be paid to them

by the company at Commencement. The scholars in general think that the government in giving them those parts write on their foreheads DUNCE in capital letters. Notwithstanding this, some of the most learned men in the country had Syllogistics when they graduated here. The good parts, as they are called, are more numerous this year than they have ever been. Before this there has been only one English and one Latin Oration, and no Poems. It is a doubt whether they intend to establish this as a precedent, or whether it is only a distinguished favor to the present class, who pretend to be the best class for learning and genius that ever graduated here. It is said that the parts have been exceedingly well distributed, and all the college are pleased. However that may be, the Syllogists all got together this evening and drank till not one of them could stand straight, or was sensible of what he did. A little after 9 they sallied out, and for a quarter of an hour made such a noise as might be heard at a mile distant. The tutors went out, and after a short time persuaded them to disperse. Mr. ——— had two squares of his windows broke.

May 24. It is feared that some bad consequences will ensue from the high-go of the Syllogists last evening. Borland, it seems, was the most active of them all; he collared Mr. ——— and threw a handful of gravel in his face, and was rather disrespectful to Mr. ———. He went this morning to the former to make an apology for his conduct, but was told it could not be received, as the matter was already laid before the government. Thus those fellows play the tyrants here; they have no regard, no allowances, for youth and circumstances. They go out when they are almost certain of being insulted, and then bring the scholar for a crime of which he knew nothing under public censure. They cannot with any face say that a scholar ought to be so severely punished for depriving himself of his senses. For there are here in college persons who have seen ——— as much intoxicated as Borland was yesterday and behaving quite as ill. But compassion is too great a virtue ever to be admitted into the breast of a tutor here. It is supposed, however, that Borland's punishment will not be very severe, because it requires a unanimous vote among the governors of the college to punish a student, and they are said to be at such variance one with the other that they can very seldom all agree.

May 25. Government met and were assembled almost all this day to determine what punishment to inflict upon Borland. He was informed of it in the evening, and the class petitioned that it might be mitigated, but probably without much success.

May 26. This morning after prayers Borland was called out to read an humble confession, signifying his repentance of his conduct, etc. The President read the votes of the government ; the affair was stated, and it was said that Borland had insulted, in a flagrant manner, two of the governors of the University. Whereupon it was voted, that he read a confession ; and secondly, that he be degraded to the bottom of his class, and that he take his place there accordingly. The other scholars were warned by this example not to run into such excesses, and to behave respectfully. I wanted, I think, neither of these warnings, but the event has warned me to alter my opinion concerning ———. I thought him the best of the tutors, but now I do not think he is a jot better than the rest.

Six weeks afterward Borland was restored to his regular place in class.

No student of a later day would have dreamed of calling such a penalty severe. Any undergraduate of the nineteenth century who indulged in the agreeable but dangerous amusement of collaring an unpopular tutor and rubbing gravel in his face, would have accepted the extremest penalty of the law without a murmur, recognizing the fundamental principle of society, that no man can violate the law and enjoy it at the same time; while the notion that drunkenness is anything but an aggravation of the offence hardly commends itself to modern New England.

Such difficulties were common under this *régime;* occasionally they were due really to the instructors. The following may have been such a case: —

May 31, 1786. *Election Day.* There is a custom among the scholars here which some of the classes follow and others do not. It is choosing a governor and lieutenant-governor for the class. They commonly take some rich fellow who can treat the class now and then. The seniors this morning chose Champlin governor, and Lowell lieutenant-governor. The lieutenant-governor treated immediately, and they chose their other officers. At Commons they all went into the hall in procession. Thomas, who was appointed sheriff, marched at their head, with a paper cockade in his hat, and brandishing a cane in his hand instead of a sword. He conducted the governor and lieutenant-governor to their seats, made his bow, and retired to the other table, for which

Jackey Hale punished him four shillings. However, he performed his part so well that the spectators were much pleased, and clapped their hands. Hale happened to see Baron, the junior, clapping, and sent orders for him to go to him after Commons. Baron, not happening to go before 2 o'clock, was punished five shillings for impudence, and four for disobedience. That is the way these modest tutors tyrannize over us. As there was a little noise in the hall, Hale struck the handle of his knife three times on the table to still it, but instead of that almost every knife in the hall was struck on the table three times. At last the tutors rose, and as they were going out about half-a-dozen fellows hissed them. They were enraged, turned round and looked as if they would devour us ; but they did not discover one person, which made them look silly enough. When they turned their backs again, there was nothing but hissing and groaning and clapping hands and stamping heard in the hall, till they got into the yard, where a few potatoes were sent out to meet them.

A difficulty of such a kind would probably in later times have been avoided by good-nature and forbearance on the part of the tutor ; but the student of 1786 cared little whether he was in the right or the wrong. The true grievance lay in the position of semi-hostility to the students taken by the college officers, who refused to acknowledge them as entitled to active assistance and sympathy. The manner, not the act, of discipline was the cause of the evil. Hence the mildest punishments were made a cause of as much complaint as arbitrary vexations.

March 14, 1787. The junior class being displeased with the distribution of parts for exhibition, so far as respected their class, assembled this evening at Prescott's chamber and made a great deal of noise.

March 17. The government met this forenoon to make inquiries concerning the noise at Prescott's and at Wier's chamber.

March 19. This morning the juniors Prescott and Wier were publicly admonished for having had riotous noises at their chambers last week. The sentence is considered all over college as uncommonly severe, and by many as wholly unmerited, at least on the part of Prescott.

March 22. In consequence of the late severity of the college governors there has been, yesterday and this day, a subscription paper handed about among all the classes to promote a meeting of the whole college to-morrow evening in the chapel, every person having a pipe, a glass, and a bottle of wine, and there to convince the government that the students are possessed of " a noble spirit, — a spirit which shall nip the bud of tyrannical oppression." They will get as drunk as beasts, and probably break every tutor's windows in college. This absurd and ridiculous plan has found so many votaries that a large majority of every class, except ours, have already subscribed; but I am happy that in our class there are but few who have joined the association, and as it is to take place only upon condition that there be a majority of every class, the plan will most probably fail.

At the risk of serious injury to the dignity of history, already compromised by this sketch, the extreme leniency of the government in the punishment inflicted in this case shall be shown by a final extract from the diary so often quoted. Some verses, not absolutely contemptible, represented the impression made by the different members of the government on the students more exactly than the regular entries of a prosaic diary could do. The verses were entitled

LINES UPON THE LATE PROCEEDINGS OF THE COLLEGE GOVERNMENT.

BY A STUDENT.

The government of college met,
And Willard ruled the stern debate.
The witty Jennison declared
That he had been completely scared.
" Last night," says he, " when I came home,
I heard a noise in Prescott's room.
I went and listened at the door,
As I have often done before.
I found the juniors in a high rant;
They called the President a tyrant;
They said as how I was a fool,
A long-eared ass, a sottish mule,
Without the smallest grain of spunk;
So I concluded they were drunk.
From Xenophon whole pages torn
As trophies in their hats were worn.
Thus all their learning they had spread
Upon the outside of the head;
For I can swear without a sin
There 's not a line of Greek within.
At length I knocked, and Prescott came;
I told him 't was a burning shame

That he should give his classmates wine,
And he should pay a heavy fine.
Meanwhile the rest grew so outrageous
That, though I boast of being courageous,
I could not help being in a fright,
For one of them put out the light,
And 't was, as you may well suppose,
So dark I could not see my nose.
I thought it best to run away,
And wait for vengeance till to-day;
For he 's a fool at any rate
Who 'll fight when he can rusticate.
When they found out that I was gone,
They ran through college up and down,
And I could hear them very plain
Take the Lord's holy name in vain.
To Wier's chamber they repaired,
And there the wine they freely shared.
They drank and sung till they were tired,
And then they peacefully retired."
When this Homeric speech was said,
With drawling tongue and hanging head,
The learned Doctor took his seat,
Thinking he 'd done a noble feat.
Quoth Joe: "The crime is great, I own.
Send for the juniors one by one!
By this almighty wig I swear,
Which with such majesty I wear,
And in its orbit vast contains
My dignity, my power, and brains,
That Wier and Prescott both shall see
That college boys must not be free!"
He spoke, and gave the awful nod,
Like Homer's Dodonean God.
The college to its centre shook,
And every pipe and wine-glass broke.

Williams, with countenance humane,
Which scarce from laughing could refrain,
Thought that such youthful scenes of mirth
To punishments should not give birth;
Nor could he easily divine
What was the harm of drinking wine.
But Pearson, with an awful frown,
Full of his article and noun,
Spoke thus: " By all the parts of speech
Which with such elegance I teach,
By all the blood which fills my veins,
By all the power of Handel's strains,
With mercy I will never stain
The character which I maintain.
Pray tell me why the laws were made,
If they are not to be obeyed."
James saw 't would be in vain t' oppose,
And therefore to be silent chose.
Read, with his two enormous eyes
Enlarged to thrice their common size,
And brow contracted, staring wild,
Said government was much too mild.
" Were I," said he, " to have my will,
I soon would teach them to be still.
Their wicked rioting to quell,
I 'd rusticate, degrade, expel;
And rather than give up my plan,
I 'd clear the college to a man."
Burr, who has little wit or pride,
Preferred to take the strongest side;
And Willard soon received commission
To give a public admonition.
With pedant strut to prayers he came,
Called out the criminals by name.
Obedient to his dire command,
Before him Wier and Prescott stand:

" The rulers, merciful and kind,
With equal grief and wonder find
That you should laugh and drink and sing,
And make with noise the college ring.
I therefore warn you to beware
Of drinking more than you can bear.
Wine an incentive is to riot,
Destructive of the public quiet.
Full well your tutors know this truth,
For sad experience taught their youth.
Take then this friendly exhortation !
The next offence is rustication."

NAPOLEON I. AT ST. DOMINGO.[1]

In his history of the Consulate and the Empire, Thiers explained how the First Consul, after finding his scheme of Egyptian and Oriental conquest frustrated by the British navy, adopted a system of compensation in the New World. " If Egypt was to be torn from us, the First Consul wished to have done something for the colonial greatness of France. If Egypt lost could no longer offer a compensation for St. Domingo, the First Consul hoped to find it in Louisiana." [2]

Thiers could not often be charged with underestimating the merit of Napoleon's schemes, but in this instance he failed to describe the First Consul's true object. Louisiana was not intended to be a compensation for St. Domingo, but was subsidiary to the purpose of recovering St. Domingo from the control of the blacks, who had held it, nominally in dependence on France, since 1791. Napoleon gave the first place in his scheme with good reason to St. Domingo, be-

[1] Originally printed in the Revue Historique, Paris, January-February, 1884.

[2] Consulat et Empire, ii. 121.

cause the island had been the centre of French colonial interests more valuable than all the other colonies of France together ; but in any case if France intended to remain a colonial and maritime power, the recovery of St. Domingo was essential. Guadeloupe and Martinique were in constant danger, and must remain comparatively worthless, until the supremacy of the whites should be re-established in the colonial centre.

France had never relinquished the hope of restoring order and prosperity to St. Domingo, and the idea of turning French energies in that direction, as soon as war in Europe should be ended, was never lost from sight by the French republic. In 1795 the Republic obliged Spain, much against her will, to cede the Spanish part of the island to France, — a measure pointing to a great extension of the French colony ; for the Spanish part, though much poorer, was much larger than the French portion of the island. After 1795 the republic waited only for peace in order to begin the task of restoring its complete authority over St. Domingo, and in the mean time encouraged Toussaint Louverture to prepare the way.

Napoleon Bonaparte obtained control of the French government by the *coup d'état* of the 18th brumaire, or Nov. 9, 1799. Toward the end of August, 1800, he sent Berthier to Madrid to prepare a large extension of the colonial scheme. Berthier was ordered to negotiate a treaty with Spain for the retrocession of Louisiana to France. The motive for including Louisiana in the scheme of which St. Domingo was the centre, was the natural result of the local and military difficulties that embarrassed the administration of St. Domingo.

Bonaparte explained the subject in confidential papers, which would not have been secret unless they had expressed his true objects. St. Domingo, like all the West Indies, suffered as a colony under a serious disadvantage, being dependent for its supplies chiefly on the United States, — a dangerous neighbor both by its political example and its commercial or maritime rivalry with the mother country. The First Consul hoped to correct the evil by substituting Louisiana for the United States as the source of supplies for St. Domingo. In case of war, either with the United States or England, St. Domingo and the other French colonies in the West Indies could be safely left to themselves, if Louisiana and perhaps also Florida could be made a certain base of supplies, — for the islands had only famine to fear.

In the words of Bonaparte's secret instructions to the captain-general whom he ordered in November, 1802, to take command over Louisiana, —

" The system of this colony, as in all those that we possess, should aim at concentrating its commerce in the national commerce. Its special function should be to establish its relations with our Antilles, with a view to take the place, in those colonies, of American commerce for all objects whose importation or exportation is permitted."

The same purpose was more concisely expressed in another draft of these instructions : —

" Its magistrates should convince themselves of the possibility of substituting this colony [Louisiana] in the place of the United States for the objects which are permitted to the commerce between the United States and the French colonies." [1]

When Bonaparte, in the year 1800, began the execution of his plan for restoring on a larger scale the colonial greatness of France, three difficulties were to be overcome or avoided. The first was the war then raging between France and England, which, owing to the superiority of the British navy, precluded the possibility of French interference in St. Domingo until peace should be made. The second was Toussaint Louverture, who maintained practical independence in St. Domingo, with the support of a black army not to be despised. The third was the possibility of trouble with the United States, where any French interference with Louisiana was likely to excite alarm.

Bonaparte rapidly restored order in Europe, and removed his first great obstacle by negotiating preliminary articles of peace with Great Britain, which were signed at London, Oct. 1, 1801, and ratified five days afterward at Paris. Without a moment's delay, the First Consul issued orders, October 7, organizing the colonial force for the service of St.

[1] Instructions secrètes approuvées par le Premier Consul le 5 frimaire, an 11 (Nov. 26, 1802). Archives de la Marine MSS.

Domingo, Martinique, and Guadeloupe. The next day, October 8, he summoned his brother-in-law General Leclerc to Paris, with his staff, to command the expedition; and the preparations were pressed with such activity that within six weeks after the signature of the preliminary articles at London, Leclerc began the embarkation of his forces at Brest. The command was regarded as a high distinction to Leclerc, who wrote to the First Consul from Brest, immediately before sailing, requesting him to soothe the feelings of Bernadotte, whose claims had been set aside.

Leclerc to Napoleon.[1]

BREST, 2 frimaire (Nov. 23, 1801).

. . . I have especial reason to be pleased with the delicate course of General Bernadotte toward me. I have been the more sensible of it because he expected to have the command of this expedition. He desires only a little ease in his circumstances; if you should give it to him, you would acquire a right to his gratitude. He is frank and loyal. He is pained to see this command pass into other hands than his own, but he is an admirer of yours; he is grateful for what you did for him after the 18th brumaire. I should like to have him know that I have spoken to you about him.

As early as July 27 the First Consul requested from the King of Spain the delivery of Louisiana, and he repeated the demand August 15; but the official order was signed by Charles IV. only a year later, Oct. 15,

[1] Archives nationales, A. F. iv. 1213.

1802, at Barcelona. The delay mattered little; for
Louisiana could not be made useful until St. Domingo
should be thoroughly subdued, and for the moment
Bonaparte's energies were turned wholly to the task
of restoring French authority in the islands., Leclerc
hastened to depart; his wife, Pauline Bonaparte, accompanied him. An immense fleet, carrying great
numbers of troops, set sail in November and December, 1801; and for the next year St Domingo became
a point of extreme interest to the world.

At that day the necessity of overthrowing the black
government of St. Domingo, and of restoring slavery
throughout the French colonies was generally admitted. Bonaparte wished to effect the result without a
violent shock to the peace of St. Domingo; but any
restoration of French authority that fell short of restoring slavery would have failed to satisfy the wishes
of the French commercial class, and would probably
have insured the ultimate failure of the whole colonial
scheme, which required a system of enforced labor
for its success. Political reasons dictated the same
course. " The interest of civilization," Bonaparte
said, required him " to destroy the new Algier which
had organized itself in the middle of America." [1] As
Leclerc set out, Bonaparte ordered Talleyrand to assure the British government that " in the resolution I
have taken to annihilate the government of the blacks
at St. Domingo, I have been guided less by considera-

[1] Napoleon to Talleyrand, Oct. 30, 1801; Correspondance, vii.
307.

tions of commerce and finance than by the necessity of stifling in all parts of the world every sort of germ of disquietude and trouble; but I am aware that St. Domingo, if reconquered by the whites, would be during many years a weak point, needing the support of peace and the parent country, while the liberty of the blacks, if recognized at St. Domingo, would be at all times a point of support for the republic in the New World." [1]

Twenty years afterward, Napoleon at St. Helena dictated four notes on the Memoirs of General Pamphile de Lacroix and the affairs of St. Domingo.[2] The subject was not agreeable to him, and he aimed only to place it in the least repulsive light; but his narrative was accepted by French authorities, and served for the next fifty years to prevent the acceptance of a truer version. As Napoleon wished to represent his action at St. Domingo, the fault and responsibility belonged in the first instance to Toussaint Louverture: —

"The prosperous situation of the republic after the peace of Lunéville, in 1801," said the Emperor at St. Helena, "foreshadowed the moment when England would be obliged to lay down arms, and when we should have power to adopt a definite course about St. Domingo. Two such policies then suggested themselves to the meditations of the First Consul. The first was to invest

[1] Bonaparte to Talleyrand, 22 brumaire, an x. (Nov. 13, 1801); Correspondance, vii. 319.

[2] Quatre Notes; Correspondance, xxx. 525–536.

General Toussaint Louverture with the civil and military authority and the title of governor-general of the colony; to trust to the black generals the command; to consolidate, to legalize the system of labor established by Toussaint, which had already been crowned with happy results; to oblige the black farmers to pay rent to the old French proprietors; to preserve to the mother country the exclusive commerce of the whole colony, causing the coasts to be watched by numerous cruisers. The second course consisted in reconquering the country by force of arms, recalling to France all the blacks who had occupied grades superior to that of major, disarming the blacks while assuring them of civil liberty, and restoring to the colonists their estates."

According to Napoleon's later recollection, he inclined as First Consul to the course of recognizing Toussaint, and legalizing the black conditions of society and property; but this plan required the concurrence of the blacks, and their loyalty to the mother country: —

" Such was the state of St. Domingo, and the policy adopted by the French government in respect to it, when Colonel Vincent arrived in Paris. He brought the constitution that Toussaint Louverture had adopted by his own authority, had caused to be printed and put in execution, and notified to France. Not only the authority, but also the honor and the dignity of the republic were outraged. Of all ways of proclaiming his independence and raising the flag of rebellion, Toussaint Louverture had chosen the most outrageous. From that moment further deliberation was impossible. The black chiefs

9

were ungrateful and rebellious Africans, with whom it was impossible to establish any system; the honor as well as the interest of France required that they should be reduced to nothing. Thus the ruin of Toussaint Louverture, the misfortunes that weighed on the blacks, were the effect of that insane step. . . . As Toussaint Louverture was the most moderate of the black generals, and Dessalines, Christophe, Clairvaux, etc. were more exaggerated, more disaffected, and still more opposed to the authority of the mother country, there was no room for deliberation. The first course was no longer practicable; and it was necessary to adopt the second, and to make the sacrifice it exacted."

The arrival of Colonel Vincent was mentioned in the "Moniteur" of Oct. 14, 1801, where he was announced as bringing "officially the constitution that is presented for the approbation of the mother country. . . . Possibly several articles of the constitution proposed by Toussaint will not be adopted in France." The next day the "Moniteur" printed the constitution and the letters of Toussaint accompanying it. The constitution was chiefly remarkable for making Toussaint governor for life, with the right to choose a successor in case of his death. It was doubtless an act of *quasi* independence; but Toussaint presented it for the approbation of the government, and in profession it assumed the continued dependence of the island upon France.

If the First Consul ever seriously thought of adopting what he described afterward as his first plan, and intrusting the colony to Toussaint and the black

generals, he had given it up before the arrival of
Vincent with the constitution.   The preliminary articles of peace with England were signed October 6;
but already, October 7, Bonaparte allotted the regi-
ments for the service of St. Domingo.   Had he
meant to leave the government to Toussaint, he would
have sent at most two thousand men, as Toussaint
wished; but his detachment of troops for St. Domingo
numbered eighteen thousand rank-and-file,[1] with his
brother-in-law in command, who could not have been
intended to serve under Toussaint.   The First Consul
wrote the same day to Decrès, the Minister of Marine,
ordering Admiral Villaret Joyeuse to leave Brest with
twelve French and five Spanish line-of-battle ships,
carrying six or seven thousand troops.   "He will pass
by Rochefort, where he will unite with the squadron
there, which will have twenty-five hundred men on
board.   He will sail directly to the Cape [Français] to
cause the rights of the mother country to be respected
in St. Domingo."

Vincent's arrival in Paris occurred nearly a week
after these orders were given.   No trace of hesitation
appeared in Napoleon's acts from the moment the
peace with England permitted him to act at all; and
his reasons for annihilating the black government, as
given to the British government in the words already
quoted, implied that he was decided in his course by
the determination to prevent the negroes from hold-

[1] Note pour l'organisation des troupes coloniales, 15 vendémiaire, an x. (Oct. 7, 1801); Correspondance, vii. 273.

ing power, because "in that case the sceptre of the New World would fall sooner or later into the hands of the blacks."

In truth, Toussaint's constitution merely added one more cause of irritation to many already existing; and the scheme which Napoleon at St. Helena affirmed to have been his preference in 1801, although it might be his secret choice, was never seriously considered as a policy of government. The recognition of Toussaint at St. Domingo, and the rule of black generals over a black society, was inconsistent with the plan of reconstructing the French colonial system, and especially with the extension of that system implied by the recovery of Louisiana.

The letter explaining to the British government the decision to "annihilate" the government of the blacks at St. Domingo was written Nov. 13, 1801; and five days afterward, November 18, the First Consul wrote a somewhat famous letter to Toussaint himself, to be taken to St. Domingo by General Leclerc.

"We send you," said Bonaparte to Toussaint,[1] "the citizen Leclerc, our brother-in-law, in the character of captain-general, as the first magistrate of the colony. He is accompanied by forces sufficient to make the sovereignty of the French people respected. In these circumstances we are pleased to hope that you are about to prove to us, and to all France, the sincerity of the sentiments which you have constantly expressed in the different letters you have written us."

[1] Correspondance, vii. 322.

With the threat to punish rebellion Bonaparte
joined the promise of honors and rewards for
obedience : —

" Assist the captain-general with your counsels, your
influence, and your talents. What can you desire, — the
liberty of the blacks? You know that in every country
where we have been, we have given it to the people who
had it not. Consideration, honors, fortune? After the
services you have rendered, and those you can render in
these circumstances, together with the particular sentiments we have for you, you should not be uncertain of
your consideration, your fortune, and the honors that
await you."

Obliged to threaten the " brave blacks " with the
consequences of rebellion, Bonaparte made an effort
to calm them on the subject of their freedom. Besides the implied pledge just quoted, the letter to
Toussaint contained another assurance, " that hence-
forward the peace and the force of the government
assure their prosperity and their liberty." In the
Exposé de la Situation de la République, dated November 22, Bonaparte sent to the legislature a third
pledge of freedom to the blacks : —

" A fleet and an army that are preparing to leave the
ports of Europe will soon dissipate all clouds, and St.
Domingo will return entirely under the laws of the Republic. At St. Domingo and at Guadeloupe there are no
longer slaves ; all is there free ; all will there remain
free. Wisdom and time will restore order there, and will
re-establish cultivation and works."

Finally, a fourth pledge was given in a proclamation to the blacks themselves, which began,[1] —

" Inhabitants of St. Domingo! whatever may be your origin and your color, you are all French; you are all free and all equals before God and before the Republic. . . . The Government sends you the Captain-General Leclerc. He brings with him great forces to protect you against your enemies, and against the enemies of the Republic. If you are told, ' These forces are intended to ravish your liberty from you,' reply, ' The Republic has given us liberty; the Republic will not suffer it to be taken from us.' "

Bonaparte's true intentions were probably expressed in his instructions to General Leclerc, but these were never made public. In the notes on Pamphile de Lacroix's Memoirs, Napoleon at St. Helena related the story of Leclerc's expedition as he wished it to be represented in history, and gavé a version of his instructions with the object of showing that Leclerc alone was to blame for his own misfortunes:[2] —

" Captain-General Leclerc had, it is true, received on his departure, from Napoleon's own hand, secret instructions on the political direction to be followed in the government of the colony. These instructions have remained unknown; at the death of General Leclerc they were transferred under seal to his successor. . . . Captain-General Leclerc would have spared himself many misfortunes, and would have avoided many troubles, had

[1] Proclamation, 17 brumaire, an x. (Nov. 8, 1801); Correspondance, vii. 315.

[2] Correspondance, xxx. 533

he scrupulously followed the spirit of these instructions. They prescribed the greatest confidence to be put by him in the mulattoes who were to be treated as equals of the whites ; marriages of mulatto men with white women, and of mulatto women with white men, were to be favored ; but a wholly contrary system was to be followed with the negro chiefs. Within the same week when the colony should be pacified, he was to notify to all the black generals, adjutant-generals, colonels, and majors, orders of service, in their grades, in the Continental divisions of France ; he was to embark them on eight or ten vessels in all the ports of the colony, and direct them to Brest, Rochefort, and Toulon ; he was to disarm the blacks, preserving ten battalions, each of six thousand men, commanded by one third black, one third mulatto, and one third white officers and non-commissioned officers ; finally he was to take all required measures to assure and secure the enjoyment of civil liberty to the blacks, by confirming the order of classes and of labor established by Toussaint Louverture."

In one respect at least this account of Leclerc's instructions, given at St. Helena from memory twenty years after they were written, must have been correct. The First Consul ordered Leclerc to lose no time in sending the black generals to Europe. The character of the instruction on that point was proved by repeated letters written afterward. The instructions were dated Nov. 10, 1801. Bonaparte's next letter to Leclerc was dated March 16, 1802,[1] and repeated the previous orders : —

[1] Bonaparte to Leclerc, 25 ventôse, an x. (March 16, 1802); Correspondance, vii. 413.

" Follow exactly your instructions ; and the instant you shall have rid yourself (*vous vous serez défait*) of Toussaint, Christophe, Dessalines, and the principal brigands, and the masses of the blacks shall be disarmed, send back to the Continent all the blacks and mulattoes who have played a part in the civil troubles."

The secret instructions certainly prescribed the arrest and exile not only of all the black generals, but also of every man, black or mulatto, who had played a part in the civil troubles. Perhaps this idea was not precisely expressed by Napoleon in the words : " Il devait faire notifier à tous les généraux des ordres de service, dans leurs grades, dans les divisions continentales de la France ; " but Napoleon seldom remembered with entire accuracy. The instructions of November 10, as repeated March 16, ordered Leclerc to send to France every man, negro or mulatto, who had taken part in the civil troubles of St. Domingo, without regard to the question whether they peaceably submitted to Leclerc's authority, or offered armed resistance.

The same instructions were repeated in Bonaparte's next letter, dated July 1, 1802 : [1] —

" I count that before the end of September you will have sent here all the black generals ; without that, we shall have done nothing, and an immense and beautiful colony would be always on a volcano, and would inspire no confidence in capitalists, colonists, or in commerce. I comprehend perfectly that this may occasion move-

[1] Bonaparte to Leclerc, 12 messidor, an x. (July 1, 1802); Correspondance, vii. 503.

ments ; but you will have the whole season before you to repress them. Whatever results the sendiug the black generals to France may produce, it will be only a small evil compared with that of their continued stay in St. Domingo. . . . From the moment the blacks shall be disarmed and the principal generals sent to France, you will have done more for the commerce and civilization of Europe than one accomplishes in the most brilliant campaigns."

Probably the original instructions left untouched the question of ultimate freedom or slavery to the black race. As a beginning, Bonaparte was satisfied to retain the severe labor-system of Toussaint. Yet the necessity of ultimate restoration of slavery was so well understood that no one in private doubted it, and the impression was so general in France that it produced a similar general impression in St. Domingo. The old colonial proprietors made no secret of their confidence. On that point, Napoleon at St. Helena preserved silence ; but his silence implied that he had never intended to deprive the blacks at St. Domingo of their freedom.

" The general law of the republic was the liberty of the blacks," said the Emperor. " Martinique, where slavery continued during British occupation, was the exception. The decree of the 28th floréal, 1801, which ordered that the slavery of the blacks should be maintained at Martinique and the Ile-de-France, as the liberty of the blacks should be maintained for St. Domingo, Guadeloupe, and Cayenne, was just, politic,

necessary." In this sentence a number of errors of
memory united to produce confusion. The decree in
question was not of the 28th floréal, 1801, but of the
30th floréal, 1802, as was correctly said in the Memoirs of Pamphile de Lacroix,[1] which Bonaparte had
been reading, and as will be shown in the course of
this story.[2] The decree did not maintain freedom at
St. Domingo and Guadeloupe, but restored slavery
there, and in principle everywhere. According to
that decree the general law of the republic became
the slavery, not the freedom, of the blacks;[3] and
Napoleon's comments proved only the wish to conceal or ignore the intention of restoring them to
slavery.

Under the version which Napoleon adopted of the
instructions he had given to Leclerc, he assumed that
Leclerc's failure to follow them was the cause of his
subsequent troubles at St. Domingo. Leclerc, he said,
offended the mulattoes ; he sent their chief, Rigaud,
out of the colony ; he gave his confidence to the negro generals Dessalines, Christophe, and others.

" When the First Consul was informed of this conduct,
he was greatly afflicted. The authority of the mother
country in the colony could be consolidated only by the
influence of the mulattoes. In postponing the sending
of the black chiefs out of the colony, there was reason to
fear losing the opportunity. It was impossible that individuals who had governed as sovereigns, whose vanity

[1] Memoirs, ii. 226.   [2] See *infra*, pp. 158–159.
[3] Pièces 6053, 6054, 6055 ; Correspondance, vii. 444–446.

equalled their ignorance, could live tranquil in submission to the orders of the mother country; the first condition for the security of St. Domingo was that of removing one hundred and fifty or two hundred chiefs. In reality the decree [of the 30th floréal] relative to the blacks was only a pretext [for their revolt]; they revolted as a result of the intrigues of England; they took arms because the cruel malady, which swept away the best of our troops, restored their hopes. It was then that the captain-general repented of having been too indulgent, — of not having executed the orders of the First Consul. All would have been well had he rid the colony of one hundred and fifty or two hundred black chiefs. In politics as in war, the lost moment never returns."

These were the opinions of Napoleon some twenty years after the event. In reality, the tale was different. As Leclerc told in his letters and despatches the story of his disasters and their cause, the true reasons for his failure were apparent, and they were not altogether such as Napoleon wished to represent them.

Leclerc landed at Cap Français, Feb. 5, 1802, and found, as he probably expected, that he must fight a campaign for the possession of the island. Christophe, who under Toussaint's orders commanded at Cap Français, burned the town, laid waste the plantations, and retired to the mountains. Leclerc began his task of conquest in a ravaged country, where the inhabitants depended on him for support. His first despatches, of which a free version was printed in the "Moniteur" of March 15, 1802, described his situation.

Leclerc to Decrès.[1]

HEADQUARTERS AT THE CAPE,
February 9, 1802 (20 pluviose, an x.).

. . . I have much anxiety on account of food ; part of the supplies on board the squadron are spoiled. Happily the Spaniards have come to our support by leaving us 2000 quintals of biscuit ; they have also left us 100,000 quintals of powder. In the city are some provisions saved from the fire. The merchants at the Cape will sell them only at excessive prices, and want ready money. Still, I will arrange so as to get them. A score of American vessels are in port, which have also some provisions. They are Jews with whom it is impossible for me to deal ; yet we shall have to deal with them notwithstanding. By adding all my resources together, I calculate that we shall be very happy to have supplies for two months and a half. I cannot depend on any commercial house here. These men are not French ; they know no country but the United States. The United States have brought here guns, cannon, powder, and all the munitions of war. It is they who excited Toussaint to defence. I am thoroughly convinced that the Americans have formed the plan of exciting all the Antilles to independence because they hoped to have the exclusive commerce, as they have had that of St. Domingo. It would not be unfortunate for me if England and France were to unite to intimidate them. . . .

Next to the hostility of the blacks, the attitude of the United States was Leclerc's chief annoyance, and

[1] Archives de la Marine MSS.

his free language on the subject, being spread in all the seaports of America, embarrassed the French chargé at Washington, who remonstrated somewhat warmly with the General.

Pichon to Leclerc.

March 30, 1802 (9 germinal, an x.).

. . . We are disposed, I fear, to find complaint with them [the United States] ; to look upon acts committed during a misunderstanding as though they had been committed in full peace ; to demand account from them, according to our own feelings, of what they could or should do consulting only their interests ; in short to exact from them what we should not exact from a nation of whose force and means we had a higher idea. At least, that is what I fear I perceive in the correspondence, the remarks and the reports that reach us from your colony.

Considering only interest, General, ours is to remove all impressions of this kind, and see only a country from which exclusively you can draw your resources, and where they can famish you. Experience proves it. Only our unfortunate misunderstanding with them caused the revolt of our colonies. We can recover our colonies only by them. These truths are weightier than the hasty satisfaction we might be able to give to national grievances that we may have, and to those that misfortune inspires in individuals. I have put you, General, on your guard. The United States have their interests, we ours ; it is our business to observe them, and as far as they act in peace with us, to live in harmony with them. Minds at this moment are much excited ; the affair of Louisiana agitates them ; the coercions applied at the Cape embitter them ; and these two incidents, I observe, indispose and embarrass prodigiously the government. A nothing would suffice to kindle a new flame. You will doubtless approve, General, of my speaking to you on this subject with all the frankness with which I speak to the government.

Leclerc was far from approving Pichon's frankness, and not only wrote to Pichon refusing to hold further relations with him, but wrote also to the First Consul that Pichon was a " fripon " and a " misérable," and demanding his recall. After this outbreak, which probably led to Pichon's subsequent disgrace, Leclerc recovered his temper, and not only forgave Pichon, but followed his advice.

Leclerc's second despatch to the government was dated February 17, when he was about to begin a formal campaign against Toussaint and the black generals. His position was still serious in regard to supplies.

Leclerc to Decrès.[1]

February 17, 1802 (28 pluviose, an x.).

. . . At every moment I learn that our position is worse in respect to provisions. The vessel which went ashore carried the provisions of the two other ships. Few American vessels were in harbor, and the resources they contained were small. Every day in ascertaining the state of supply of the vessels, damage is discovered. Our hospital effects were disembarked to-day. They were on the ' Danae.' They are all damaged. I know not how we shall manage. Come quick to our aid. We are bare-foot. Send me thirty thousand pairs of shoes.

[1] Archives de la Marine MSS.

The campaign was short, vigorous, and successful, but not without efforts and losses severely felt by the army. Leclerc wrote ten days later to report the result at that moment.

Leclerc to Decrès.[1]

February 27, 1802 (8 ventose, an x.).

. . . Here is the actual situation of the colony : I am master of the northern part, but nearly everything has been burned there, and I can expect no resources from it. Cultivators are assembled behind at a score of different points. . . . The rebels are still masters of a part of the west, and have burned the points they no longer occupy ; I can expect no resources from there for the moment. The south is in part preserved. . . . As for the Spanish part, it has been so squeezed by Toussaint that we must rather give to it than demand of it. I am nearly master there. . . . In order to appreciate the work of the brave army I have the honor to command, you must know that I entered the campaign without horses, without cavalry, without means of transport. The soldiers filled their knapsacks with cartridges and biscuit. On leaving Brest, I was given a statement which assured me that I had fifteen thousand pairs of shoes on board ; on arriving at St. Domingo I found only four thousand bad pairs. I was assured that I had camp effects, but I have not found a kettle to give to a soldier, nor a single can. According to my lists, these things should have been brought by the "Fidèle," but they have not been found in her. The hospital effects were so badly stowed on the "Danae" that they arrived altogether damaged. Yet I have thirty-five hundred men in hospital whom I know not how to care

[1] Archives de la Marine MSS.

for, the burning of the cities having deprived me of all resources. . . . In the different combats I have had to fight I have lost six hundred men killed and fifteen hundred wounded ; I have two thousand sick. . . . My military position is not bad, as you see, citizen Minister, but it would become so if you should not come promptly to my aid.

The winter passed before Leclerc had succeeded in bringing the colony to complete submission. Toussaint and his generals, with a few troops, still held out, and occupied refuges in the mountains. Leclerc reported to the government in sombre colors the difficulties he foresaw.

Leclerc to Decrès.[1]

April 21, 1802 (1 floréal, an x.).

. . . Toussaint still holds the mountains. He has under his orders about four thousand colonial troops and a very considerable quantity of armed cultivators. . . . I cannot terminate this war without occupying in force, after having conquered them, the mountains of the north and those of the west ; and in attacking these points I shall always need to occupy all that I now hold where the cultivators are beginning to return. I need twenty-five thousand effective troops to complete the conquest of St. Domingo, and restore it wholly to France. I have for the moment eleven thousand European troops, and seven thousand colonial troops on whom I am very far from relying entirely. As long as I am successful they will remain with me, and if I have a reverse they may well serve to double the enemy's means. I have already made several attempts to

[1] Archives de la Marine MSS.

induce Toussaint and all the black generals to surrender, but without success.   I am going to busy myself seriously with that affair.   I believe dissensions exist among the chiefs by which I can profit; but yet, citizen Minister, though I should succeed in causing the submission of these men, I could not take the measures of rigor which would assure to France the fixed possession of St. Domingo until I shall have twenty-five thousand Europeans present under arms.

A few days afterward Christophe made submission, and came to a meeting with Leclerc.   "After the assurance which I gave him that we had not come to destroy liberty," reported Leclerc, May 6, " he declared to me that he was ready to execute all my orders." The defection of Christophe obliged Toussaint to ask terms, and Leclerc reported to the government the terms offered.

Leclerc to Decrès.[1]

May 6, 1802 (16 floréal, an x.).

. . . Two days afterward General Toussaint sent me his adjutant-general with a letter that meant little, but in which I saw a very pronounced desire to surrender.   I replied to General Toussaint that I would receive his surrender, but that if he did not yield promptly I would march on him ; and that he had best send me some confidential agent to tell me what he wanted to obtain.   He sent me his private secretary, with one of his aids, to let me know that he wanted the grade of lieutenant-general and a particular command ; that each of his generals should resume the command he had at the time of my

[1] Archives de la Marine MSS.

10

arrival; and that he should have troops alone under his orders. I answered that he would not be employed; that he would retire to one of his residences, and could not leave it without permission; that his generals would be employed as well as his troops, but where I should think proper and useful; as for him, he must surrender to me at the Cape, and I would give him my word of honor that after the conference he should have the liberty to go where he would; finally, that his troops should be all united and ready to execute my orders within four days. I wrote this last letter only two days ago. . . .

Such leniency was contrary to the spirit of Leclerc's instructions, and he closed his letter by saying, —

" If circumstances force me sometimes, citizen Minister, to appear to deviate from the end of my instructions, believe me that I do not lose them from sight, and that I yield something to circumstances only to master them afterward and make them serve the execution of my plans."

Toussaint appeared within the term fixed, and had an interview with the captain-general. Unquestionably he asked for conditions and received them, — probably those prescribed in Leclerc's letter to him; but Leclerc made no report of what passed. He announced very briefly Toussaint's submission.

Leclerc to Decrès.[1]

May 8, 1802 (18 floréal, an x.).

General Toussaint has been here. He went away perfectly content with me, and ready to execute all my

[1] Archives de la Marine MSS.

orders. I believe that he will execute them, because if he did not I should make him repent it. I must have inspired him with great confidence, since he slept at the headquarters of one of my generals, and had with him only a few men. I lose not an instant to restore tranquillity, and to have nothing to fear in the colony from any cause whatever.

According to the First Consul's instructions the time had come when Leclerc should at once — within a week — order the black generals to Europe, or send them there by force. Leclerc would have been glad to do so, but the pacification had consumed three months, from February 5 till May 8, and the summer had begun with disastrous effects on his army, as he notified the government on the same day with Toussaint's surrender.

Leclerc to Decrès.

May 8, 1802 (18 floréal, an x.).

Sickness makes frightful ravages in the army that I command. You will be convinced of it when you look at the accompanying army report. You will see that the army which you calculated at twenty-six thousand men is reduced at this moment to twelve thousand. . . . I have at this moment thirty-six hundred men in hospital. In the last fortnight I have lost from thirty to fifty men a day in the colony, and there is no day when from two hundred to two hundred and fifty men do not enter the hospital, while more than fifty never come out. My hospitals are crowded. I give every care to them, — but observe that I arrived in a colony where the principal establishments were burned; that my hospital effects were all left behind; that the garrisons I have in the cities suffer much because there are no barracks; that the soldiers want hammocks, the fleet having carried them almost all away. If my men fall ill, it is not for want of being well nourished, for the composition of the ration is excellent. . . . This consumption of men is truly appalling, and I am assured that it will only increase. To be master of St. Domingo I need twenty-five thousand men present under arms. You see that I have only the half. Not an instant should be lost in sending me reinforcements whatever may be my actual position. . . .

Although Leclerc did not arrest at once all the black generals, he began the deportation of the less important negroes, sending them by hundreds to the various prisons or galleys of France, while he made his arrangements for seizing Toussaint. He explained to the First Consul the reasons why he was obliged to spare for a time the other black generals.

Leclerc to the First Consul.[1]

June 6, 1802 (17 prairial, an x.).

My position becomes worse from day to day. Sickness carries away men. . . . Toussaint is treacherous, as I expected; but I have gained from his submission the end I intended, which was to detach Dessalines and Christophe with their troops from him. I am going to order his arrest, and I believe I can count on Dessalines, whose spirit I have mastered, sufficiently to charge him with the errand of arresting Toussaint. I do not think I shall fail; but if I should miss him, I will have him pursued by Christophe and Dessalines. The season does not permit

[1] Archives nationales MSS.

of my making war with European troops, and I can still
use the blacks to advantage. What makes me take this
resolution, citizen Consul, is my need of raising in the
colony by some act of vigor the idea of my strength. I
shall sustain it well for the first moment, but if I should
not receive reinforcements my position would become
bad. As soon as I have received four thousand men,
whom I will give out for six thousand, I count on undertaking the disarmament of the cultivators by means of the
black generals. These measures are always subordinate
to those I shall be obliged to take either after Toussaint's
arrest or his escape. Do not be surprised if I say I may
miss him. Within a fortnight the man has become extremely suspicious. Not that I have given occasion for
his distrust, but he regrets his power ; and his regrets, frequently expressed, give rise to the idea of renewing his
party. By my course in regard to his followers I have
left him very few partisans. As soon as I have secured
his person, I shall send him to Corsica, and I will give
orders for imprisoning him in one of the castles of that
island. I shall send there a great part of those I mean
to get rid of. I despatch fifty to-day on the "Maizon."
I write to citizen Miot that he can employ them on public works. I send only men who might be dangerous to
the colony.

Soon every prison in the seaports of France was
filled to overflowing with negroes from St. Domingo,
until the ports remonstrated strongly against the
stream of naked, diseased, and helpless barbarians
that poured into them. In this respect Bonaparte's
orders were carried out, but the exile of subordinate
negro officers or officials did not relieve the least of

Leclerc's difficulties. On the day when he announced to Bonaparte the intended arrest of Toussaint, he wrote to Decrès in discouragement.

Leclerc to Decrès.[1]

June 6, 1802 (17 prairial, an x.).

. . . The month of germinal cost me twelve hundred men dead in hospital; the month of floréal cost me eighteen hundred, and I fear much that this month will cost me two thousand. This mortality will last another three months. I have at most only ten thousand Europeans present under arms at this moment. My position, citizen Minister, becomes every day worse owing to the way I am neglected by government. . . . Every day the blacks recover audacity. I am not strong enough to order the disarmament, nor the necessary measures. If the war begins again here, as is possible, it will not be my fault, who have done more than my physical strength permitted from me ; it will be the fault of the government, which does not come to my aid. . . .

Decrès was obliged to admit that the extraordinary burden of these colonial expeditions, falling suddenly on the navy, had overtasked its resources. Leclerc had not received the reinforcements or outfit he had been promised.

Weak though Leclerc was, and burdened with increasing anxieties, he took the step of arresting Toussaint. His report to Decrès on the subject was printed, with variations, in the "Moniteur" of the

[1] Archives de la Marine MSS.

28th messidor, July 17, 1802. His letter to Bona-parte was never printed.

Leclerc to the First Consul.[1]

June 11, 1802 (22 prairial, an x.).

I have taken a step that will do much good to the colony. I have, as I warned you, arrested General Tous-saint, and I send him to France to you with all his family. This operation was not easy ; it has succeeded as happily as possible. Within some days he had collected near him six or seven hundred cultivators and a number of desert-ers. He had refused to go to two rendezvous that Gen-eral Brunet gave him. Some days before, he had written me to complain of my having stationed troops at Dennery, which he had chosen as his residence. I answered that to remove all ground for complaint I authorized him to confer with General Brunet on the station of the troops in that canton. He went to General Brunet. There he was arrested and embarked. A score of his adherents were arrested in the neighborhood. I shall send them to Cayenne. I have issued a proclamation to make his con-duct known ; nevertheless assemblages have taken place. I am making the black generals march against them, and I hope to restore order. The blacks are without a com-pass ; they are divided among themselves. . . . Tous-saint is removed ! It is a great point, but the blacks are armed, and I must have forces to disarm them. Sickness makes frightful progress here, and it is impossible to calculate where it will stop. Possibly less than four thousand French troops will remain in St. Domingo by October. Judge what will then be my position. . . . My health is still bad, and if my position were sufficiently

[1] Archives nationales MSS.

secure to cause me no anxiety, I can assure you that I should demand my successor at once; but I will do my best, by sparing myself, to last six months more here. By that time I shall have completed everything, if the minister of marine does not neglect me as he has done till now. . . . Toussaint must not be free. Imprison him in the interior of the republic, so that he shall never see St. Domingo again.

To Decrès the captain-general wrote, supplicating assistance more earnestly than ever.

Leclerc to Decrès.[1]

June 11, 1802 (22 prairial, an x.).

. . . I send to France this man, so dangerous to St. Domingo. The government, citizen Minister, must have him put in a strong place situated in the middle of France, so that he can have no means of escaping and returning to St. Domingo, where he has all the influence of a religious chief. If within three years that man should reappear at St. Domingo, perhaps he would destroy all that France should have done there. . . . I have taken from the blacks their rallying point, but I am very weak, and supply my physical strength only by moral force. For pity's sake send me aid; without it I cannot undertake the disarmament, and without the disarmament I am not master of the colony. Send me money; my penury is extreme. Do something for us, and do not leave us abandoned as you have done till now. This is, I assure you, the only motive for disgust I encounter in the difficult enterprise with which I am charged.

[1] Archives de la Marine MSS.

Before pursuing further the story of Leclerc, the fate of Toussaint merits attention. In the painful history of St. Domingo, Toussaint was the most interesting actor, and his sudden disappearance from the public view invested his life with a mystery that added to his fame.

The First Consul received the news of Toussaint's arrest, July 22, and immediately wrote to Leclerc approving the measure and announcing reinforcements. " We wait with impatience the arrival of Christophe and Dessalines in France. The arrival of Toussaint has been extremely honorable to you, and is a subject of tranquillity and hope for our commerce." [1] The next day he signed a secret decree ordering Toussaint to be taken as a prisoner to the Fortress of Joux, to be kept in secrecy without power of writing or communicating with any one but his domestic.[2] Apparently the First Consul intended to bring Toussaint to trial and punish him by legal methods, for Decrès wrote to Leclerc requesting him to forward proofs of Toussaint's guilt; but Leclerc replied that he had no proofs.

Leclerc to Decrès. [3]

Sept. 26, 1802 (4 vendémiaire, an x.).

. . . I have proof enough to serve for his trial if recourse be had to what was done before the amnesty I

[1] Bonaparte to Leclerc, July 22, 1802; Correspondance, vii. 529.

[2] Dècret, July 23, 1802 ; Correspondance, vii. 533.

[3] Archives de la Marine MSS.

granted him ; since then I have none. In the actual
situation of affairs his trial and execution would merely
embitter the minds of the blacks. . . .

Obliged to abandon the design of punishing Toussaint according to law for crimes he had not committed, the First Consul was still able to inflict equal
punishment on him for the crimes for which he had
been pardoned. Toussaint was taken, with every
precaution of secrecy, to the Fortress of Joux in the
Jura mountains, and every week the commandant
of the Fortress reported to Decrès the condition of
the captive. As the cold weather of autumn set in,
Toussaint began to fail in health.

The Commandant Baïlle to Decrès.[1]

CHÂTEAU DE JOUX, Oct. 30, 1802.

. . . Since my last I can say nothing of Toussaint
Louverture except that he has continual indispositions
caused by internal pains, headaches, and some attacks
of fever which are not continuous. He complains
always of cold, though making a great fire. Heretofore
the officer on guard could see him, without power of
speaking to him except of matters regarding his usual
wants, and then only during the time when his food
or firewood and other needs were supplied ; but now
no one is allowed to see him but myself ; and when he
is obliged to enter his chamber I make him pass to the
next room, formerly occupied by his domestic. He can
shave himself only before me, who give him his razor,
and take it back when he has finished. The constitution

---

[1] Archives de la Marine MSS.

of negroes resembling in no respect that of Europeans, I dispense with giving him either physician or surgeon, who would be useless for him.

The Commandant Baïlle, whose acquaintance with negro physiology dispensed him from providing a physician for Toussaint, was succeeded by another commandant, Amiot, who gave still better reasons for not calling medical aid.

The Commandant Amiot to Decrès.[1]

CHÂTEAU DE JOUX, March 19, 1803.

Since my letter of the 13th instant the situation of Toussaint is always the same. He complains continually of pains in the stomach, and has a continual cough ; for some days he has kept his left arm in a sling on account of pains. I perceive that in the last three days his voice is much changed. He has never asked for a physician.

Nine months of this treatment sufficed. Toussaint grew steadily weaker, and his cough grew constantly worse, until April 7. Major Amiot's reports ceased with one dated the 19th germinal, or April 9, 1803.

The Commandant Amiot to Decrès.

April 9, 1803.

I had the honor to render you an account of Toussaint's condition by my letter of the 16th germinal. The 17th, at eleven and a half o'clock in the morning, on carrying his food to him, I found him dead, seated on his chair, near the fire. . . . I have caused him to be

[1] Archives de la Marine MSS.

interred by a priest of the commune, in the vault under the old chapel, lettered G, in the Fort of Joux, where formerly the soldiers of the garrison were buried.

The commandant directed an autopsy to be made by the surgeon and physician of Pontarlier, Tavernier, who reported on the 18th germinal, that " apoplexy-pleuro-peripneumonia " caused Toussaint's death.

The severity with which Toussaint was treated in prison, without pretence of authority in law, resulted from the orders of the First Consul, given through Decrès to the commandant. These orders had some historical interest, showing the system under which prisoners of state were managed during the consulate.

Decrès to the Commandant Baïlle.

Oct. 27, 1802 (5 brumaire, an xi.).

. . . The First Consul has charged me to inform you that you are responsible for his [Toussaint's] person with your head. I have no need to add anything to an order so formal and so positive. Toussaint Louverture has no right to other consideration than such as humanity commands. Hypocrisy is a vice as familiar to him as honor and loyalty to you, citizen Commandant. . . . Toussaint's only means of seeing his lot ameliorated would have been to lay aside all dissimulation. His personal interest, the religious sentiments with which he should be penetrated to expiate all the evil he has done, imposed on him the duty of truth; but he is very far from performing it, and by his continual dissimulation he dispenses those who approach him of all interest in his lot.

The French people prided themselves on their keen sense of the ridiculous, and in that respect, as in others, Bonaparte was not French, else he would never have preached to Toussaint a sermon so grim in its defiance of absurdity. Between Toussaint, De-crès, Leclerc, and Bonaparte, critics might perhaps differ in establishing the correct order in dissimulation and hypocrisy ; but the position of Toussaint at Joux proved decisively that he was the least proficient of the four.

As the First Consul recorded his opinion of Toussaint, Toussaint's opinion of the First Consul and his agents should be allowed expression. The Commandant Baïlle was obliged to report it.

The Commandant Baïlle to Decrès.

Nov. 6, 1802.

I have the honor to observe to you that Toussaint is naturally quick and passionate, and when I make observations to him on the complaints of want of justice which he pretends to suffer here, he stamps his feet, and strikes his head with his two fists. . . . When he is in this state, which seems to me a sort of delirium, he says the most indecent things of General Leclerc ; and as he has gall in his heart, and has in his retreat time to color his lying impertinences with a certain substratum of intelligence, and lacking judgment (in my opinion), he colors his sayings with insidious motives which have an appearance of truth. . . . Three days ago, my General, he was impudent enough to tell me that in France there were none but men wicked, unjust, calumniators (those were his terms), from whom justice could not be had.

The life of Toussaint, after his arrest in June, 1802, was short; that of Leclerc was still shorter, and quite as tragic. In any case the situation of Leclerc in the summer of 1802 was desperate, and even though his government had given him all the support he expected, he must probably have perished; but the First Consul needlessly overloaded him with trouble. Exhausted by the unnecessary efforts imposed upon him by the neglect of his appeals, Leclerc began the summer enfeebled and discouraged. His arrest of Toussaint was a desperate step, but had he not arrested Toussaint, he knew that Toussaint would soon arrest him; and only a few days before he decided at St. Domingo to risk the danger of a new revolt, Bonaparte at Paris took a measure that made revolt inevitable. As early as April 6, a month before the black generals accepted Leclerc's amnesty, and while Leclerc was still struggling with every sort of difficulty, the First Consul ordered Decrès to organize a commission to discuss and draft a plan " to fix the status of the blacks " in the colonies.[1] About three weeks later, five projects were referred to the consuls for selection and approval.[2] According to the general scheme, the colonies were to be divided into two classes, — those in which the blacks had been freed since 1789, and those in which slavery had been preserved. St. Domingo and Guadeloupe belonged

[1] Arrêté, 16 germinal, an x.; Correspondance, vii. 430.
[2] Bonaparte to Cambacerès, 7 floréal, an x. (27 April, 1802); Correspondance, vii. 444.

to the first class; Martinique, Sta Lucia, Tabago, and the Ile-de-France belonged to the second.

In all colonies of the second class the blacks, having never been freed, were to remain slaves, and all laws regarding these colonies passed by different legislatures since 1789 were annulled at a single stroke, while the slave-trade was restored.

For colonies of the first class — St. Domingo and Guadeloupe — slavery was also to be restored, but the freedom of individuals was to be maintained. Lists were to be made of all blacks who were free before the 26 [16?] pluviose, an II.[1] (Feb. 14, 1794), when the republic decreed the general liberty of all the slaves, and declared St. Domingo an integral part of France; lists were also to be made of blacks who had defended or served the state. All these individuals were to be declared free; the rest, comprising in effect the entire black population, were to be replaced under the slave code of 1789, and the slave-trade was to be restored.

The First Consul signed, May 20, 1802 (30 floréal, an x.), the necessary decree restoring slavery in certain specified colonies, but it was not published in the "Moniteur," nor was the decree avowedly applicable to St. Domingo, but only to colonies of the second class. St. Domingo and Guadeloupe remained apparently exempt from its operation. The news of Toussaint's submission and the restoration of order in St. Domingo arrived in France three weeks after-

[1] Article 1er. Pièce 6054; Correspondance, vii. 445.

ward, and was published in the " Moniteur " of June
12. Without delay the First Consul ordered the
minister of marine to send the law of May 20 (30
floréal) to General Richepanse commanding at Guadeloupe, and to General Leclerc commanding at St.
Domingo, with instructions to regulate their conduct.
These letters, which were never made public, possess much historical interest.

Decrès to Richepanse.[1]

PARIS, June 14, 1802 (25 prairial, an x.).

I send you, General, some printed copies of the law
of May 20 (30 floréal), concerning slavery and the slave-
trade. It is textually applicable only to the colonies
named in it. You will easily penetrate the motive for
this. The state of crisis existing at St. Domingo and
the troubles that continued at Guadeloupe did not allow
of irritating by direct provisions the spirit of resistance
and rebellion. Already the valor of our troops and the
courage of the chief who commands them have subjected
the insurgents of the Leeward Islands. We should not
be long in hearing of equally happy success on your part,
either by force of arms or by that of persuasion, against
the insurgents of your island [Guadeloupe]. Yet in
order to run no risk in a matter so serious, the government prefers to trust only to your wisdom for the publication or the non-publication of the law in question,
according as you shall think it suitable, and especially
on the weight you shall place on its explanation according to circumstances which you, better than any one, are
able to appreciate. But whatever course you may take,

[1] Archives de la Marine MSS.

he recommends to you two things that he regards as being of the greatest importance. The first is to establish in the *ateliers* a police for order and labor so vigilant as to resemble the discipline of the old slavery, and reassure the neighboring colonies against the dangers of an incongruous régime ; by that means you will prepare the way for a return of legal uniformity as soon as prudence shall permit its establishment. I need not impress on you that good treatment by the masters will be the most powerful vehicle for it. The second will be to favor the markets for the slave-trade by giving every guaranty to buyers for the state of servitude of the blacks bought of French or foreign shippers. I do not doubt that your confidence in the Colonial Prefect will cause you to invite the aid of his counsels in a conjuncture so delicate. The uncertainty about the resolution you may think proper to take, prevents me from writing directly to him on this occasion.

Decrès to Leclerc.

PARIS, June 14, 1802.

The text of the law of the 30th floréal, several printed copies of which I am ordered to address to you, could not and should not, when it was made, contain mention of the colony of St. Domingo ; it is nominally applicable, as concerns slavery, only to the establishments which we recover in consequence of the peace, and to the eastern colonies. But it re-establishes the slave-trade, and all our colonial possessions have need of it. On these two intimately connected points, equally delicate and important, I have to send you to-day the instructions of the government. As far as concerns the return to the old régime of the blacks, the bloody struggle from

11

which you have just emerged, glorious and conqueror, commands the greatest caution. Perhaps we should only plunge ourselves into it anew if we tried to break precipitately that idol of liberty in whose name so much blood has flowed till now. During some time yet vigilance, order, and a discipline both rural and military must replace the positive and pronounced slavery of the colored people of your colony. Especially the good treatment of the master must attach them to his rule. When they shall have felt by comparison the difference between a usurping and tyrannical yoke and that of the legitimate proprietor interested in their preservation, then the moment will have come to make them return to their original condition, from which it has been so disastrous to have drawn them. As for the slave-trade, it is more necessary than ever to recruit the *ateliers* after the immense void that ten years of trouble and stoppage of supply have made there. So you should undoubtedly favor it, encouraging the buyer by the formal assurance of the right he will acquire to full proprietorship. For the rest, General, all is subordinated to your wisdom, even the publication of the law in question. You will suspend it if you think proper ; circumstances will determine you. Nobody knows better than you how to estimate them. In the uncertainty of your decision I abstain from writing to the citizen Prefect of the colony ; but I doubt not that your confidence in him will cause you to consult him on an object of such high importance.

These letters were duly forwarded to Guadeloupe and St. Domingo. General Richepanse at Guadeloupe, feeling confidence in his entire control of the colony, published the decree, and announced the res-

toration of slavery in that island.   The story of
Leclerc's experiences in St. Domingo is best continued in his own words.

Leclerc to Decrès.

July 6, 1802 (17 messidor, an x.).

After the embarkment of Toussaint some men wanted
to make trouble.   I have had them shot or sent off.
Since then some colonial troops have had the air of
revolting.   I have ordered the chiefs to be shot, and at
this moment those troops hide their discontent; but the
disbanding operates.   The black generals now see clearly
that I am going to destroy wholly their influence in this
country; but they dare not raise the standard of rebellion,
first, because they all detest each other, and know well
that I would destroy one by means of another; second,
because the blacks are not brave, and this war has terri-
fied them; third, because they fear measuring themselves
with one who has destroyed their chief.   In the circumstances I move steadily with long steps toward my end.
The south and west are nearly disarmed; the north will
begin to be so in a week.   The gendarmerie is organizing,
and as soon as the disarmament is finished and the gendarmerie placed, I will strike the last blows.   If I succeed, as is probable, St. Domingo will then be truly restored to the republic. . . .   The mortality continues, and
at present makes its ravages through the whole colony.
The month of prairial may have cost me three thousand
men; the month of messidor will cost me more; till now
it has cost me one hundred and sixty men a day.   I
have ordered a review of the army by corps.   I have
hardly more than eight thousand five hundred men now
present under arms, not including the two thousand I

have just received. My troops are nevertheless as well nourished as it is possible for them to be, and they suffer no fatigue. . . . Since the 21st germinal (April 11) I have received no letter from you. I have corresponded with you very exactly, and you answer none of my letters. The abandonment you leave me in is cruel. I have asked you for money, clothes, hospital effects, artillery effects, workmen. You have sent me nothing; you announce to me nothing. . . .

The same day Leclerc wrote to the First Consul in a hopeful tone: [1] "In two months I will declare St. Domingo restored to France. I count on making this declaration on the 1st vendémiaire (September 23). Then I will celebrate the fête of the general peace. At that epoch no one will annoy me more at St. Domingo, and you will be satisfied." Yet the captain-general's situation had never been more critical, and the air was almost as full of conspiracy as of pestilence. His next letters, only a week later, showed incessant anxieties.

Leclerc to Decrès. [2]

July 12, 1802 (23 messidor, an x.).

I have not yet been able to order the disarmament of the north. That operation is very delicate. It is impossible for me to think of marching European troops now. A battalion of the Legion of the Cape lost three hundred men in six hundred after three days' march. My black troops are very weak, and the reformed officers agitate

[1] Leclerc to Bonaparte, 17 messidor, an x. Archives nationales MSS.

[2] Archives de la Marine MSS.

them.   My garrison at the Cape is very weak, and I cannot increase it without exposing myself to lose the half of the troops I shall place there.   I am obliged to use much circumspection to succeed. . . . Within a week assemblages by night have taken place in the plain and even in the city.   I do not yet know the chiefs, but I watch them.   The conspirators' object is the massacre of the Europeans.   They are to begin with the generals.   I will leave them no means of executing their designs.   I press the organization of the gendarmerie and the disarmament.   I shall not be at ease till these two operations are finished.

The next despatch, ten days afterward, announced the outbreak of new revolt.

Leclerc to Decrès.

July 23, 1802 (4 thermidor, an x.).

Just now I learn a disagreeable incident; the disarmament at La Tortue has been badly ordered; the blacks have revolted and have burned some houses.   I am going to send troops there.   At the Port de Paix a similar insurrection has occurred.   I have no details.   It is impossible for me to make the European troops march; they break down on the way.   I have few colonial troops; I have given many leaves of absence; it did not suit me to keep a great number of them.   I will advise you hereafter about these insurrections within a few days.   That at Port au Paix might be serious, but I hope to suppress

Leclerc to the First Consul.

August 9, 1802 (21 thermidor, an x.).

My situation since my last despatch is the better for the arrival of about two thousand men from Genoa and

Toulon. I have put these troops to use at once, and their presence has arrested the progress of the insurrection, which is much, in present circumstances. To-morrow I mean to move on different points all the forces I can assemble, both European and colonial. I expect happy results from this operation. I shall have the honor of telling them to you as soon as the operation is finished ; but from now until the 1st vendémiaire (September 23) I expect to be annoyed by handsful of brigands. At that date I shall destroy everything that will not obey me. I am content with Dessalines, Christophe, and Morpas. These three alone have influence ; the others are null. Christophe and Morpas especially have served me much in the late circumstances. Christophe and Dessalines have begged me not to leave them here after my departure ; by that you can judge the confidence they have in me. I hope in the last days of brumaire (November 10–20) to be able to send to France or elsewhere what is in my way here. I hope to leave in ventose (February-March, 1803) ; without doubt you will have sent me a successor by that time. I can assure you that I shall have well deserved rest, for I am nearly crushed here, being almost alone. When I depart, the colony will be ready to receive the régime you shall wish to give it, but it will be for my successor to take the last step. I will do nothing contrary to what I have printed here.

The " last step," the restoration of slavery, was far beyond Leclerc's power to effect, apart from his scruples of consistency. Richepanse had already made the experiment at Guadeloupe, and the mere rumor alarmed Leclerc for the safety of St. Domingo. The blacks became frantic with despair.

Leclerc to Decrès.[1]

August 9, 1802 (21 thermidor, an x.).

I have united all the disposable troops I have, colonial and European. To-morrow I shall attack the rebels on all points. The black generals conduct the columns; they are well surrounded. I have ordered them to make terrible examples, and I always use them when I have to do much harm. This battle will last at least ten days; I will let you know the results. . . . The decrees of General Richepanse circulate here and cause much evil. That which re-establishes slavery, on account of having been published three months too soon, will cost many lives to the army and colony of St. Domingo. I learn news of a bloody combat fought by General Boyer at the Gros Morne. The rebels have been exterminated; fifty prisoners have been hung. These men die with incredible fanaticism; they laugh at death; it is the same with the women. The rebels of the Moustique have attacked and carried Jean Rabel; it should be retaken by this time. This fury is the work of General Richepanse's proclamation and the inconsiderate talk of the colonists.

At last Bonaparte's incessant orders to send the black generals to Europe, as though Leclerc were not the best judge of the situation, irritated the captain-general; and he wrote expressly to explain that the black generals had nothing to do with his troubles; on the contrary they were his only support.

[1] Archives de la Marine MSS.

Leclerc to Decrès.[1]

August 25, 1802 (7 fructidor, an x.),

It appears to me that you have no exact idea of my position, by the orders you send me. You order me to send the black generals to Europe. It is very simple to arrest them all the same day; but these generals serve to arrest the insurgents who are always at work, and who have taken an alarming character in certain cantons. Morpas is treacherous; he serves me now, but he will be arrested shortly. Charles Belair has revolted; I am marching troops against him. Dessalines and Christophe do well, and I am under veritable obligations to them. I have just discovered a great plot which aimed to revolt the whole colony at the end of thermidor (August 15), but was executed only partially for want of a single head. It is not everything to have removed Toussaint; there are two thousand chiefs here to be removed; there is not an overseer but has influence enough to raise his *atelier* at will. Nevertheless, as I take away the arms, the taste for insurrection diminishes. I have already brought in about twenty thousand guns; about as many more remain in the hands of the cultivators. I must certainly have them. . . . I long for the moment when I can send away those who trouble me here, and they will mount to two thousand; but I cannot do it without having enough troops to enter at once into the campaign and march on all the points where I shall find rebels.

Sept. 13, 1802 (26 fructidor).

This is my position! Of the twelve thousand three hundred and two men you announce as to arrive from

[1] Archives de la Marine MSS.

different points, I have received . . . . six thousand
seven hundred and thirty-two. I have received nothing
more. As these troops arrived I have been obliged to
put them into the field to repress the general' insurrections of which I have given you account in my last despatches. During the first days the troops have acted and
have obtained success ; but sickness has affected them,
and with the exception of the Polish Legion, all the
reinforcements yet arrived are destroyed. . . . I cannot give you an exact idea of my position. Each day
makes it worse. . . . If I can have by the 15th vendémiaire (October 7) four thousand Europeans in condition to march, including all you have sent me, and all
I brought with me, I shall be very fortunate. . . . To
give you an idea of my loss, know that the Seventh of
the line arrived here thirteen hundred and ninety-five
strong ; it has now eighty-three sickly men, and one hundred and seven in the hospitals ; the rest have perished.
The Eleventh light regiment arrived with nineteen hundred men ; it has one hundred and sixty-three men in
the corps and two hundred and one in the hospitals.
The Seventy-First, which has received about a thousand
men, has nineteen men with the flags and one hundred
and thirty-three in the hospitals. It is the same with the
rest of the army. So make yourself an idea of my position in a country where civil war has existed for ten
years, and where the insurgents are persuaded that we
mean to reduce them to slavery. . . . During four
months I have snstained myself only by address without
having real strength. Judge whether I can carry out the
instructions of the government.

Leclerc to the First Consul.

Sept. 16, 1802 (29 fructidor).

. . . Immediately on arrival of the news of the re-establishment of slavery at Guadeloupe, the insurrection which till then had been only partial became general, and being unable to make face on all sides, I was obliged to abandon certain points which have suffered. Happily reinforcements arrived in my greatest difficulties. I employed them with success; but after twelve days campaign these corps were annihilated, and the insurrection recovered strength for want of means of repression. . . . Yesterday I caused La Grande Rivière, Ste Suzanne le Dondon, and La Marmalade to be attacked. We succeeded on some points, but the principal positions could not be carried. I had united all my troops for that attack, which renders my position so much the more unpleasant. Here I am, once more obliged to remain on the defensive in the plain of the Cape until the arrival of new reinforcements. My troops are discouraged by effect of climate. This is the condition of my black generals. Morpas is a dangerous rascal. Within a few days I will have him arrested and will send him to you. I am not strong enough just now to arrest him, because his arrest would produce an insurrection in his quarter, and I have already enough for the present. Christophe, to repair the folly he committed in uniting with the blacks, has so maltreated them that they execrate him, and I shall send him to you without fear that his departure will make the least insurrection. I am not satisfied with his conduct yesterday. Dessalines is at this moment the butcher of the blacks; I cause all odious measures to be executed by him. I shall keep him as long as

I need him. I have attached two aides-de-camp to him, who watch him, and talk constantly of the happiness one has in France in having fortune [*du bonheur qu'on a en France d'avoir de la fortune*]. He has already begged me not to leave him behind in St. Domingo. Laplume, Clairvaux, and Paul Louverture are three imbeciles, of whom I will rid myself at my pleasure; this will be as soon as I can. Vernet is a cowardly knave; I shall send him off shortly. Charles Belair has been condemned and will be shot. . . . Yes, citizen Consul! such has been my position; there is no exaggeration. Every day I have been occupied in discovering means of remedying yesterday's evils. Never a consoling idea has come to efface or diminish the cruel impressions of the present and the future; and since the departure of Toussaint, the preservation of St. Domingo is a thing more surprising than my first appearance in this island and the removal of that general.

Leclerc to Decrès.

Sept. 17, 1802 (30 fructidor).

. . . The failure of my attack of the 28th (September 15) renders my position bad in the north. I am going to keep the defensive in the plain of the Cape. . . . I shall be able to protect the plain, supposing always that the sickness stops in the first ten days of vendémiaire. . . . To curb the mountains when I shall reach that object, I shall be obliged to destroy all the provisions and a great part of the cultivators, who, accustomed to brigandage for the past ten years, will never submit to work. I shall have to make a war of extermination, and it will cost me many men. A great part of my colonial troops have deserted and gone over to the enemy. . . .

During this cruel malady, I have sustained myself only by my moral strength and the rumors I have spread of the arrival of troops ; but the news of the re-establishment of slavery at Guadeloupe caused me to lose a great part of my influence over the blacks, and the troops which have already arrived are destroyed like the others. . . .

Leclerc to the First Consul.

Sept. 26, 1802 (4 vendémiaire).

My position becomes worse every day. . . . Every day the insurgents' party increases, and mine diminishes by the loss of whites and the desertion of blacks. Dessalines, who till then had not thought of revolt, is now thinking of it ; but I have his secret, — he will not escape me. This is how I discovered his idea. Not being strong enough to dismiss Dessalines, Christophe, and others, I hold them, the one by the other. All three are suited to be party chiefs ; none will declare himself as long as he has the others to fear. In consequence, Dessalines has begun to make reports to me against Christophe and Morpas, insinuating that their presence is harmful to the colony. He has under his orders a remnant of the Fourth Colonial, which has always been the corps devoted to him ; he has just asked me to let him raise it to a thousand men. A month ago, in the expeditions I ordered him to make, he destroyed the arms ; to-day he destroys no more, and does not maltreat the blacks as he did then. He is a rogue ; I know him. I cannot have him arrested to-day ; I should terrify all the blacks who are with me. Christophe inspires me with a little more confidence. I send to France his eldest son, whom he wants to give an education. Morpas is a scamp ; but I cannot yet have him carried off. I may cause Morpas to be first taken, but Christophe and Dessalines will follow the same day. Never did a general find himself in a more trying position. The troops arrived within a month no longer exist. Every day the rebels make attacks in the plain; they burn, and their musketry is heard at the Cape. I cannot possibly take the offensive; it crushes my troops, and I have not enough means for taking it and following up the advantages that I could obtain. . . . I have told you my opinion of the measures taken by General Richepanse at Guadeloupe. Unfortunately the event justifies it; the last news announce that colony in flames. . . .

Leclerc to Decrès.

Sept. 26, 1802 (4 vendémiaire).

. . . All my army is destroyed, even the reinforcements you have sent me. . . . Every day the blacks quit me. The unfortunate decree of General Richepanse, which restored slavery at Guadeloupe, is the cause of our evils.

The last letter from Leclerc that threw light on his situation was written a fortnight after these, and seemed written purposely to answer the complaints of his conduct which were to be made by Napoleon at St. Helena.

Leclerc to the First Consul.

Oct. 7, 1802 (15 vendémiaire).

. . . The sickness continues, . . . and I estimate my loss every day at one hundred and thirty men in the whole colony. . . . During messidor and a part of thermidor, I held the country without real force. At the end of thermidor the war began, and doubled my losses in men. At the end of fructidor my army and my reinforcements were destroyed. Then the blacks, witnessing my weakness, became bold. However wise my decree for the raising of sequestrations may have been, the farmers, who saw that at the expiration of their leases they would lose their farms, believed that if they took advantage of our disasters they would end by driving us out of the colony. The black generals, who had been till then held back by fear, fomented these insurrections. They spread among the colonial troops the rumor of our approaching embarkation to induce those to desert who were still faithful to us. Their plan succeeded only too well; very few colonial troops remain with me. A battalion of the Eleventh Colonial, which had been united with the Legion of the Cape, having furnished a number of deserters, one hundred and seventy-six men of this battalion were embarked from Jacmel for Port Republican; of this number, one hundred and seventy-three strangled themselves on the way, their major at their head. These are the men we have to fight! . . . I have ordered the arrest of Morpas and Dessalines, who have much to do with all this; I will also arrest Vernet. I have no occasion to spare the blacks further; they are all in insurrection. You will perhaps blame me for not having sooner got rid of the black chiefs; but bear in mind that I have never been in a position to do it, and that I had expected to be able at this season to act against them. I have no false measure here to reproach myself with, citizen Consul; and if my position, from being a very good one, has become very bad, no blame can be attached here to anything except the sickness that destroyed my army, the premature re-establishment of slavery at Guadeloupe, and the journals and letters from France which talked only of slavery. . . .

The despatches of October 7 were the last that Leclerc sent home. Worn out and disheartened, he was attacked by a slow fever which gradually reduced his strength, until he died November 2, leaving the colony in a condition of revolt more obstinate than he had found on arriving.

During all this time Bonaparte seemed to have but one idea, — "Get rid of these gilded Africans, and there will be nothing more to desire." [1] Christophe, Dessalines, and their lieutenants represented to him the whole revolt, when in truth the revolt began in spite of them, and received no considerable support from them until it had succeeded. "The decree of the 28th floréal, 1801 (30 floréal, 1802)," said Napoleon at St. Helena, "was only a pretext; the blacks revolted as a consequence of the intrigues of England. . . . Then the captain-general repented having been so indulgent, and not having executed the orders of the First Consul. All would have passed very differently had he disembarrassed the colony of one hundred and fifty or two hundred black chiefs." The clinging to one small idea in an analysis of such vast errors marked a feature of Napoleon's character.

The idea that leaders were everything and masses without leaders were nothing, was a military view of society which led Napoleon into all his worst miscalculations. The tragedy of Toussaint at Dennery was repeated six years afterward at Madrid by different actors with identical results, — the same revolts, the

[1] Bonaparte to Leclerc, July 1, 1802; Correspondance, vii. 503.

same massacres, the same want of leaders up among the insurgents, the same frightful waste of life on both sides, and the same miserable failure, concealed less successfully by the same effort to throw blame on subordinates. Unfortunately for Napoleon, he could not abandon Spain as he abandoned his colonies; he could only shut his eyes to his own errors, and hurry to repeat the same mistakes in Germany and Russia, until he had roused to desperation the masses of all Northern Europe as he had roused the negroes of St. Domingo and the peasantry of Spain.

Even the death of Leclerc did not necessarily cost France her colony. The sickly season was then passed; a new army of sixteen thousand men was on its way to St. Domingo, which raised the force above twenty thousand men, and a competent general, well supported, might have made short work of resistance. Nothing less than extermination would have suppressed the revolt; but Leclerc and his officers expected and intended to exterminate, until the entire male population of certain districts, capable of bearing arms, should be killed. Leclerc was on the point of beginning operations on this plan when he died. He meant to isolate one district after another, and apply, in succession to each, a process resembling extermination.

Had Bonaparte followed Leclerc's repeated advice, by sending officers competent to relieve his cares or to succeed him, and had the French government adhered obstinately to its colonial policy, giving to the captain-general the support he wanted, the negroes must have succumbed. None of the French generals doubted that, with time and means, the military result could be attained. Instead of following Leclerc's wishes, Bonaparte neglected the colony, except by fits and starts; he sent out no competent officer to aid or succeed Leclerc, but busied himself with European quarrels, and showed that the colonial scheme was little to his taste. As Leclerc had foreseen, the command fell at his death on General Rochambeau, an incompetent officer, who began his administration, December 7, by writing a demand for thirty-five thousand men, and then introduced a period of senseless and debauched cruelty and violence without a parallel even in the history of the Empire. He was in the midst of a frantic career, when the First Consul suddenly began a new war with England, which served the double purpose of hiding from France the loss of St. Domingo and Louisiana, and of restoring to Bonaparte his freedom of action on the only field where he could display his true instincts without restraint.

12

THE BANK OF ENGLAND RESTRICTION.

1797–1821.[1]

DURING the eighteenth century the mechanism of trade was elaborated in Great Britain to a high point of perfection. London became in a great degree the centre of commerce for the world, while the Bank of England was the business centre of London. The Bank had a double sphere of usefulness. As a private corporation it exercised, not less by the high character of its directors than by the amount of its capital and the privileges of its charter, great influence over all foreign and domestic trade. By common agreement, its notes circulated within London to the exclusion of other bank-paper. Its discounts represented a great proportion of the active capital of England. Its operations were not restricted within the limits of ordinary banking; it was also a recognized official agent. As a national establishment, it issued the coin, managed the debt, took charge of government deposits, and made advances to the Exchequer and the Treasury, on security of Exchequer

[1] From the North American Review for October, 1867.

bills. In the same capacity it was expected to maintain a supply of gold, not merely for circulation, but in anticipation of any sudden drain which might cause a run upon the other banking institutions of the country. It was obliged, therefore, to purchase at a fixed rate all the gold brought to its counters. Thus as a bank of discount it held the exclusive privilege of discounting government paper; as a bank of deposit it held the public balances; as a bank of issue, its circulation alone passed through the hands of the government as well as of the public. Its notes, when not issued in loans on Exchequer bills to the government, or in payment for the precious metals, could pass into circulation only through discounts furnished to merchants. At no time has the Bank had other than these three means of issuing its paper; and as no notes could be paid for bullion which did not represent their equivalent in bullion brought in, the only modes of issuing an excess of paper were either by loans to the government on security of Exchequer bills, or in regular and legitimate commercial discounts.

All foreign and most provincial payments were ultimately settled by drafts on London; but the country merchants and others, who had occasion to extend their connections beyond the limits of a district, found it convenient to deal through the local bankers of their neighborhood rather than to draw upon correspondents of their own. In 1797 about three hundred and fifty such country banks existed in England

and Wales, most of which were banks of issue ; and as they were always obliged to redeem their notes either in gold, in Bank of England notes, or in bills of exchange drawn on London, their circulation was subject to the variations of the London money-market.

Besides this practical check, another control was exercised by the Bank of England over the credit operations of the country. Every private banker naturally felt that his credit depended upon the solvency of his customers ; and he was obliged, by the nature of his business, to acquire accurate knowledge of the people who dealt with him. In the same way the London banker, his correspondent, looked carefully to the country client's credit, and to the character of the bills in which he dealt ; while the London banker was subjected to the scrutiny of the business community of London, whose opinions, centring upon one point, guided the policy and the particular discounts and accommodations of the Bank of England. Thus again the Bank was at once the head and heart of English credit ; it exercised a controlling influence even upon the remote provincial trader.

So far as concerned the currency, the Bank could by contracting its issues affect in a short time the whole circulation of England ; and naturally, when such a contraction had taken place, a renewed expansion on its part would be likely to result in a similar movement on the part of private bankers. The antiquated and mischievous legislation of Parliament still maintained, and in spite of practical lessons long continued to maintain, a legal maximum of interest at five per cent, even when the government itself was borrowing at six. At present the Bank regulates its discounts by raising or lowering its rate according to the value of money in the open market; but while the usury laws were in force, the Bank continued to lend its credit at five per cent, whether the market value was at two or at twenty; and it possessed no means of restricting its discounts and contracting its circulation other than that of refusing a certain proportion of each applicant's paper, without regard to his solvency or credit. Such a measure was seldom resorted to, since it was calculated to aggravate the evils of a financial pressure by sacrificing the public in order to save the Bank. In practice, the Bank avoided the exercise of any other control over its discounts and circulation than was implied by a proper regard for the soundness of the bills it discounted. The directors might exercise more or less caution in their loans, according as individual credit varied; but they never during the restriction attempted to act upon exchange or general credit, either by contracting or by expanding their issues.

The average amount of Bank of England notes in circulation during ten years before the restriction, was £10,800,000. The best authorities estimate that the coin in circulation may have then amounted to about £20,000,000, or somewhat more. A large quantity of country bank-paper was also circulated; while certain wealthy districts, as Lancashire for example, used no other currency than bills of exchange, which were passed from hand to hand, and in every case indorsed by the holder. No reasonable confidence can be placed in any estimate which assumes to establish a fixed sum representing the value of English currency previous to the restriction. Perhaps £40,000,000 would be a moderate value to assign for it; and from this calculation Scotland and Ireland are excluded, since their currency systems were independent of England, and exercised no more influence upon hers than those of Holland or Hamburg.

The great war, which continued, with only a few months' intermission, for upward of twenty years, began in February, 1793. It was preceded and accompanied by a commercial crisis throughout Europe, which caused in England a great number of bankruptcies and a fall in prices, the country banks suffering especially; but the Bank of England succeeded in maintaining its credit unimpaired under the shock, and in spite of every difficulty continued its specie payments and its ordinary discounts, to the relief of the mercantile community. Two years of the war passed without altering this position of affairs. Not until 1795 did a drain of bullion to the Continent begin, which obliged the Bank directors to contract their issues by rejecting a certain proportion of the applications made upon them for discounts, without regard to the credit of the applicants. During the next two years the Bank circulation was steadily diminished, as the supply of gold became smaller; but the policy of contraction was hampered by the necessities of Mr. Pitt, then prime minister, who insisted upon advances, which the directors could not properly furnish. The Bank records were filled with repeated remonstrances addressed to Pitt on this account, and in February, 1796, these were carried to the extent of an absolute refusal to discharge the bills drawn; while again, in July of the same year, a similar refusal was overcome only by the positive assurance of Pitt that the most serious and distressing embarrassments to the public service could not be avoided unless advances to the extent of £800,000 were made. The Bank yielded, but only under protest, declaring that nothing but the extreme pressure and exigency of the case could justify the directors in acceding.

Whether this source of difficulty was due to bad management on the part of Pitt, or whether he had no choice but to lean upon the Bank, is of little consequence. The directors carried out their policy of contraction. While the drain of gold continued, and their treasure fell from £6,000,000 in 1795 to £2,000,000 in August, 1796, the circulation was simultaneously reduced from £14,000,000 to £9,000,000. Violent as this contraction was, it failed to counteract the causes of the drain. Foreign subsidies, the payment for large quantities of imported grain, and of articles the price of which had been enormously increased by the war demand, prevented the exchanges from rising. For three years, from 1794 to 1796, these extraordinary payments were estimated at £40,000,000, — a calculation certainly not extravagant, if compared with the length of time and the amount of pressure required to restore the exchanges.

The Bank could hardly do more to preserve the country from the evils of an inconvertible currency. The directors might have refused to advance another shilling in loans, and in order to save themselves might have forced a national bankruptcy, as well as general private ruin ; but they could scarcely have reduced their issues more resolutely than they did, or resisted more obstinately the entreaties of the merchants. These last were sacrificed; and their fate was especially hard, since the crisis was caused by no act of theirs, but by a combination of political and natural agencies, by bad harvests and foreign wars, over which they could have exercised no control, and on the occurrence or the cessation of which they could not have calculated.

The measures thus taken by the Bank were successful. Early in 1797 the tide had already turned; the foreign exchanges began to improve ; and had the Bank been able to stand another month or two of pressure, gold would probably have flowed into its coffers. Precisely at the time of extreme exhaustion, after the foreign drain had been checked, but when the Bank was too weak for further resistance, a sudden panic seized the people of England. An ungrounded alarm of French invasion caused a run upon the banks of Newcastle, and obliged them to suspend payment. From Newcastle the panic spread in all directions. Every country banker rushed to the Bank of England for assistance or for gold. The Bank responded by forcing its issues down to £8,640,000, while its treasure fell to £1,200,000, and the panic naturally grew more and more violent. Hopeless of averting their fate, the directors at last sent word to Pitt that suspension was inevitable; and on the morning of Monday, the 27th of February, an Order in Council, issued the preceding day, was posted on the doors of the Bank, forbidding further payments in cash.

The policy of the Bank throughout the crisis has been since that day generally criticised; and the directors themselves afterward expressed the opinion that the contraction had been pressed too far, until it contributed to bring about the difficulty it was intended to preclude. A bolder course might have been adopted; the discounts might have been liberally increased, and the gold paid out to the last guinea. In support of this policy is instanced the celebrated crisis of 1825, when the Bank, in face of a drain which reduced its stock of gold to £1,027,000, increased its issues from £17,000,000 to £25,000,000, and succeeded in restoring confidence and maintaining its payments. However this may be, Pitt should not have sanctioned suspension before exhausting every alternative. At the worst, the Bank could only have refused to redeem its notes. While a chance of escap-

ing this final disaster remained, neither Pitt nor the
Bank directors were justified in neglecting it. The
mere political consequences of suspension, in that
disastrous year, were a triumph to the enemy as important as the mutiny at the Nore or the Treaty of
Leoben.

Pitt felt only the necessity of maintaining the
credit of the Bank, and thought that this might be
done by giving to the suspension an official appearance, throwing upon it the character of a compulsory
act of government. He represented the Bank as a
passive, or even unwilling, instrument in the hands
of the Privy Council. The expedient was unlikely to
deceive any person, however dull of comprehension,
but its result was fortunate; for while Pitt declared
that the affairs of the Bank were in the most affluent
and flourishing condition, and that the restriction
was only a precautionary government measure, which
in a few weeks would be removed, he established a
legal fiction of some value. Parliament never recognized any incapacity on the part of the Bank to meet
its obligations, but only a temporary restriction, created by Parliament itself, and limited by law to a certain period. A distinction favorable to national pride
and private credit was involved in this idea that no
actual bankruptcy existed, but that the government
had seen fit, for the public convenience, to relieve
the Bank for a time from a duty which it was still
ready and able to perform.

Pitt was glad to use this or any other device in

order to quiet the general alarm. The idea of inconvertible currency was, in 1797, associated with the Continental paper of the American Congress, and with the assignats of the French Directory. Men like Fox and Lord Lansdowne supposed that the mere fact of inconvertibility must soon destroy that confidence in paper which enabled it to represent values. A few months were believed sufficient to bring about this decay of credit. To provide against such a disaster, extraordinary efforts were required. On the day of suspension, a great meeting was held at the Mansion House, the Lord Mayor presiding; and more than three thousand business men pledged themselves, by resolution, to receive and to make their payments in bank-notes, as equivalent to coin. A nearly similar paper was signed and published by the Lords of the Council. In modern times such a pledge would, in similar circumstances, be considered superfluous; but in that day it had a value, and tended to restore public confidence. Had the foreign drain still continued, bank paper would no doubt have fallen to a discount, in spite of all the resolutions that could be passed; but this cause of difficulty had ceased to act. The only effect of suspension was to lower the exchanges for a few days, after which they again rallied, and before the close of the year they rose to the highest point ever known. The Bank increased its issues, and commerce returned to its regular routine.

The suspension having taken place, Parliament was

obliged to intervene, not merely to legalize the act, but to establish the new condition of the Bank. A secret committee was appointed, which made elaborate investigations, and concluded by reporting a bill indemnifying the governor and directors for all acts done in pursuance of the Order in Council, superseding all actions which might have been brought against them for refusing payments, prohibiting them from issuing cash except in sums under twenty shillings, sheltering them from prosecutions for withholding payment of notes for which they were willing to offer other notes in exchange, restricting them from advancing to the Treasury any sum exceeding £600,000, obliging the collectors of revenue to receive bank-notes in payment, protecting the subject from arrest for debt unless the affidavit to hold him to bail contained a statement that the amount of debt claimed had not been tendered in money or bank-notes, and limiting the duration of the restriction to the 24th of June following.

The policy of Pitt may not have been bold or necessarily correct, but it was at least free from the mistakes which ruined or dishonored almost every other country where an inconvertible currency existed. He began by treating the suspension as a temporary difficulty, and limiting its duration. In this respect, his successors followed his example ; and never, during the next twenty-three years, did Parliament allow the country to consider the restriction as other than a temporary measure, for the termination of which a provision was made by law. Pitt further pledged the government not to make an improper use of the Bank resources, or to tamper with the currency by obtaining excessive advances; and this pledge he observed. Finally, he refused to make the bank-note a legal tender except between the government and the public, still allowing the creditor to insist upon payment in coin if he chose to do so, and leaving open to him his ordinary process in law, except only the power of arrest in the first instance. England probably owed much to Pitt for his forbearance in regard to the currency. His necessities were great, and his power was unlimited. He might have used paper money as was done by contemporary financiers; but the example he set became a law for his successors, so that whatever mistakes he or his imitators made, they did not tamper with the currency.

The Restriction Act passed without opposition, and in June was continued till one month after the commencement of the next session. In the mean time gold began again to flow into the Bank, which held in August treasure to the amount of £4,000,000, against a circulation of £11,000,000. When Parliament again met in the autumn, the Bank directors announced themselves ready to resume payments, " if the political circumstances of the country do not render it inexpedient."

Had Pitt been able to foresee the course of events during the next ten years, he would surely have acted upon this opportunity. The dangers and temptations of irredeemable paper were too obvious for any statesman to incur them unless under necessity. Pitt probably foresaw something very different from what actually occurred. He had reason to expect a series of monetary convulsions and commercial misfortunes, such as had harassed him since 1792. On the other hand, he saw that none of the prophesied evils followed restriction. Bank-paper did not depend for its credit merely on its convertibility. Month after month passed, not only without bringing depreciation, but even rapidly increasing the stream of precious metals which flowed toward England, so that people were little inclined to dwell upon the dangers or temptations of restriction, and probably overestimated its value as a safeguard against panic. They were already demoralized. Pitt was not ashamed to fall back upon the hint given by the Bank directors, and to declare " that the avowal by the enemy of his intention to ruin our public credit was the motive for an additional term of restriction," — thus, as Tierney rejoined, in order to leave the enemy no credit to attack, destroying it himself ; for France was prevented by the restriction from no action upon public credit, except that of causing another restriction.

The bill by which the measure was continued till one month after the conclusion of peace passed with little opposition, Fox and his friends having ceased to take part in the debates. Had the Bank been obliged to resume its cash payments, it would have had no great difficulty in maintaining them till 1808 or 1809 when it must, from political causes have again broken down; but the occasion was lost, and from that time the restriction took its place among the permanent war-measures of the government.

Previous to the suspension, no bank-note of less than five pounds in value was allowed to circulate. Under the new state of affairs this prohibition was removed, and notes of one and two pounds began to drive gold from ordinary use. With this exception, the public was unaffected by the change in the currency. Throughout the year 1798 the Bank continued to receive treasure and the foreign exchanges continued favorable, until at the end of February, 1799, more than £7,500,000 had accumulated in the Bank vaults, against a note circulation of less than £13,000,000. Apparently nothing could be more solid than such a position. No expansion of consequence occurred in the Bank circulation; yet by the close of 1799 the exchanges turned against England, and the gold began to disappear almost as rapidly as it had accumulated. The explanation of this sudden revolution was simple. A deficient harvest had caused large importations of corn; a severe commercial crisis at Hamburg produced a pressure for the immediate transmission of funds from England; and the war on the Continent created a perpetual demand for gold to supply the armies. Had the Bank been obliged to redeem its notes, it might probably have contracted its issues. Instead of doing so, it extended them in proportion to the increased demand for discounts thrown upon it by the rise in the market-rate of interest, and the circulation rose till in the first quarter of 1801 it averaged nearly £16,500,000. The price of gold also rose, until it stood at a premium of ten per cent.

These events naturally caused uneasiness; they gave rise, indeed, to the first currency controversy. Mr. Boyd, a member of Parliament, published a pamphlet with the object of proving that the depreciation was due to the excess of bank-notes. He was answered by Sir Francis Baring and Mr. Henry Thornton, whose work remains to this day a standard authority. The question then raised was practically identical with that which ten years afterward excited elaborate and earnest discussion. Events soon decided in favor of Boyd's opponents. The Bank continued its policy undisturbed; the pressure ceased; during 1801 and 1802 the foreign exchanges again rose, and gold fell almost to par. The temporary depreciation of 1801 was preceded by the fall of exchange and was caused by it; and when the accidental foreign demand for gold had been satisfied, the currency returned to its natural value, without effort on the part of the Bank, or artificial pressure on credit or on circulation.

The Treaty of Amiens was signed in March, 1802; and the interval of peace allowed Great Britain a momentary relief of inestimable value. The Restriction Act was again continued for another term, and the Bank circulation rose to nearly £17,400,000,

without producing any sensible effect on exchange or
on the price of gold. War was resumed in May,
1803, but without affecting the currency, which during the next five years remained stationary in its
amount, or varied slightly between £16,000,000 and
£17,000,000. The Bank, anxious to maintain its reserve of bullion, offered a standing premium of about
three per cent for gold, which caused a common belief that bank-notes were depreciated to that extent.
This was not the case. Under such circumstances
the exchanges became the only true standard, and in
those days the quotations of exchange included any
existing depreciation of paper; the nominal, not the
real, exchange was always given, so that in the want
of fair quotations of gold, its fluctuations in value
were recorded only by the recorded fluctuations in
exchange. These were slight, and rather in favor of
England than against her, so that the Bank had
accumulated in 1805 the unusual sum of £7,600,000,
— a result showing that the bank-notes with which
this treasure was bought could not have been depreciated to the full extent of the three-per-cent bonus
offered as an inducement to the seller. During the
whole of this period from 1803 to 1808, Bank paper
was in fact at par, or not enough below it to make
the exportation of gold profitable in a time of specie
payments. At intervals no doubt the Bank lost gold,
but if the average of each year be taken, the exchanges were uniformly favorable.

No comparison can be just between such a state of

things and the ordinary forced issues of government
paper, known in most countries suffering under prolonged difficulties.　A distinct difference exists between the two cases, which removes the English
currency from the same class with ordinary instances
of depreciation.　Usually the issue of paper has been
assumed by governments, and such issues have been
made directly in payment of expenses, without providing on the same scale for a return of the paper put
out, or consulting the wants of the people.　Bank of
England paper was in no sense a government issue.
It was not even government paper, but merely that
of a private banking corporation, conducted on strict
banking principles, whose notes, so far as they were
in excess of public wants, were inevitably returned at
once to the Bank counters.　The government was not
to blame if paper was issued in excess; in such a case
the Bank directors must have failed to observe proper
rules in their extensions of credit either to the government or to individuals.

It is necessary, therefore, to turn aside for a moment in order to examine the Bank rules of that day
in their ordinary action upon circulation, since there
the secret will be found, not only of the steadiness
which marked the currency during the first ten years
of war, but of its extraordinary fluctuations afterward, — fluctuations quite inexplicable on the suppo-
sition of a forced issue.　The usury laws fixed the
highest legal rate of interest at five per cent.　The
Bank rule during the whole period of restriction

was to discount at that rate all good mercantile bills offered, having not more than sixty-one days to run; and in making these advances the only duty which the directors considered themselves obliged to observe was that of throwing out, so far as possible, all bills which were believed to represent speculative transactions. In other respects the Bank was passive, neither contracting nor expanding its issues, but allowing the public demand to contract or expand the currency, in the conviction that the public would not retain more notes than were actually required. Naturally the demand for discount at the Bank varied according to the market-rate of interest outside; and when private bankers lent money at three per cent, comparatively few persons cared to pay five to the Bank of England. During the early part of the war the Bank-rate was in fact almost always higher than that in the open market, and consequently the Bank issues were moderate. By a regularly self-balancing principle, the advances made to government in an ordinary state of affairs diminished the private demand, since the government at once paid away to the public the notes it received from the Bank, — and this money coming back to the private bankers, enabled them to extend their discounts and to accommodate those merchants who would otherwise have been obliged to apply to the Bank. The theoretical question what would have been the result had government obliged the Bank to make excessive advances on its account, requires no reply. In point of fact the case did not occur, and government contented itself with moderate accommodation; while, as a rule, private demands were greatest when the advances to government were at the lowest point.

Thus the Bank was a mere channel of credit. It did not, and under these rules it could not, exercise direct control over its issues, and it conducted its business upon much the same principles as would have regulated any sound private banker, whether he issued notes or not. The Bank thought itself in no way bound to regard the exchanges or the price of gold, or to interfere with the course of business. Its sole duty was to lend capital; the public and each individual merchant must see that his affairs were in a proper condition, that speculation was avoided, that the exchanges were watched, or take the consequences of neglecting such precautions.

So long as each individual did observe a proper degree of precaution, or until political difficulties or some other accidental cause deranged the ordinary state of credit, these rules of the Bank answered the purpose for which they were made; but while the usury laws remained in force, any rise in the market-rate of interest was certain to precipitate the whole body of merchants upon the Bank of England; and any crisis which obliged private bankers to seek instead of furnishing credit, was sure to bring the whole nation to the counters of the Bank. In either of these cases the Bank was liable to be driven into an excessive issue of its paper and extension of its credit; but such an expansion did not necessarily lead to a permanent increase of the circulation. On the contrary, whenever the crisis was over, and the rate of interest again had fallen below the Bank standard, the demand for discount would naturally decline, and the circulation would return to its normal state.

For two or three years after the war had been resumed, everything continued in a sound and regular course. Great Britain might have carried on hostilities indefinitely, had she been subjected to no greater pressure. The currency retained its value and trade its regularity, but taxation was greatly augmented and the cost of production increased. Prices steadily rose, until they attained in 1805 almost as high a range as ever afterward. With the exception of grain, an article peculiarly liable to be affected by accidental causes, almost the whole rise in prices — afterward attributed to depreciation of currency — took place during the first twelve or fifteen years of the war, when no depreciation existed. Much of it occurred at a time when paper was highest in credit, and the same thing would probably have happened if the Bank had continued its specie payments.

This comparatively happy and prosperous state of affairs was not destined to continue. While the English waged a cheap and effective war on the ocean and in the colonies; while Nelson crushed the combined navies of France and Spain at Trafalgar, and Wellington subdued the Mahrattas in India, Napo-

leon reached Vienna, and turning from Austerlitz to
Berlin, swept the whole of Germany into the hands
of France. From Berlin he turned to Russia, and at
Friedland stopped for want of other countries to
conquer.

Such successes promised little good to England.
Napoleon hastened to turn his new power against her.
From Berlin, in November, 1806, he issued the famous decree declaring the British Islands in a state
of blockade, confiscating English property wherever
found, and prohibiting all intercourse with the British
nation. Russia joined the coalition in the following
year, and Sweden in 1809. Thus the Continent was
closed to English commerce.

Napoleon's Continental system was a prodigious
shock to Great Britain. There seemed no end to the
losses and complications which it caused. Yet one
country remained beyond its reach, whose commerce
was of inestimable importance. The United States
of America continued to be an open market, and the
Berlin Decree almost forced the United States into
the arms of England. Yet the British government
actually assisted Napoleon to extend his Continental
system even to America. The Berlin Decree, and
that of Milan which followed it, declared the British Islands to be in a state of blockade, and ordered
that no ship should enter any port under the control of France if she came from England, or had
touched at England, or if any part of her cargo was
English. The British government retaliated in Jan-

uary, 1807, by issuing an Order in Council interdicting the passage of vessels between any two ports not open to British commerce; and in November it declared all ports closed to the British flag to be in a state of blockade, and all vessels trading to or from such ports, or carrying any produce of such countries, to be, with their cargoes, lawful prize. The American government responded to these outrages by interdicting commerce with both England and France.

No ordinary review can undertake so difficult and complicated a labor as that of examining the various effects of these measures on English credit and currency. That British trade with the Continent was annihilated, that the course of exchange was for a time impossible to determine, and indebtedness beyond reach or recovery was but the most obvious and immediate result. No sooner were the decrees enforced, than all articles for a supply of which England depended on the Continent rose to speculative prices. Flax, linseed, tallow, timber, Spanish wool, silk, hemp, even American cotton, advanced in 1807 and 1808 to prices two or three times those till then prevailing. While one class of imports was thus thrown into the hands of speculative holders, another class, consisting of colonial produce, underwent an opposite process. The European market was closed to it. Sugar and coffee sold at Calais for three, four, and five times their price at Dover. Meanwhile the almost omnipotent naval force of

Great Britain contributed under the Orders in Council to aggravate the evil, and to pile up still vaster quantities of unsalable goods in British warehouses, by compelling every neutral ship to make for an English port.

A wild spirit of speculation then took possession of the British people. Brazil and the South American colonies of Spain happened to offer a new market, and merchants flung themselves into it as though it had no limit. The beach at Rio Janeiro was for a time covered with English merchandise, with no warehouses to hold and no chance of selling it. In London, a rage for visionary joint-stock enterprises characterized the years 1807 and 1808. None of the symptoms were wanting which long experience has shown to be precursors of commercial disaster.

The Bank of England still preserved its steady and conservative routine. The issues were not increased, the price of gold did not vary, the exchanges had not fallen below par, as late as September, 1808. So far as concerned the Bank, no unusual speculation existed. It neither lent itself nor was asked to lend itself to speculative objects. Speculators did not act through the Bank ; but if one turns to the private and country bankers, and out of the almost impenetrable obscurity in which this part of the subject is hidden attempts to gather evidence of their condition, one will find, not indeed that their paper was depreciated, — for that it could not be without immediately bankrupting the issuer, — but that their credit had been extended beyond moderate limits. The number of country banks had been more than doubled in ten years, but of greater consequence than this was the change which had gradually crept into their mode of conducting business. Originally their rules of discount had been the same as those of the Bank of England ; they accepted only short bills, representing, so far as they could judge, real transactions. They gradually began to make advances upon bills of longer date, and then to lend money without security of any kind. Paper which could not be discounted in London was sent down to them by their London agents. Their West Indian bills had from twelve to thirty-six months to run. They made little inquiry as to what might be accommodation paper, and still less about the speculative transactions of their customers. The reaction which ultimately followed, at the time when the Bank circulation was greatly increased and increasing, proved the extent to which private credit had been abused.

To this point the subject offers comparatively few difficulties. Beyond it, the whole region has been a favorite battle-ground for armies of currency theorists. Only within the last thirty years a fair comprehension of the matters in dispute has been made possible through the great work of Thomas Tooke. The opinions first advocated, and the facts first proved by the author of the " History of Prices," have since been accepted by some of the highest authorities in political economy, of whom John Stuart Mill stands at the head. That they are still contested in England only adds to the interest of the inquiry.

Until September, 1808, the exchanges remained favorable to England, and the price of gold continued firm. During the first half-year, the average Bank circulation had been £16,950,000 ; at the end of August, £17,200,000 were in issue. These sums were not excessive. If the small notes — which merely supplied the place of coin withdrawn — are deducted, the real circulation was but £12,993,000, less than had frequently been in issue before, and considerably less than has always been in issue since.[1] The prices

[1] BANK CIRCULATION.

Date.	Total.	Notes of £5 and upward	Bank Treasure.	Price of Gold
1797, 28 February	£9,674,780	£9,674,780	£1,086,170	100
31 August	11,114,120	10,246,535	4,089,620	100
1798, 28 February	13,095,830	11,647,610	5,828,940	100
31 August	12,180,610	10,649,550	6,546,100	100
1799, 28 February	12.959,800	11,494,150	7,563,900	100
31 August	13,389,490	12,047,790	7,000,780	100
1800, 28 February	16,844,470	15,372,930	6,144,258	109
31 August	15,047,180	13,448,540	5,150.450	109
1801, 28 February	16,213,280	13,678,520	4,640,120	107.85
31 August	14,556,110	12,143,460	4,335,260	106.5
1802, 28 February	15,186,880	12,574,860	4,152,950	106.2
31 August	17,097,630	13,848,470	3,891,780	103
1803, 28 February	15,319,930	12,350,970	3,776,750	103
31 August	15,983,330	12,217,390	3,592,500	103
1804, 28 February	17,077,830	12,546,560	3,372,140	103
31 August	17,153,890	12,466,790	5,879,190	103
1805, 28 February	17,871,170	13,011,010	5,883,800	103
31 August	16,388,400	11,862,740	7,624,500	103
1806, 28 February	17,730,120	13,271,520	5,987,190	103
31 August	21,027,470	16,757,930	6,215,020	103
1807, 28 February	16,950,680	12,840,790	6,142,840	103
31 August	19,678,360	15,432,990	6,484,350	103
1808, 28 February	18,188,860	14,093,690	7,855,470	103
31 August	17,111,290	12,993,020	6,015,940	103

of all commodities, except grain, had already reached
their highest point, or reached it within six months
afterward.   At this time, when no change except
ordinary fluctuations had occurred in the currency for
seven years, the exchanges suddenly turned, and the
price of gold rose.

The Continental system had begun to act.   The
mercantile ventures of the last year proved ruinous ;
the enormous importations at fabulous prices required
to be paid for ; the unfortunate military expeditions
which Great Britain was renewing against the Continent demanded the transmission of gold.   England
was paying money in every direction, and she was
selling her goods nowhere.   No one watched this
process of exhaustion more carefully, or understood
its consequences better, than Napoleon.

The Bank, following its invariable routine of business, took no notice of the sharp fall in exchanges, or
of the heavy drain which rapidly reduced its treasure,
and instead of contracting its issues, allowed them
slowly to expand, according to the demand for discount.   From £13,000,000 in 1808, the circulation
in notes of £5 and upward rose to £14,325,000 in
November, 1809.   The exchanges indicated already
a difference of about fifteen per cent between paper
and gold.   Meanwhile the government expenses requiring transmission of coin abroad had increased
to above £10,000,000 for the year.   The excessive
prices of that class of goods which could be obtained
only from the Continent stimulated merchants to

procure them. Ships' papers were regularly forged as a matter of business ; licenses for trading were obtained at great expense from both governments. Importations were by these means greatly increased, and large quantities of grain were bought to supply an unusual deficiency in the harvest. The receipts of cotton were more than doubled, and the market was again overwhelmed with colonial produce. Thus no opportunity was allowed for a recovery of the exchanges, and the country continued to be drained steadily of its gold.

Throughout the year 1810 the same process was continued. Again the importations were greatly increased, and the quantity of grain brought from abroad was far in excess of what had been imported in any year since 1801. Wellington was in the lines of Torres Vedras, requiring continual supplies of gold ; the military efforts made by England on the Continent were greater than ever before, and the foreign expenditure rose beyond £12,000,000 for the year. The exchanges continued to fall, although at one time there was a tendency to recovery ; gold remained at about the same premium as in 1809, while the government and the public equally increased their demands on the Bank, until in August the circulation of large notes rose to £17,570,000.

If irredeemable government paper had been forced upon the public without regard to its wants, until within a space of two years the currency had swelled from a total of £17,000,000 to one of £24,500,000, the result would have been a rise in prices and an increase of speculation. According to old currency theories, such ought to have been the case with England. In fact, the contrary result took place. During the last months of 1809 and the whole of 1810 a fall of prices and a destruction of private credit occurred, which for severity remains perhaps to this day without a parallel, as it was then without a precedent. Half the traders in the kingdom became bankrupt, or were obliged to compound. Country banks by dozens were swept out of existence. Rich and poor alike were plunged in distress, while the crash extended to the Continent and to America. This universal collapse of credit, by driving the whole trading-class for assistance to the Bank, obliged the Bank to increase its issues. Nothing but an absolute refusal of discounts could have prevented suspension, had the Bank been paying its notes in specie. According to one theory, the withdrawal of so much country bank-paper should have restored gold to par, since the Bank issues supplied only a part of the vacancy. This would no doubt have been the case if the depreciation had been the result of over-issue; but the depreciation was due to unfavorable foreign exchanges, and England had not the means of correcting it. The foreign debt of England was enormous; its immediate payment was necessary; gold was the only exportable commodity, and gold was not to be had. Alexander Baring declared in the House of Commons, that, if his firm wished to obtain fifty thousand pounds sterling for transmission abroad, he did not know how such a sum was to be procured even at a premium of fifty per cent. The export of more bulky goods was impossible. The British merchant was sending sugar by sea to Salonica, and thence on horseback through Servia and Hungary, in order to reach Vienna; one parcel of silk sent from Bergamo to England, by way of Smyrna, was twelve months on its passage; another, sent by way of Archangel, was two years. The British government attempted to establish a smuggling depot at Heligoland, in order to overcome the obstructions caused by the Continental system. A single licensed cargo to a French port cost for freight alone twenty times the cost of the vessel which carried it. Gold alone was comparatively easy to export, and naturally bullion rose in value.

All this was clear evidence of a terrible convulsion in commerce and, no doubt, of a previous expansion in credit, followed by excessive contraction; but nothing indicated an excess of currency in the sense commonly ascribed to the effect of forced issues on prices. Undoubtedly a depreciation of ten or fifteen per cent, or even more, occurred in paper compared with gold, and perhaps the Bank was bound to restrict its issues till that difference was removed; but so long as the usury laws remained in force, the Bank could not act upon the exchanges by raising its rate of interest, and its refusal of accommodation would have ruined such merchants as had hitherto succeeded in surviving the shock. Even had the Bank resorted to this desperate measure, such was the preponderance of foreign payments over receipts from abroad that no possible pressure could have immediately restored the balance of exchange. In ordinary times a monetary crisis effects this result by reducing prices, and thus making it possible to export goods at a profit; but no reduction of prices could well have had such an effect in 1810, since for years before that time Holland and Hamburg could not obtain, even at three and four times their English price, the goods which overwhelmed the British market. The only result of Bank contraction must have been to stop importations; but the general fall in prices was alone sufficient to produce that result, as was proved in 1811; grain was at famine rates; the people must be fed; the foreign expenditure of the government also defied laws of political economy, and Wellington's army in Portugal required millions in gold. If the Bank had attempted to put a still more severe pressure on the exchanges, it would have found itself paralyzed by the government at its first step; and in the struggle which must have followed, the people would have been ground into the dust. Even under the liberal system adopted, there was a time, in 1811 and 1812, when the general distress shook society to its foundations. Had the Bank wilfully intensified and prolonged this distress, not improbably Napoleon's Continental system might have proved the greatest success of his life.

The fall in foreign exchange during 1808 and 1809 did not attract very much public attention until Ricardo published a pamphlet on the subject, — " The High Price of Bullion a Proof of the Depreciation of Bank-notes." Shortly after the meeting of Parliament in 1810, a committee was appointed, at the instance of Francis Horner, to investigate the causes of the high price of gold bullion. This was the famous Bullion Committee, whose report made so marked an era in currency problems that it might almost be called their *pons asinorum*. Its doctrines, rejected by Parliament in 1811 only to be triumphantly adopted in 1819, acquired through the conversion of Sir Robert Peel an overruling ascendency, and embodied in the Bank Charter Act of 1844 still hold sway in England, although more liberal economists have long since protested against the application given to them.

The bullion report was based upon three propositions : first, that Bank paper was depreciated as compared with gold ; second, that this depreciation was caused by over-issues ; third, that the price of gold and the state of foreign exchange should regulate the issues of paper. The report closed by recommending that the Bank should be obliged to resume payments within two years.

Had the government been in the hands of able or dextrous men, Horner's resolutions, in which the substance of his report was embodied, need not have been so difficult to deal with as they proved. The first proposition was indeed incontrovertible, and no sensible being could have fallen into the blunder of disputing it; the third was, if not indisputable, at least not necessary to dispute under certain limitations; but the second was far from evident in the sense which Horner gave to it, and Thornton, perhaps the highest authority in the House, appears to have understood it as not inconsistent with the idea that the depreciation might be due to a deeper cause; while the concluding practical measure was supported by scarcely any one besides Mr. Horner, its author.

The government was held by a class of men equally incapable of seeing their own mistakes, and of profiting by those of their opponents. The ministers began by plunging into the grossest absurdity they could have found, — they denied that Bank-notes were depreciated at all. Assuming that the sale of coin for more than its nominal value in paper was forbidden by law, they undertook to affirm that the Bank-note and the guinea still maintained their relative worth in regard to each other. They denied that bullion was the true standard of value, and they affirmed that it was the stamp and the stamp alone which made the guinea a standard. They denied that the amount of circulation affected the price of gold, or that the Bank issues had anything to do with the course of exchange. Yet at intervals they were obliged practically to admit the conclusions which they were so eager to contest, until their accurate statements and

14

forcible reasoning became inextricably entangled in a mass of inconsistent arguments.

On the other hand, they had as opponents some of the ablest men whom England has produced. Mr. Vansittart, Mr. Rose, and Lord Castlereagh were helpless in the grasp of Mr. Horner, Mr. Huskisson, and Mr. Canning. The mistakes of the bullionists are hidden by the brilliancy of their oratory, the sparkle of their wit, the vigor and solidity of their genius. Sympathy is attracted to their side, when they are shown exercising magnificent powers to convince an unreasoning majority of the simplest principles in practical business. After all these efforts, they thought themselves fortunate in being defeated by a vote of only two to one.

Vansittart and his associates would have done well to rest satisfied with this negative upon the resolutions offered by Horner. Victorious in defence, they thought it necessary to establish their advantage permanently by a vigorous assertion of what they deemed the true principles of credit and currency. Vansittart accordingly moved, in his turn, a long series of resolutions.

The third of these has been the chief means of preserving Vansittart's memory. It was worded as follows : —

" *Resolved*, That it is the opinion of this committee that the promissory notes of the Bank of England have hitherto been, and are at this time, held in public estimation to be equivalent to the legal coin of the realm, and generally accepted as such in all pecuniary transactions to which such coin is lawfully applicable."

This position was beyond the reach of argument, but not of ridicule. In the range of Parliamentary oratory, few examples of sarcasm were so happy as that which Canning poured upon this unfortunate resolution in his speech of May 13, 1811. Although the House sustained Vansittart by a vote of 76 to 24, from that day to this the resolution has stood,· an object of laughter and wonder to each succeeding generation.

Thus the Bullion Committee was disposed of, but the subject was further than ever from a satisfactory settlement. Within two months of the passage of this resolution, in which Parliament gravely pledged the people to believe that Bank-notes were equivalent to coin, two events almost simultaneously occurred, which obliged the government to take active measures in order to compel the people to accept these Bank-notes. The first of these difficulties was due to an unexpected interpretation of the law. Two obscure individuals — one a Jew pedler named De Yonge, the other a guard on the Liverpool mail-coach — had been taken in the act of buying guineas at a premium, — an act supposed to be illegal, and, like the exportation of coin, subjecting the delinquent to the penalties of a misdemeanor. Government determined to make an example of these persons, and they were accordingly indicted under an obsolete statute of Edward VI.; and the facts being clearly proved, they were duly

found guilty of the acts charged in the indictment.
Their counsel raised the point of law, that the act
as laid in the indictment and proved in evidence was
not an offence in law, inasmuch as the statute of
Edward VI. was intended to apply only to the exchange of one sort of coin for another. Judgment
was respited until the opinion of the twelve judges
in the Court of the Exchequer Chamber could be obtained on this point; but at length, July 4, 1811,
Lord Ellenborough pronounced the unanimous decision of the Court, that the exchange of guineas for
Bank-notes, such guineas being taken at a higher
value than they were current for under the King's
proclamation, was not an offence against the statute
upon which the indictment was founded. Thus the
government theory in regard to paper money was
at once overthrown.

Almost at the same time with this blow, the famous
third resolution was attacked from another side with
a vigor more alarming. The law of 1797 had by no
means made Bank paper a legal tender. The case
of Grigby v. Oakes, in 1801, established the principle
that Bank of England notes might be refused by the
creditor, and the debtor must in that case discharge
his debt in coin. In usage the Bank-note had been
received as equivalent to coin, except in some remote
districts of Ireland, where the unfortunate peasants
were obliged to buy guineas at a premium from the
landlord, in order to discharge their rents.

The government policy seemed calculated to challenge attack, and the bullionists, who saw no limit to the possible depreciation, naturally resorted to the last means left for compelling government to check it. Lord King, a nobleman of high character and strong liberal principles, issued a circular to such of his tenants as held leases dated before the depreciation began, requiring them in future to pay their rents either in gold or in Bank paper representing the market value of gold. Even the dignity of the House of Lords was almost overthrown by this unexpected attack. A storm of indignation burst on the head of Lord King, whose practical sarcasm was more exasperating to the Ministry than the satire of Canning; but Lord King was in his right, — he was acting from conscientious motives, and he would not yield. Yet after the passage of Vansittart's resolution, this act tended to bring Parliament into public contempt. " My Lords," said Lord Grenville, in opening his speech on the subject, " it is painful to me to observe, that I cannot remember in the course of my life to have ever seen the ministers of this country placed in so disgraceful a situation as that in which they appear this night." Obviously some action had become necessary, but ministers hesitated, in the hope that Lord King's example would not be followed. The judges' decision in De Yonge's case turned the scale; but even then, such was the general dislike to a law of legal tender, and such was the difficulty of forcing a contraction in the Bank discounts, that ministers were placed in an embarrassing situation. There was apparently a third alternative, — that of allowing Lord King to proceed ; but this would have established two scales of prices throughout the country, and the result would ultimately have been that the Bank rather than endure the discredit thus attached to its paper, would have preferred to withdraw it.

Ministers were saved from this dilemma by Lord Stanhope, one of their ordinary opponents. He invented one of the curiosities of legislation, — a measure which disposed of Lord King, and established the law for such cases as that of De Yonge, but neither made paper a legal tender, nor contained the trace of a legal principle. The Act, which has since been commonly known as Lord Stanhope's, made the purchase or sale of coin for more than its legal value in Bank-notes or other lawful money a misdemeanor, as also the reception or payment of notes for less than their nominal value; and it further deprived the creditor of the power of distraining, in case a tender in Bank-notes to the amount of the debt had been made.

Strange to say, this preposterous statute answered its purpose. The courts seem never to have been asked to interpret it, nor did any creditor attempt to enforce his rights. The law officers of the Crown did not venture to express an opinion upon the bill while on its passage through Parliament. During the ten years that the Restriction Act still remained in force, with Lord Stanhope's measure as its supplement, no man in England knew what the law was, or the extent to which Bank-notes were recognized as the lawful equivalent of coin. In the failure of any judicial declaration on the subject, one can only refer to an opinion expressed in debate by Sir Samuel Romilly. That eminent lawyer pointed out to Parliament, that, if the object of government were to prevent Lord King or any other landlord or creditor from insisting upon payment in coin, the bill was far from answering its purpose. Creditors would still have the right to demand gold, and no court could refuse in such a case to give judgment against the debtor, who was yet apparently debarred by the Act from obtaining gold without incurring the penalties of a misdemeanor. The creditor having obtained his judgment, need not, and probably would not, proceed by way of distraint upon the goods of his debtor. If a landlord, he would resort to an ejectment. In any case, however, he might proceed against the person, and shut up the debtor in jail indefinitely, or until he made himself liable to further imprisonment by purchasing coin. One means of escape alone seemed open to him. The law prohibited the trade in coin, not that in bullion. If the debtor chose to purchase bullion, and have it coined at the mint, he might so evade the law.

Ministers gave it to be understood that if creditors pressed their rights to this point, Parliament would intervene by making Bank-notes a legal tender. It is difficult to see what was gained by a resort to these subterfuges, or why a legal-tender act should not have been passed outright, since Lord Stanhope's bill was intended to have, and did in fact produce, the same effect, except that it went beyond the limits of reasonable legislation, and accomplished its purposes only by creating a new offence hitherto unknown to the law. The plea that it successfully met the emergency was an excuse for slovenly legislation.

This Act, hurried through Parliament in July, 1811, just at the close of the session, was the sole result of the currency controversy, unless Vansittart's resolutions shared its credit. From that time no interference by government in monetary matters was to be looked for, but the Bank retained that exclusive control which it had hitherto possessed. This result was probably fortunate for the country. The Bank directors, if not great masters of statesmanship, were at least convinced that arbitrary action would aggravate the evils of the situation, while if the foreign and domestic policy of the government in other respects gave an idea of the probable result of its interference in Bank affairs, it might have brought inextricable confusion upon the credit and resources of the community.

The financial crash of 1809 and 1810 threw the country into profound distress and depression, but it prepared the way for a rapid change at the first sign of military success. The year 1811 marked perhaps the lowest point of England's fortunes; but in the autumn of that year the prospect became brighter. Napoleon had broken with Russia, and was preparing his great campaign to Moscow, while Wellington achieved unusual success in Portugal. There was hope that both the Russian and the Spanish ports would soon be reopened, while the colonies and South America were again consuming large quantities of British goods. Importations into England had meanwhile fallen to a low point, and the exchanges were slowly creeping upward. The pressure upon the Bank for assistance and for discounts fell off as credit recovered, until the circulation, which had reached £17,570,000 in August, 1810, contracted itself to £15,365,000 in August, 1812, the small notes excluded.

What was only hope in 1811 became certainty in 1812. Napoleon was driven both from Russia and from Spain. In another year all Europe was again open to British commerce, and in April, 1814, peace was restored. During this period, many of the dangerous symptoms of 1807 and 1808 again made their appearance. The circulation had become much smaller, but nevertheless prices rose; speculation was as general, if not so desperate, as in 1808; the Continent was flooded with English goods, while in England the price of wheat rose in 1812 to nearly one hundred and sixty shillings the quarter; but although the circulation was diminished by £2,000,000, and although the exchanges became considerably more favorable, still gold showed no sign of falling in value. The premium had risen to forty-two per cent in September, 1812, and after various fluctuations it was again forty-two per cent in the autumn of 1813. Then at last the fall began, and for a twelvemonth gold continued to decline steadily, until at the close of 1814 the premium was less than twelve per cent.

The rise in value of Bank-paper was coincident with another very large extension of issues, which reached £18,700,000. This extension was due partly to government, but partly, as in 1810, to the private demand. The fabric which speculators had raised for themselves on the apparently solid basis of supposed European necessities, crumbled to pieces at the first shock. Europe was too poor to buy or too thoroughly plundered to pay for English merchandise. The speculations abroad failed at the time when a prodigious fall in the price of grain ruined the English farmers and the country bankers, who depended upon agricultural prosperity. The collapse was general and disastrous; England was again plunged into distress at the time when her success was most brilliant; for two years after 1814 trade stagnated and merchants became bankrupt, without reference to the price of gold or the amount of circulation; nor could the Bank have prevented, or even shortened, the distress by any action upon the currency.

However devoted might be the adherence of theorists to their favorite currency dogma, the most ardent follower of Horner could scarcely have regretted that the Bank followed its own course during the year 1815. The evils of inconvertible paper were no doubt many, but there were also advantages in the system during times of political trouble; and the violent convulsions of 1815 would have proved too severe a trial for any but the most elastic form of credit. During January and February gold stood at about 115, compared with paper. The Emperor returned from Elba and arrived in Paris on the 20th of March. At the next quotation of gold, April 4, at one leap it rose to 137, — almost as high a point as it had reached during the war. The exchanges went down with almost equal violence; but the Bank circulation remained absolutely stationary.[1] After the first panic was over, gold began again to fall slowly, and on the news of Waterloo it declined to 128. On the 1st of September gold resumed the position it had held in January; but instead of resting there, it continued to fall, until at the close of the year the premium was only five per cent; and in July, 1816,

[1] BANK CIRCULATION.

Date.	Total.	Notes of £5 and upward.	Bank Treasure.	Price of Gold.
1809, 28 February	£18,542,860	£14,241,360	£4,488,700	115.5
31 August	19,574,180	14,393,110	3,652,480	115
1810, 28 February	21,019,600	15,159,180	3,501,410	115
31 August	24,793,990	17,570,780	3,191,850	115
1811, 28 February	23,360,220	16,246,130	3,350,940	118.75
31 August	23,286,850	15,692,490	3,243,300	125
1812, 29 February	23,408,320	15,951,290	2,983,190	122
31 August	23,026,880	15,385,470	3,099.270	128.5
1813, 27 February	23,210,930	15,497,320	2,884,500	130
31 August	24,828,120	16,790,980	2,712.270	142
1814, 28 February	24,801,080	16,455,540	2,204,430	140
31 August	28,368,290	18,703,210	2,097,680	115.5
1815, 28 February	27,261,650	18,226,400	2,036,910	115
31 August	27,248,670	17,766,140	3,409,040	115

it was nothing at all, or at most only about one per cent. The Bank circulation meanwhile expanded or contracted itself according to the demand, averaging rather more than £17,500,000, exclusive of the small notes.

The equilibrium was therefore restored, and it was restored without interference by government. The system vindicated itself, and was entitled to the high credit that properly belonged to so brilliant a success. Unfortunately, this success gave occasion for another dispute among currency writers, involving the whole question in its historical as well as in its theoretical bearings.

There were in 1816, and there still are, two classes of political economists, so far as the currency is concerned. The one has found in bank paper and its over-issues an explanation for every rise or fall in prices, and for every financial disaster. The other has denied to such a medium of exchange any influence whatever upon prices, and insists that if every bank-note were destroyed, speculation and abuses of credit would flourish not less than now. The bullionists of 1810 and their successors were strong in the belief that the Bank issues did control prices, and the price of gold especially. They were obliged to explain how it happened that gold fell about forty per cent to par, while the Bank issues were actually increased. Obviously the dilemma was serious.

The bullionists had a reply, and a reasonable one.

McCulloch argued that although no contraction of Bank issues occurred which could explain the fall in gold, yet such a contraction did occur in the entire circulation, taking the country banks into the calculation; and that the rise in value of Bank of England paper was in fact due to the destruction of country bank-notes during the disastrous years of 1814, 1815, and 1816. If the inquiry be carried a step further by seeking the cause of the disasters, McCulloch explained that the fall of grain from 155 shillings the quarter, in 1812, to 67 shillings in 1814 spread universal ruin among the agricultural class.

So obvious an explanation as this may well be sufficient; yet the view taken by Tooke and Fullarton appears more philosophical and more exact than that of McCulloch. They maintained that the fall in gold was due simply to the fact, that with the final turn of exchange in favor of England gold ceased to be an object of demand, and, like other commodities in the same position, rapidly fell to its ordinary value.

McCulloch's facts are unquestioned, but they appear to be only a part of the truth. The prodigious decline in the price of grain was coincident with a general decline in prices, which naturally checked importations and stimulated export. The grain alone imported in 1814 was estimated at £2,800,000 in value; in 1815 it was but £800,000, and in 1816 only £940,000. Silk and wool, coffee, flax, linseed, and most of the great staples of import fell off between 1814 and 1816. Under any circumstances the exchanges must have risen without regard to the currency, and gold must have fallen, since considerable sums were actually brought from abroad during 1815 and 1816.

The force of this argument becomes evident by comparison with previous cases. If the rise in exchange and the appreciation of paper in 1815 and 1816 were caused by the withdrawal of private banknotes, the same reason should hold good for the similar events in 1814. If at the later time the currency were so depreciated from excess as to regain its value only by contraction, it was certainly more in need of that relief at the earlier period; yet a fall of thirty per cent in gold was then coincident with an increase of paper throughout the country.

Allowing that McCulloch was right, and that the restoration of paper was caused by involuntary contraction, that contraction was at all events only temporary, and the re-establishment of the credit of the country banks of issue should have renewed the depreciation. The Bank issues rose in 1817 and 1818 to a higher point than ever before, and the country banks again extended their credit in every direction. Under these circumstances, the depreciation should have been great, even after every reasonable allowance had been made ; yet in fact gold was at a premium of only about five per cent, and this slight advance appears to have been caused merely by a temporary pressure on the foreign exchanges.

If these arguments seem still insufficient to show

that the theory of excessive issues fails to meet the
difficulties of the case, the circulation of 1814 and
1815, which is said to have lost twenty per cent or
more of its value through its excess, may be compared with that which existed after specie payments
were resumed. Such comparisons are not a fair
proof of either excess or deficiency, since the public demand varies, and the same amount of circulation is at one time less and at another more than is
required. Allowing for such variations, one may com-
pare the three different periods of general expansion
between 1813 and 1825. The small notes having
been withdrawn at the resumption and their place
supplied by coin, must be excluded in each case.

The highest point reached by the Bank circulation
in any quarterly average between 1812 and 1815 was
£19,067,000, in the third quarter of 1814; the price
of gold being about 112. Between 1816 and 1822
the highest average was in the second quarter of 1817,
or £21,517,000; and it remained above £20,000,000
until July, 1818, the country banks expanding generally. Gold was then at about 105. Between 1823
and the close of 1825 the highest average was in the
first quarter of 1825, a time of universal expansion,
when it reached £20,665,000, the Bank redeeming its
notes in coin.

If, then, two thirds or three fourths of the whole
depreciation was removed in 1814 without withdrawal of paper; if the circulation was restored to
its widest range in 1818 without any effect of conse-

quence upon the price of gold; and if after the resumption the circulation remained undiminished in amount, and its issue subject to the same general laws as before, — there seems to be no necessity for resorting to the theory of involuntary contraction in order to explain the fall of gold in 1816. That theory needs no dispute, if it means merely that the contraction was itself a part of a general movement of trade and credit, and as such contributed to hasten the result; but if more than this is intended, the effect produced was out of proportion to the cause assigned.

The whole subject of private banking, for many years assigned as the source of all financial troubles, has in fact very little to do with the question of depreciation during the French wars. The country banks held then precisely the same position they had held before suspension, nor did the resumption change it. They never suspended payments. At any time gold might have been demanded for their notes. At all times they did in fact redeem their notes on demand, by exchanging them for those of the Bank of England. Their circulation was limited by that of the Bank, and the same general laws controlled the whole.

Country bank-paper could not have been in excess of the public wants then, any more than it could now be, although the credit of such banks might be and no doubt was abused then, as it may be now. On the other hand, the Bank of England was not obliged to redeem its notes. Through the channel of permanent loans to government, it might have forced any given amount of paper into circulation had it chosen to do so; but it did not force a single note upon the public. It lent notes, but never paid them away. At the end of two months every such loan had to be paid back into the coffers of the Bank by the borrower; and although the advances to government were to some degree permanent, they were not excessive, and, as has been already shown, they tended to lower the private demand. Whatever action may have been caused by the restriction was upon credit in the first place, and not upon currency. The encouragement it may have afforded to speculation could not have been very great, or ten years would not have passed without showing it; but when taxes, bad seasons, or the operations of war, or other causes, combined to raise prices and to stimulate speculation, the credit system was not then, nor is it now, adapted to check the rise. When a stagnation in business and a fall in prices followed, as must ultimately be the case, the circulation contracted as a necessary consequence; but in every instance, before the resumption and since, the rise in prices has preceded the expansion, and the fall has preceded the contraction.

In the early part of 1817 the supply of bullion in the Bank had risen to £10,000,000, the average total circulation for the quarter being somewhat in excess of £27,000,000, while the exchanges were considerably above par. The directors considered the experiment of partial resumption to be safe, and by a series of steps taken during that year they undertook to redeem all notes dated previous to the 1st of January. This was, in fact, resumption. During the next two years any holder of Bank-notes could obtain gold for them at the Bank, either directly, or by exchanging them for such as were dated previous to January 1, 1817. Had the exchanges remained firm, there would have been no further question of an easy and regular return to the normal condition of the currency.

Unfortunately, the year 1817 was one of renewed speculation, and the imports again rose to an extravagant point. Grain alone to the value of £17,300,000 was brought into England in the two years 1817 and 1818. Another cause which could not well have been foreseen, tended powerfully to depress the exchanges and to carry gold abroad. Nearly all the governments of Europe were borrowing large sums of money, and the English capitalists negotiated several of their largest loans. How much money was sent abroad for this purpose is not easily said, but certainly not less than £10,000,000. The effect upon exchange was immediate; yet the extreme variation in gold was not more than five per cent, although no effort was made to counteract the pressure. So far from resorting to the theory of excessive issues for an explanation of this temporary rise in gold, one may well feel surprise that under the circumstances no greater disturbance of the market occurred. The return of peace must have largely increased English resources, to enable them to bear so easily the pressure of enormous foreign payments.

The slight variation of five per cent was not of long duration Again in 1819, as before in 1816 and in 1814, the system vindicated itself without artificial pressure, by the mechanical operation of its own laws. The excessive importations of 1817 and 1818 resulted in stagnation of business and decline in prices. The foreign loans were discharged. The exchanges, relieved from pressure, rose. The demand for gold ceased, and in July, 1819, the Bank-note was again at par. There it remained thenceforward; and from that day to this there has been no depreciation in the value of Bank of England paper.[1]

[1] BANK CIRCULATION.

Date.	Total.	Notes of £5 and upward.	Bank Treasure.	Price of Gold.
1816, 29 February	£ 27,013,620	£ 18,012,220	£ 4,640,880	105
31 August	26,758,720	17,661,510	7,562,780	101.5
1817, 28 February	27,397,900	19,261,630	9,680,970	100.8
30 August	29,543,780	21,550,630	11,668,260	103
1818, 28 February	27,770,970	20,370,290	10,055,460	104.5
31 August	26,202,150	18,676,220	6,363,160	104.5
1819, 27 February	25,126,700	17,772,470	4,184,620	104
31 August	25,252,690	18,017,450	3,595,360	100
1820, 29 February	23,484,110	16,794,980	4,911,050	100
31 August	24,299,340	17,600,730	8,211,080	100
1821, 28 February	23,884,920	17,447,360	11,869,900	100
31 August	20,295,300	17,747,070	11,233,590	100
1822, 28 February	18,665,350	17,290,500	11,057,150	100
31 August	17,464,790	16,609,460	10,097,960	100

Average circulation of bank-notes of £5 and upward for the years

1823.	1824.	1825.
£ 18,033,635	£ 19,927,120	£ 19,679,120

In the mean while Parliament had taken alarm. The Bank directors, after paying out £4,000,000 in redemption of their notes under the conditions specified in 1817, seeing no immediate prospect of a rise in exchange, and fearful of the entire exhaustion of their treasure, applied to Parliament early in 1819 to be relieved from the further performance of their own promises of redemption. Committees were appointed by both Houses, whose first act was to renew the restriction in its whole extent. Then, with a view to the final establishment of a fixed government policy in regard to resumption, the two committees entered into a separate and extended investigation of the whole subject, resulting in two reports made in the course of April and May, which with the accompanying evidence fill a volume, and furnish a mass of readable matter not less interesting than bulky.

Robert Peel, afterward the celebrated Prime Minister, was chairman of the House committee. Hitherto an opponent of the bullionists, his opinions were changed by the testimony offered before his committee, and he became a convert to the doctrines which Horner and his friends advocated in 1810. He carried almost his whole party with him. Bank-paper was generally acknowledged in Parliament to be depreciated in regard to gold, and a forcible contraction would restore the equilibrium. This principle was the foundation of his report.

The most serious resistance to resumption came from a new party, which made an alarming use of

the doctrine of depreciation. The trifling difference
between paper and gold was affirmed, and probably
with truth, to be no measure of the actual depreciation in paper as compared with commodities generally.
The rise in prices during the war had been as much
as fifty or one hundred per cent upon the old scale.
A return to the original standard would be a flagrant
injustice to the community. The fund-holders alone
would be benefited by it, and the people would be
ground by additional taxes solely to pamper the capitalist. If Parliament determined to restore specie
payments, it should at least create a new standard,
and reduce the value of sterling money by twenty-
five per cent; or it should accompany the resumption by allowing an equivalent deduction to every
debtor on the amount of his debt. In other words, a
general repudiation to the extent of twenty-five per
cent was demanded by a party which contained some
leading and influential members of Parliament not
inclined to act the part of demagogues.

The House of Commons was faithful to one principle, in which it justly considered the national honor
to be involved. The restriction had been a war
measure merely. Since peace had been restored, Parliament, while consenting to renew the law from year
to year, had repeatedly pledged itself to ultimate resumption. Every government loan had been raised
on the faith of these pledges; the interest of the
national debt had been paid in paper, on the ground
of its equivalence to gold; every public or private

debt since 1797 had been contracted under the influence of Acts of Parliament prescribing the time of resumption; every Bank-note bore a promise to pay upon its face. Four years had already been allowed to pass, and nothing had yet been done. Further concession, either to public timidity or to class interests, would endanger the national credit, if indeed it did not proclaim criminal dishonesty in those to whom the duties of legislation were intrusted.

Resistance to the principle of resumption in its purest and simplest form was summarily swept aside, yet Peel thought necessary to invent a clumsy and ponderous engine to bring about a simple result. At the time when his committee was sitting, there was a premium of about five per cent upon gold, and his first object was to restore the equilibrium between paper and coin. Beyond that comparatively easy result, he aimed to create a system under which paper could not fall again below par. The latter purpose could, as he believed, be effected by requiring that the circulation should be forcibly contracted as the exchanges became unfavorable; or, in other words, that the Bank should diminish its issues whenever its treasure was diminished. As the Bank directors obstinately denied the efficacy of this contrivance, Peel undertook to frame his bill in such a manner as to leave them no option but to follow his theory.

The project began by an order for the repayment by the government of ten millions out of the twenty-three millions advanced to it by the Bank. This repayment was not made for the purpose of necessarily contracting the Bank loans or issues, but because the Bank could more easily control its circulation when made in short private loans than when made in more permanent advances to government, and would therefore be more able to act energetically should a fall in the exchanges threaten the success of the plan.

Having thus removed one possible impediment, Peel's next step was to propose the following resolution: "That from the 1st of February, 1820, the Bank shall be liable to deliver on demand gold of standard fineness, having been assayed and stamped at his Majesty's mint, a quantity of not less than sixty ounces being required in exchange for such an amount of notes by the Bank as shall be equal to the value of the gold so required, at the rate of £4 1s. per ounce;" that is to say, any person presenting Bank-notes to the amount of £243 at the Bank counter should receive in return a bar of gold worth £233. After the 1st of October he was to pay only £238 for the same quantity of gold, and after May 1, 1821, the ingot of sixty ounces was to be purchasable at its par value in notes. After this experiment had been fully tried during a space of two years, May 1, 1823, the Bank was to redeem its notes in coin.

Such was Peel's famous bill, which excited warm controversies during a whole generation. So far as its ultimate purpose of effecting an unconditional return to specie payments was concerned, it deserved all praise; but the merits of Peel's bill as a practical measure were hardly great, nor apart from its general tendency could it exercise any great influence on the result. A simple resolution requiring the Bank to resume on a certain day would have answered the purpose better.

The elaborate mechanism by which the price of gold was to be forced down involved an official acknowledgment of depreciation, the Bank-note being made the legal equivalent of a smaller sum in gold than that named upon its face. No actual coin was to pass, but the gold ingots were as much coin as if they had been guineas. To reverse the policy of the war, and at that late moment to proclaim that the government had for years cheated its creditors by paying them in depreciated paper, was unnecessary, and doubtful in principle.

In the second place, had Peel's bill been tested, — had the event occurred for which it was designed to provide, — it would probably have proved useless. Few admirers of that Act can deny that the theory of regulating the currency by the movements of exchange does not and cannot exclude violent fluctuations in credit, — in fact, that it for the time aggravates them. Had the exchanges become unfavorable in 1820, as they did in 1825, no amount of contraction could have saved the specie of the Bank. If in the face of such a drain the Bank had undertaken to increase it by selling gold two per cent cheaper than before, as Peel's Act required, it would have again broken down.

As Ricardo pointed out to Parliament, its duty was to establish the principle; the Bank was to carry that principle out in action. Peel's Act provided not merely for the resumption of specie payments, but also for the regulation of commerce and credit; it undertook to control both the currency and the exchanges. Such efforts have hitherto failed. The valuable part of the bill was that which fixed a day for the resumption, and that which repealed the penal statutes against melting or exporting coin. Had the rest been omitted, the measure would have been improved.

Whatever may have been the theoretical merits or demerits of the scheme, in practice it was inoperative. Within a few months of its adoption, and without operation upon the currency, gold again fell to par, and there it has since remained. The Bank prepared its bars of bullion, but no one would have them. On the contrary, large amounts of gold were brought into its vaults. Weary of prolonging an obviously useless delay, the directors applied to Parliament early in 1821, and procured the passage of a new Act, under which cash payments were at length resumed on the 1st of May of that year. The public was unconscious of the event. The Bank system was not altered, nor was the circulation diminished, except so far as sovereigns were substituted for notes of one and two pounds; and after twenty-four years of an irredeemable paper

currency, Great Britain returned smoothly and easily
to its ancient standard, and redeemed its pledged
honor.

Yet between the years 1818 and 1822 a general
and severe fall in prices occurred, which was then,
and is still, commonly referred to the action of Peel's
bill; but in truth, other causes tended much more
strongly to produce the same result. The agricultural class, which uttered the loudest complaints, had,
under the influence of an excessive stimulus, brought
more land under cultivation than was required by the
public wants, and a long time passed before a proper
equilibrium was again established. The shipping
interest was in much the same condition. The population at large did not suffer; on the contrary, the
condition of the mass of Englishmen steadily improved after 1817. At the time when prices were
falling, the manufacturing interests were rapidly extending and enriching themselves; less and less was
heard of political discontent and internal disorder,
as reviving prosperity brought with it social repose,
while even among the bankers and traders fewer
bankruptcies occurred during the three years ending in 1821 than in any similar period since 1809.
If the resumption was to be held responsible for the
misfortunes of certain branches of industry, justice
required that the general prosperity of others should
outweigh the complaint; but both complaint and
praise were equally thrown away. The system after
resumption was identical with that which had existed

before. The only effect of the long suspension was to breed a race of economists who attributed an undue degree of power to currency, and who delayed for years a larger and more philosophical study of the subject by their futile experiments upon paper money.

Without applying England's experience to other cases of depreciation, though no richer field could be wished, a wide distinction must be drawn between inconvertible bank-notes, issued on good security merely as loans payable within a short definite period, and inconvertible government paper, issued like so much gold or silver, yet not capable of being melted like the precious metals into an article of commerce, nor of being returned to the issuer and not again borrowed, like bank-notes. In one case the public regulates the supply by its own wants; in the other, it is compelled to regulate prices by the supply. No country laboring under the latter difficulty can draw consolation from England's example. If in addition to the £60,000,000 which may have circulated in British paper during the last ten years of restriction, there had been another £60,000,000 of government currency forced upon the public, and if the private banks of issue had been under a less rigorous central control, some parallel might be drawn between the difficulties of resumption in 1821 and those under which other nations have been weighed down. In this case, too, the return to cash payments on the old system would not have been so easily brought about; and if England had succeeded in ultimately restoring her credit, if she had redeemed her pledges and vindicated her honor, she would have accomplished more than any nation has done down to the year 1867, although many have been placed in a similar situation.

THE DECLARATION OF PARIS. 1861.

AT the outbreak of the Crimean War in 1854, Great Britain and France agreed to respect neutral commerce, whether under its own flag or under the flag of an enemy. Great Britain expressly limited the concession to the special emergency: "To preserve the commerce of neutrals Great Britain is willing for the present to waive a part of the belligerent rights appertaining to her by the law of nations. . . . Her Majesty will waive the right of seizing enemy's property laden on board a neutral vessel unless it be contraband of war."

At the close of the Crimean War the Congress of Paris adopted, April 16, 1856, a Declaration embracing four heads, —

1. Privateering is and remains abolished.

2. The neutral flag covers enemy's goods, with the exception of contraband of war.

3. Neutral goods, with the exception of contraband of war, are not liable to capture under enemy's flag.

4. Blockades in order to be binding must be effective; that is to say, maintained by forces sufficient really to prevent access to the coast of the enemy.

Great Britain, France, Prussia, Russia, Austria, and Turkey adopted this mutual agreement, and pledged themselves to make it known to States not represented in the Congress, and invite their accession to it, on two conditions, — (1) That the Declaration should be accepted as a whole, or not at all; and (2) That the States acceding should enter into no subsequent arrangement on maritime law in time of war without stipulating for a strict observance of the four points. On these conditions every maritime power was to be invited to accede, and had the right to become a party to the agreement. Accordingly nearly all the States of Europe and South America in course of time notified their accession, and became, equally with the original members, entitled to all the benefits and subject to the obligations of the contract.

The government of the United States was also invited to accede, and like the other Powers had the right to do so by simple notification. Secretary Marcy notified the French government, July 28, 1856, that the President could not abandon the right to use privateers, unless he could secure the exemption of all private property, not contraband, from capture at sea; but with that amendment the United States would accede to the Declaration. The French government made no objection to the Marcy amendment; Russia favored it; Prussia, Italy, and the Netherlands were friendly to it. Great Britain was understood to oppose it.

Before the negotiation was fairly begun, President

Pierce was succeeded, March 4, 1857, by President Buchanan, who directed the negotiations to be arrested for the purpose of enabling him to examine the questions involved. During the four years of Buchanan's administration the subject remained untouched; and when, March 4, 1861, President Lincoln began his term of office, his Secretary of State found the Declaration of Paris among the most important of the unsettled subjects calling for attention.

At that anxious moment, when the fate of the Union depended on many uncertain forces, any step which promised to conciliate Europe and convince Great Britain and France of the advantages they might expect from a Northern rather than a Southern influence in the United States, seemed to President Lincoln and his Cabinet good policy.[1] They decided to give the accession of the United States to the Declaration of Paris. The decision was taken early, and promptly acted upon. About six weeks after the inauguration, Secretary Seward sent a circular despatch, dated April 24, 1861, to the American ministers in Great Britain, France, Russia, Prussia, Austria, Belgium, and Denmark, instructing them to ascertain whether those governments were " disposed to enter into negotiations for the accession of the government of the United States to the Declaration of the Paris Congress, with the conditions annexed by that body to the same ; and if you shall find that government so disposed, you will then enter into a convention to

[1] Seward to Dayton, July 6, 1861.   Infra, p. 257

that effect, substantially in the form of a project for that purpose herewith transmitted to you, — the convention to take effect from the time when the due ratifications of the same shall have been exchanged."

Meanwhile the subject attracted the attention of the British government. Lord John Russell, the Foreign Secretary in Lord Palmerston's Ministry, wrote to Earl Cowley, the British ambassador at Paris, May 6, an important despatch,[1] which began by announcing that her Majesty's government considered the Confederacy of the Southern States as a belligerent, invested with all a belligerent's rights and prerogatives. As both belligerents, North and South, were about to enter on maritime operations, Lord John Russell suggested to the Emperor Napoleon that they should be invited " to act upon the principles laid down in the second and third Articles of the Declaration of Paris of 1856, which relates to the security of neutral property on the high seas."

The form thus suggested was somewhat peculiar. Scarcely five years had then elapsed since April 16, 1856, when the plenipotentiaries at the Congress of Paris, including the representative of England, signed the protocol to the proceedings of that day : —

" On the proposition of Count Walewski and recognizing that it is for the general interest to maintain the indivisibility of the four principles mentioned in the Declaration signed this day, the plenipotentiaries agree

[1] Russell to Cowley, May 6, 1861 ; Papers presented to Parliament, 1862 ; North America, No. 3, p. 1.

that the Powers which shall have signed it, or which shall have acceded to it, cannot hereafter enter into any arrangement in regard to the application of the rights of neutrals in time of war, which does not at the same time rest on the four principles which are the object of the said Declaration."

In 1856 England and France pledged themselves to enter into no arrangement with each other or any third Power unless it started from the indivisible four Articles. In 1861 England invited France to do the thing which both Powers had pledged themselves not to do.

The act was the more significant, because under ordinary circumstances, as a matter of courtesy, the adhesion of both belligerents to the Declaration as a whole should have been first invited, previous to suggesting their adhesion to half the principles involved. The discourtesy was not due to any peculiar interest of England in the two principles thus put in the foreground. Russell's wish went no further than to secure the immunity of the British flag when covering belligerent goods, and of British goods under the belligerent flag. The abandonment of privateering and the definition of a binding blockade seemed equally important to neutrals, but to these points Russell made no allusion.

Earl Cowley had an interview, May 9, with M. Thouvenel, then Foreign minister of Napoleon III., and wrote [1] the same day to Lord John Russell that

---

[1] Cowley to Russell, May 9, 1861. Papers No. 3, p. 3.

16

the Imperial government concurred entirely in the views of the British government, and was prepared to act jointly in asking from the belligerents " a formal recognition of the second and third Articles of the Declaration of Paris." Thouvenel suggested that a friendly communication should be made to both governments in the same language, " that the governments of Great Britain and France intended to abstain from all interference, but that the commercial interests of the two countries demanded that they should be assured that the principles with respect to neutral property laid down by the Congress of Paris should be adhered to, — an assurance which the two governments did not doubt they should obtain, as the principles in question were in strict accordance with those that had been always advocated by the United States."

Lord John Russell acknowledged the receipt of Cowley's despatch May 13, and on the same day the new minister of the United States to England arrived in London. A few days intervened before Mr. Adams could begin upon business,[1] and these were actively employed by Russell in fixing the attitude of England beyond remonstrance. The Proclamation of Neutrality, recognizing the Confederate States of America as belligerents, was signed May 13, and published May 15 ; while Russell wrote to Cowley, May 16, transmitting to the French government the draft of a des-

[1] Adams to Seward (No. 1), May 17, 1861 ; Papers relating to Foreign Affairs; Diplomatic Documents, p. 69.

patch requesting the accession of the belligerents to
the second and third Articles of the Declaration of
Paris.[1] The draft sketched the history of the subject, showing that the United States government had
in principle acceded to the second, third, and fourth
Articles of the Declaration, and withheld its assent
only from the first, which regarded privateering. On
that point, Russell announced that Great Britain must
hold any government issuing letters of marque responsible for losses sustained in consequence of privateers
which did not respect the established laws of war.

Lord Cowley reported, May 17, that Thouvenel
concurred entirely in the draft, and had already
written in the same terms to the French minister at
Washington, M. Mercier.[2] Cowley's report reached
Russell May 18, and Russell immediately, on the
same day, sent the despatch to Lord Lyons, the British minister at Washington, together with instructions for his action.[3] The personal instructions contained matter not included in the formal despatch
intended for communication to the United States
government : —

" I need not tell your Lordship that her Majesty's government would very gladly see a practice which is calculated to lead to great irregularities, and to increase the
calamities of war, renounced by both the contending

[1] Russell to Cowley, May 16, 1861; British Papers, No. 3,
p. 3.

[2] Cowley to Russell, May 17, 1861; Papers No. 3, p. 4.

[3] Russell to Lyons, May 18, 1861; Papers No. 3, pp. 4–6.

parties in America as it has been renounced by almost
every other nation in the world; and therefore you will
not err in encouraging the Government to which you are
accredited to carry into effect any disposition which they
may evince to recognize the Declaration of Paris in
regard to privateering, as her Majesty's government do
not doubt that they will, without hesitation, recognize
the remaining Articles of the Declaration to which you
are now instructed to call their attention. You will
clearly understand that her Majesty's government cannot
accept the renunciation of privateering on the part of the
government of the United States if coupled with the
condition that they should enforce its renunciation on
the Confederate States, either by denying their right to
issue letters of marque, or by interfering with the belligerent operations of vessels holding from them such letters of marque, so long as they carry on hostilities
according to the recognized principles and under the
admitted liabilities of the law of nations."

At noon, Saturday, May 18, before these despatches
could have left the Foreign Office, Adams appeared at
Pembroke Lodge, Lord John Russell's country house
nine miles from London, to claim an interview with
the minister.[1] Their conversation was long and
serious; not till toward its close did Adams reach
the subject of the Declaration of Paris. Then he
said that he had the necessary powers to negotiate,
"together with a form of a convention" which he
would submit if the British government was disposed

[1] Adams to Russell, May 21, 1861; Diplomatic Documents,
p. 74.

to pursue the matter. Lord John Russell did not
express a wish to pursue the matter in London, nor
did he ask to see the draft of convention, " but he
seemed to desire to leave the subject in the hands
of Lord Lyons, to whom he intimated that he
had already transmitted authority to assent to any
modification of the only point in issue which the
government of the United States might prefer. On
that matter he believed there would be no difficulty
whatever." Under these circumstances Adams postponed further action until he should receive new
instructions.

Russell reported the substance of this conversation
in a short despatch to Lord Lyons,[1] dated May 21,
that may be quoted in full: —

" In the course of our conversation on the 18th, Mr.
Adams told me that his Government was disposed to
adhere to the provisions of the Declaration of Paris,
and that he had powers to negotiate upon that question ;
but upon my saying that both Great Britain and France
had given instructions to their ministers at Washington
upon this subject, he thought it would be well not to
pursue the matter here, but to leave it in the hands of
the Secretary of State."

These two reports of what was apparently a brief
and clear exchange of views, differed in effect. Russell understood Adams to suggest leaving the subject
to be treated at Washington. Adams understood
Russell to prefer that course, with the addition that

[1] Russell to Lyons, May 21, 1861 ; Papers No. 3, p. 6.

the British government had already transmitted "authority" to assent to any modification of the article on privateering, "the only point in issue," which the United States government might prefer. "On that matter he believed there would be no difficulty whatever." That Adams should have misunderstood Russell was highly improbable, the more so because Russell's language, as reported, harmonized with the language of his despatch to Lord Lyons, which he signed only an hour or two before or afterward.

The next step was taken by Mr. Dayton, the United States minister at Paris. Dayton notified the French government, May 25, that he was fully authorized to enter into a convention on the points of the Declaration of Paris. In conversation, May 28 or 29, Dayton added that he was authorized to accept the four Articles, although he preferred to make the offer in the first place with the addition of Marcy's amendment.[1] Thouvenel, according to his own report to the British *chargé*, replied that the imperial government would be glad if that of the United States acceded "purely and simply" to the Declaration of Paris.[2] He gave Dayton no reason to suppose that France was opposed to the Marcy amendment; but after three weeks of delay and consultation with the British government he replied that the American proposition must be addressed jointly to all the

[1] Dayton to Seward, May 30, 1861; Diplomatic Documents, p. 200.

[2] Grey to Russell, June 14, 1861; Papers No. 3, p. 7.

Powers associated in the treaty. In other words, Thouvenel, like Russell, evaded the offer of the United States government. After consulting Russell, Thouvenel no longer wished that the United States should simply accede to the four Articles.

Between May 18, when Lord John Russell had his first interview with Adams, and June 20, when Thouvenel made his reply to Dayton, the governments of England and France changed their attitude. Before learning that the United States offered pure and simple adhesion, both Governments expressed a wish or willingness for that result; after learning it, both Governments evaded an answer.

The misunderstanding in the case of Thouvenel was greater than in the case of Russell. Thouvenel sent word to the British government that Dayton had made him two propositions,[1] —

1. That the United States should adhere to the four Articles with the addition of the Marcy amendment. To this, Thouvenel replied, according to his story to the British government, that it was out of the question. Dayton on the contrary affirmed that Thouvenel never made such a reply.

2. Thouvenel represented Dayton as asking " that privateering being abolished by the adoption of the first Article of the Declaration of Paris, amended as proposed, the privateers sent out by the so-called Southern Confederacy should be considered as pirates."

[1] Russell to Grey, June 12, 1861. Grey to Russell, June 14, 1861. Papers No. 3, p. 7.

Dayton declared that he never made such a proposition. He certainly never did make it.

Another complication then occurred. Lord Lyons wrote from Washington, June 4, a letter received June 17, saying that Adams would propose adhesion to all the Articles of the Declaration of Paris.

" There is no doubt," added Lyons,[1] " that this adherence will be offered in the expectation that it will bind the Governments accepting it to treat the privateers of the Southern Confederacy as pirates. . . . It seems to be far from certain that the United States Congress would ratify the abolition of privateering, nor do I suppose that the Cabinet will abide by its proposal when it finds that it will gain nothing toward the suppression of the Southern privateering by doing so."

The animus of Lord Lyons's remarks was evident; and he was clear in the opinion that President Lincoln, after the recognition of Southern belligerency, would not renew his offer to accept the four Articles.

Ten days afterward, June 15, Lord Lyons and M. Mercier waited together on Secretary Seward at the State Department, to communicate the joint action of their Governments in regard to neutral flags. As their proposed communication was founded on the assumption that the Southern States were to be regarded as belligerents, Seward declined to receive it, and complained that England and France should concert, and announce their concert of action on such a sub-

[1] Lyons to Russell, June 4, 1861; Papers No. 3, p. 8.

ject. He asked them to leave their instructions with him informally, that he might understand the views of the two governments and found his despatches on clear apprehension. They did so, and the discussion closed. Lyons reported the result to his Government, June 17, and in another despatch of the same day added that Secretary Seward seemed to have concluded, from a despatch he had received from Minister Adams, that Lyons had received authority to enter into a separate negotiation on the offered adhesion to the treaty or Declaration of Paris. When Lyons undeceived him, Seward said he thought he had reason to complain of the want of notice taken by the governments of Europe of the offer to adhere ; but he should authorize Adams to renew it without delay.[1]

Few Secretaries of State would have borne such treatment with such temper. When Minister Adams in London learned what had occurred at Washington, he was still less favorably impressed by the manner in which he and his Government had been treated by Lord Russell and M. Thouvenel. He too kept his temper, but the affair made a lasting impression on his mind, and shook his faith in the straightforwardness of the British government. When he received renewed instructions from Secretary Seward, dated July 1, repeating the order to accede to the Declaration of Paris, he wrote to Seward expressing his "profound surprise" at the remarkable se-

[1] Lyons to Russell, June 17, 1861; Papers No. 3, p. 10.

ries of misunderstandings that had occurred, of which he then knew only a part; and he added that he had already written to Lord John Russell a letter intended " to bring this matter to a distinct issue." [1] He meant to trust no longer to oral communications.

The note was dated July 11, and brought the matter " to a distinct issue."

" I certainly understood your Lordship to say that the subject had already been committed to the care of Lord Lyons at Washington with authority to accept the proposition of the government of the United States, adopting three Articles of the Declaration of Paris, and to drop the fourth altogether."

As Lord Lyons was not authorized to enter into a convention, Adams offered to present his own project of convention to Russell at any moment he should appoint.[2]

To this letter Russell replied, July 13, in language undoubtedly chosen with care : —

" In the first conversation I had the honor to hold with you, on the 18th of May, I informed you that instructions had been sent to Lord Lyons to propose to the government of the United States to adopt the second, third, and fourth Articles of the Declaration of Paris, dropping the first altogether. You informed me that you had instructions on the same subject; but I understood you to

[1] Adams to Seward, July 12, 1861; Diplomatic Documents, p. 97.

[2] Adams to Russell, July 11, 1861; Diplomatic Documents, p. 99.

express an opinion, in which I fully concurred, that it would be well to leave the question in the hands of the Secretary of State at Washington. Lord Lyons had instructions to make an agreement with the government of the United States, but he had no express authority to sign a convention."

Lord John next said that the States which had adhered to the Declaration of Paris had done so by notes or despatches. He did not expressly say that the United States had, by the terms of the Declaration, the same right to adhere to the four Articles by a simple notification, — no such admission was required, since no one questioned the right; but, he added, as Mr. Adams was instructed to present a convention, he might do so the same day at the Foreign Office at three o'clock.

Evidently Lord John, with his usual spirit, meant to meet Adams's issue as distinctly as it was made; but the note of July 13 was still an extremely curious paper, and caused Adams much perplexity, which time increased rather than diminished.

Comparison of the note to Adams of July 13 with the despatch to Lyons of May 21 shows that Russell evidently referred to the earlier paper to refresh his memory while writing the later. He could hardly have done otherwise. No minister could venture to write a second report of conversation without referring to his first. The despatch of May 21 was before Russell's eyes when he wrote the note of July 13; but the despatch of May 21 was unknown to Adams, and could not at that time be appealed to. Russell was at liberty to make any changes that suited his purposes or position, without immediate danger of criticism. Conversely, every change he thought proper to make must have been made with the object of suiting some purpose.

In the letter of May 21, Russell began by saying: "Mr. Adams told me that his Government was disposed to adhere to the provisions of the Declaration of Paris." In the letter of July 13 he represented that the subject was not introduced by Adams, but by himself: "I informed you that instructions had been sent to Lord Lyons. . . . You informed me that you had instructions on the same subject." In the letter of May 21, Russell said that both Great Britain and France "had given instructions" to their ministers at Washington. In the letter of July 13 he said that instructions "had been sent to Lord Lyons." In strictness, the instructions dated May 18 might perhaps be said to have been "given," but they had certainly not been "sent;" and in both cases the intention was obvious to conceal from Adams that the instructions were not yet sent. In those days the Foreign Office despatch-bag, like the despatch-bag at the United States Legation, was closed and sent Saturday evening to go by messenger to Queenstown for Sunday's steamer. Russell could hardly have said at three o'clock Saturday afternoon, May 18, that despatches had been "sent" which were still in the Foreign Office, if not on his own table, and could not start for America till nine o'clock that night or thereabout.

The next divergence was more significant. The note of May 21 gave Adams's words: " Mr. Adams told me that his Government was disposed to adhere to the provisions of the Declaration of Paris, and that he had powers to negotiate upon that question." The note of July 13 ignored Adams's proposal. " You informed me that you had instructions on the same subject." For some reason not expressed, Lord John preferred that the nature and extent of Adams's proposal should not be repeated to Adams in the note of July 13.

At three o'clock the same afternoon of July 13, Adams promptly appeared at the Foreign Office with the draft of a convention in his hand. Lord John took and examined it; then, in the language of Adams's report, —

" The first remark which he made was that it was essentially the Declaration of Paris. He had never known until now that the government of the United States was disposed to accede to it. He was sure that I had never mentioned it. To this I assented."

Apparently Adams's memory deceived him, and he allowed too much credit to that of his opponent. Russell's report of May 21 proved that Adams had mentioned it, and Russell's suppression of that report, only two or three hours before he made the assertion, proved that Russell had motives for not recalling it to memory. Within two or three hours of writing

to Adams the note of July 13, which was but a copy
of the despatch of May 21, with the inversion of one
fact and the suppression of another, Russell affirmed
that he never had heard of the fact he himself
suppressed.

If this were all, Lord John's reputation would
repel the charge; but this was not all. Russell told
Adams, July 13, that "he had never known until
now that the government of the United States was
disposed to accede" to the Declaration of Paris, —
he had never known a fact of newspaper notoriety.
A few months afterward he himself published for Parliament a blue-book containing the official letters on
this subject, and among these was the despatch from
Lord Lyons, dated June 4, marked as received June
17, and containing the passages already quoted: —

"It is probable that Mr. Adams may, before this despatch reaches your Lordship, have offered, on the part
of his Government, to adhere to Article 1 of the Declaration of Paris as well as to the others, and thus to declare
privateering to be abolished. There is no doubt that this
adherence will be offered in the expectation that it will
bind the government accepting it to treat the privateers
of the Southern Confederacy as pirates. . . . It seems
to be far from certain that the United States Congress
would ratify the abolition of privateering; nor do I suppose that the Cabinet will abide by its proposal when it
finds that it will gain nothing toward the suppression
of the Southern privateering by doing so."

Lord John Russell was then near his seventieth
year, and at that age failure of memory is common;

but whatever was the true cause of his inversion and perversion of truth in this instance, no European diplomatist with whom he had ever come in contact during his long public career, would have hesitated in regard to the interpretation to be put on his conduct. Diplomacy cannot afford, and never has admitted, the possibility of accidents like these. Statesmen who made such slips were always, in European diplomacy, understood as meaning to deceive. American diplomatists in Europe could do nothing else than accept European rules. When Adams learned these contradictions, as he did within a few months, he was obliged to infer that Russell had intended to mislead him.

Two months had then elapsed since Adams's arrival in London, and during that time the British government had done no act which impressed him as honest or straightforward. Russell's reception of the project of convention, July 13, was as little calculated as all the other acts of the British government to inspire confidence.

An American would have supposed that any British minister must welcome an offer from the United States government to adhere to the Declaration of Paris. So great was the concession, that, as Lord Lyons justly said, Congress would probably have rejected it. So strong was the feeling against it among Americans abroad that Dayton, the United States minister in Paris, refused to carry out Secretary Seward's order, and gave the British and French governments a pretext for a misunderstanding, by coupling the Marcy amendment to the offer of adhesion. By no device could Great Britain have gained so much from the United States, at so little cost, as by accepting on the spot Adams's offer of adhesion pure and simple. Had Russell signed Adams's convention on the spot, he would have gained what nine Americans in every ten regarded as a great advantage over the United States.

Russell showed no such understanding of the matter. Taking the copy of the project " for the purpose of submitting it to the consideration of his colleagues in the Cabinet," he said he would let Adams know when he should be ready for another meeting. There the matter rested five days, till July 18, when Lord John wrote a formal note, beginning with two remarks : (1) That hitherto States had adhered to the Declaration by simple notice of adherence ; and (2) That the Declaration was not an insulated engagement between two Powers only. Her Majesty's government were willing to waive objection to the form, but should be assured that the United States were ready to contract with all the parties to the Declaration as well as with Great Britain. As much time would be required for these communications, " her Majesty's government would deem themselves authorized to advise the Queen to conclude a convention on this subject with the President of the United States so soon as they shall have been informed that a similar convention has been agreed upon, and is ready for signature, between the President of the United States and the Emperor of the French, so that the two conventions might be signed simultaneously and on the same day."

Once more the British government insisted upon acting only in union with France, on a matter that concerned France much less than England. The persistency of this attitude of suspicion or compulsion toward the United States could not be mistaken. Adams felt it, as it was meant to be felt, but wrote immediately to Dayton at Paris, asking to know whether the joint action was within Dayton's authority. This letter was sent July 19, and on the evening of July 24 Dayton himself arrived in London to help Adams in solving the mystery that had hitherto baffled comprehension.

Meanwhile Seward at Washington made every effort for the same object. He wrote a long despatch[1] to Dayton, July 6, to overcome Dayton's objections, and gave him the positive order to make the offer of adhesion to the four Articles, without raising a question about the belligerent rights of the Union over the States in rebellion. Dayton had feared that after the recognition by France and England of belligerent rights in the rebel States, accession to the Declaration of Paris would cause a serious injury to the Union and a sacrifice of considerable advantages, not merely for the benefit of England and France, but especially

[1] Seward to Dayton, July 6, 1861; Diplomatic Documents, p. 215.

for the rebel government. " If I understand the view of these foreign governments," wrote Dayton,[1] " such accession by us would merely bind our hands as respects privateering ; it would not at all enlarge our rights as against a belligerent power not a party to the treaty. If they admit the Confederate States as a belligerent power, and recognize them for even commercial purposes, which, I take it, is what they mean to do, our accession to the Treaty of Paris will not change their action on this question." The soundness of this opinion was obvious ; but Seward's action rested on different views.

" The United States," wrote Seward to Dayton, " have never disclaimed the employment of letters of marque as a means of maritime war. The insurgents early announced their intention to commission privateers. We knew that friendly nations would be anxious for guarantees of safety from injury by that form of depredation upon the national commerce. We knew also that such nations would desire to be informed whether their flags should be regarded as protecting goods, not contraband of war, of disloyal citizens found under them, and whether the goods, not contraband, of subjects of such nations would be safe from confiscation when found in vessels of disloyal citizens of the United States."

The object to be gained by Seward was evident, but it had nothing to do with Dayton's fears. Seward wished to quiet foreign Powers and exclude them from interest in the war. He regarded the abandon-

[1] Dayton to Seward, June 7, 1861 ; Diplomatic Documents, p. 204.

ment of privateering as not practically important to the United States, and he was undoubtedly right; but he believed that the Union was vitally interested in precluding every excuse for interference by Europe. The conduct of Great Britain was already demonstrating to him, and every other American, that there again he was right, and that at any sacrifice of small interests the vital interest of the Union must be protected, — if, indeed, protection was still possible. The attitude of England and France became more equivocal every week.

On the same day of writing the long despatch to Dayton, Seward called on Lord Lyons and tried to remove obstacles on that side. Lyons, like his French colleague Mercier, made little disguise of his leanings, and no one was ignorant that the whole social weight of both Legations was thrown in the scale against the Union. Lyons had no faith in the success of the national government, or in its professions; and his influence with his own government was exercised in that sense. Seward struggled to win him over. The visit of July 6 had no other object than if possible to draw Lyons into a friendlier attitude.

Seward had been obliged to take a strong measure in refusing to receive the joint action of the two Powers, or to recognize their concession of belligerent rights to the rebel States. He exerted himself to assure the two ministers that the United States government, though evidently unable to admit or even to discuss a denial of its own sovereignty, would ignore the action of England and France. Seward asked only that England and France should not insist on forcing their measures upon the attention of the United States government. He assured Lyons that if Europe would but consent to let the President shut his eyes, the President would not open them. The Declaration of Paris was the test. Evidently to influence British opinion, Seward told Lyons of Dayton's fears and of his own course, and in effect begged him to prevent the raising of obstacles.

" Now," Mr. Seward went on to say, " if, on the one hand, the government of the United States declared that they held their accession to the Paris Declaration to impose an obligation on France with regard to all the States of the Union, the disloyal as well as the loyal; or if, on the other hand, the government of France announced that it did not intend, by accepting the accession of the United States, to contract any engagement affecting the States in revolt, — then Mr. Dayton's apprehensions might be well founded.   But if nothing was said on either side concerning this particular point, the accession of the United States might be given at once, and accepted, and the effect of it in regard to the States in revolt be determined afterward."

Lyons understood, as he was intended to understand, that Seward wished his assistance to deter the governments of England and France from preventing the adhesion of the United States by imposing any condition that should imply recognition of the Southern Confederacy.   Everything else the United States would do to please England, but recognize the rebels they could not.

Lyons listened to Seward's remarks without further comment than to say that he supposed the accession of the United States would be received with great satisfaction by every government.   He then reported the conversation to Lord John Russell.   His report, dated July 8, closed with the following paragraph : [1]

" Notwithstanding the opinion expressed by Mr Seward, I continue to think it very important, with a view to preventing serious disputes in future, that Great Britain and France should not accept the accession of this government to the Declaration of Paris without stating to it, formally and distinctly beforehand, the effect which their so doing is intended by them to have with regard to the seceded States."

Lord Lyons knew that his advice, if followed, would prevent the United States from acceding to the Declaration of Paris.   His motive, as he explained it, was to prevent serious disputes in future. In his mind the advantages to be gained by the adhesion of the United States were outweighed by the risk of disputes.

In these complications certain points gradually became clear.   That the governments of Great Britain and France were unwilling that the United States should accede to the Declaration of Paris pure and simple, was evident.   Under the Declaration of Paris they were bound to invite the United States govern-

[1] Papers No. 3, p. 14.

ment to adhere to the four Articles in their entirety, and were especially pledged to enter into no other arrangement. In violation of the pledge, they invited the United States government to enter into another arrangement, and did not invite it to accede " purely and simply." They persistently ignored, evaded, and postponed attention to the offer of pure and simple adhesion. Lord Lyons, when requested by Seward to use his influence to facilitate the accession pure and simple, acted in the opposite sense, and pressed his Government to impose a condition which he was warned would prevent accession. France acted only as the ally of England, and was guided by the wishes of the British cabinet. Palmerston and Russell were the chief agents in the affair, and their wish to prevent the United States from acceding was the cause of the whole difficulty. The mystery that neither Seward nor Adams could penetrate was the motive that actuated the British cabinet. To that point Adams directed his attention.

Dayton having arrived in London, July 24, had an interview with Adams, July 25, and " under the circumstances felt it his duty to say to Mr. Adams that there need be no delay on his account." [1] Dayton asked only that before offering accession pure and simple, Adams should obtain from Russell a distinct refusal to entertain the Marcy amendment. Adams accordingly wrote to Russell, July 29, informing him

[1] Dayton to Seward, July 30, 1861; Diplomatic Documents, p. 220.

of Dayton's wish to be assured on that point, and promising that as soon as he should receive an explicit assurance that the Marcy amendment was inadmissible, Dayton would apprise the French government of his intention to accede to the Declaration of Paris pure and simple.

Russell replied July 31, giving the required assurance, and adding that he was ready to carry on the negotiation so that the convention should be signed simultaneously at London and Paris. His note closed with a significant phrase: " I need scarcely add that on the part of Great Britain the engagement will be prospective, and will not invalidate anything already done." [1]

In transmitting this note to his Government, August 2, Adams said: " I must frankly admit that I do not understand the meaning of the last paragraph." [2] The persistent creation of difficulties by Russell caused in Adams an equally persistent determination to force Russell into an avowal of his true position. Adams took no notice of the reservation, and waited for Russell to take the next step. If Russell wished only to reserve the right to disregard future complaints or claims of the United States, this formal notice seemed sufficient. He would in that case sign the convention without more delay.

[1] Russell to Adams, July 31, 1861; Diplomatic Documents, p. 110.

[2] Adams to Seward, Aug. 2, 1861; Diplomatic Documents, p. 108,

Russell waited until August 19. Then he wrote to Adams a note enclosing a formal declaration which he meant to make on signing the convention.[1]

"In affixing his signature to the convention of this day between her Majesty, the Queen of Great Britain and Ireland, and the United States of America, the Earl Russell declares, by order of her Majesty, that her Majesty does not intend thereby to undertake any engagement which shall have any bearing, direct or indirect, on the internal difficulties now prevailing in the United States."

On the same day Russell transmitted a copy of this declaration to Paris, and it was adopted by Thouvenel for communication to Dayton.

To Russell's note of August 19 Adams replied in a long and carefully prepared note,[2] dated August 23, recapitulating the story of the negotiation down to the actual moment, when the "novel and anomalous proceeding" of Earl Russell arrested it.

"Obviously," said Adams, "a consent to accept a particular exception, susceptible of so wide a construction of a joint instrument, made by one of the parties to it in its own favor at the time of signing, would justify the idea that some advantage is, or may be suspected to be, intended to be taken by the other. The natural effect of such an accompaniment would seem to be to imply that the government of the United States might be desirous

[1] Russell to Adams, Aug. 19, 1861; Diplomatic Documents, p. 118.

[2] Adams to Russell, Aug. 23, 1861; Diplomatic Documents, p. 120.

at this time to take a part in the Declaration, not from any high purpose or durable policy, but with a view of securing some small temporary object in the unhappy struggle which is going on at home. Such an inference would spoil all the value that might be attached to the act itself. The mere toleration of it would seem to be equivalent to a confession of their own weakness. Rather than that such a record should be made, it were a thousand times better that the Declaration remain unsigned forever. If the parties to the instrument are not to sign it upon terms of perfect reciprocity, with all their duties and obligations under it perfectly equal, and without equivocation or reservation of any kind on any side, then it is plain that the proper season for such an engagement has not yet arrived. It were much wiser to put it off until nations can understand each other better."

To this note Russell replied at equal length, August 28,[1] evidently feeling that his position was seriously assailed. His defence of the proposed declaration was contained in a few sentences : —

" It would follow from the position taken by the United States that the privateers of the Southern States might be decreed to be pirates ; and it might be further argued by the government of the United States that a European power signing a convention with the United States declaring that privateering was and remains abolished, would be bound to treat the privateers of the so-called Confederate States as pirates. Hence instead of an agreement, charges of bad faith and violation of a convention might be brought in the United States against

[1] Russell to Adams, Aug. 28, 1861; Diplomatic Documents, p. 128.

the Power signing such a convention and treating the privateers of the so-called Confederate States as those of a belligerent power. . . . It is in this spirit that her Majesty's government decline to bind themselves, without a clear explanation on their part, to a convention which, seemingly confined to an adoption of the Declaration of Paris of 1856, might be construed as an engagement to interfere in the unhappy dissensions now prevailing in the United States."

This explanation was remarkable for admitting the correctness of Adams's criticism; but it raised doubts of another kind, which could not but strengthen the growing conviction in the minds of all Americans who followed the negotiation, that behind the British evasions and excuses some unavowed motive was still concealed.

The ostensible plea was clear. Lord - Russell wished to avoid the vortex of American wars. Equally clearly the proposed declaration would not answer that purpose, even though the American government had accepted it. It could not be a part of the four Articles of the Declaration of Paris. The United States government could at any moment, by merely writing a formal note, accede to those Articles as they stood, and Great Britain was pledged to accept the adhesion unconditionally. Adams asked for a convention because the Senate must have some instrument to ratify in order to make it valid at home; but had the United States government chosen to act directly, it could have done so, as far as regarded

foreign Powers, without the possibility of condition
or refusal from Great Britain.

The proposed declaration was merely a notice given
by Earl Russell that the British government would
follow a certain course; but the notice would bind the
United States in no way, and left President Lincoln
still free to call upon Great Britain to fulfil all the
obligations of the four Articles, whatever they were.
In that case the British government, with or without
the declaration, stood in the same attitude. The
declaration merely warned the United States that
Great Britain, in case of a demand to fulfil certain
duties resulting from the treaty, meant to refuse
compliance; but it could not prevent the demand
if the United States government chose to make it.

Lord Russell knew that the United States always
had considered Great Britain bound to treat the Southern cruisers, whether public or private, as pirates, on
grounds altogether separate from the Declaration of
Paris, though in American eyes much stronger. The
British ministry had emphatically refused to do so by
recognizing them as belligerents. The act, unfriendly
to the United States at best, had been made more so
by its adoption on the day when Adams reached
London, as though Russell wished to preclude discussion. President Lincoln had not acquiesced in that
decision, but had not made it ground of quarrel.
Russell showed extravagant bias against the United
States government if he supposed that President Lincoln meant to seek a contest over the Declaration of

Paris, when Lincoln had made every effort to prove that he did not mean to quarrel over the proclamation of Southern belligerency. The Declaration of Paris was a side issue. The main issue was the belligerency of the rebel States; and the British government had already by proclamation given formal and sufficient notice, by creating them belligerents, that Great Britain did not intend to treat Southern privateers as pirates.

The proposed declaration was superfluous as far as concerned its ostensible object; it was discourteous, for it implied that the United States government was laying a trap for Great Britain; it had no binding power on the United States; and it was a measure which Russell knew, through the warning of Seward to Lyons, would prevent further proceedings on the part of the United States.

As a matter of history the story stops there. The motives of the British government were not further avowed, and its action led to no apparent consequence. Earl Russell's course in 1861 was all of one character; and whether in a single point it was controlled by fear of Seward's supposed tricks or by unavowed motives, is immaterial. In either case it was equally unfriendly. History abstains from imputing motives and adopting uncertain conclusions; but what history avoids, diplomacy is obliged habitually to do. No diplomatist in the service of a European government ever received such treatment as was received by **Adams and Dayton** without searching for unavowed reasons to account for it.   Least of all would an English diplomatic agent have been satisfied with the official explanations in this case; for among diplomatists the English, not without excuse, were always most prone to act on the assumption that truth was an English virtue, and that falsehood was a diplomatic profession.   During the year 1861 the United States Legation in London stood in an attitude of anxiety not easy to realize; and in the face of hostility or distrust so openly avowed by Earl Russell, no member of that Legation could afford to pass over so extraordinary an experience without framing some explanation that could be used for guidance through the darkness and danger that surrounded him.

When Adams arrived in London, May 13, 1861, the American Union was universally supposed to be at an end.   Not one Englishman in a hundred took a different view.   The possibility of a civil war, believed to be necessarily futile, irritated Englishmen against President Lincoln and his supporters.   Never in the history of human events had a revolt of such a nature and extent been repressed by force; and even the friends of America shrank for a moment from the realization that a million lives might have to pay the price of Union.   This state of public opinion was natural, and not a subject for complaint so much as for correction.   Within a few months it was corrected, and within a year the British government could have adopted no unfriendly measure without meeting vigorous resistance from its own ranks; but during the summer of 1861 the United States government could count on no support in England. Not until Bright, Cobden, and Forster had fully entered the lists and shown a temper almost resembling that of the American combatants, did the American Legation in London draw a free breath.

The conviction that the Union was at an end lay at the foundation of every act adopted by the British government during the spring and summer of 1861. The assumption that the United States government existed only in form was evident in Russell's attitude toward Adams from the moment of his arrival until the following year. Russell intentionally fixed, as far as he was concerned, the position of Adams before he arrived, as the representative of half an empire, and afterward showed without concealment his intention to hold Adams in the position fixed for him.

The Declaration of Paris was the first battle-ground between Russell and Adams. For the Declaration itself Adams cared as little as Russell or Dayton; but the evident intention to prevent Adams from giving his Government's adherence to the Declaration of Paris, and the extraordinary equivocations to which Russell resorted in the effort to take from his course the appearance of outrage, exasperated Adams to the point of pressing the British government as far as it could be induced to go in discovering its true intentions. Evidently the British government, for some reason not clearly understood, shrank from saying

how far it meant to go. Russell said only enough to
show that in due time he meant to say more.

The story has shown that Russell and his colleagues
recognized the rebels as belligerents before Adams
could arrive to remonstrate; that they effected a
practical alliance with France against the United
States at the same time; that they induced the French
government to violate the pledge given in the protocol
of the Declaration of Paris in order to offer to both
belligerents a partial adhesion, which must exclude
the United States from a simple adhesion, to the
Declaration of Paris, while it placed both belligerents
on the same apparent footing.   These steps were
taken in haste before Adams could obtain an interview.   When Adams by an effort unexpected to Russell obtained an interview at Pembroke Lodge at
noon of Saturday, May 18, and according to Russell's
report of May 21 said that the United States were
" disposed to adhere to the Declaration of Paris,"
Russell evaded the offer, saying that he had already
sent sufficient instructions to Lyons, although the instructions were not sufficient, nor had they been sent.
When this evasion was afterward brought to his notice by Adams, Russell, revising his report to Lyons,
made such changes in it as should represent the first
proposal as coming from himself, and the evasion to
have come from Adams.   When at last obliged to
read the American offer, Russell declared that he had
never heard of it before, although he had himself reported it to Lyons and Lyons had reported it to him.

When compelled to take the offer for consideration, Russell, though always professing to welcome adhesion pure and simple, required the co-operation of Dayton. When Adams overcame this last obstacle, Russell interposed a written proviso, which as he knew from Lyons would prevent ratification. When Adams paid no attention to the proviso, but insisted on signature of the treaty, Russell at last wrote a declaration in the nature of an insult, which could not be disregarded.

Lord Russell's motives for this conduct were his own affair. The United States Legation in London could not undertake to say certainly what they were, nor did it greatly care for an explanation, since no conceivable explanation could have excused the Legation for acting on any principle but one of distrust. By the necessities of the case, Adams had no choice. Russell's acts, whether straightforward or not, bore every external appearance of covert hostility. Adams could do nothing else than draw inferences from every step in Russell's progress. From the first, — Russell's disregard of the pledge of indivisibility in the protocol to the Declaration of Paris, — the American minister was obliged to infer that England no longer thought her interest to require that the United States should be a party to the whole Declaration. From the second, — Russell's wish for accession to the second, third, and fourth Articles, — it was clear that the first Article, or the whole in conjunction, in some manner clashed with British interests after

the dissolution of the Union.   From Russell's evasion
of Adams's offer, May 18, Adams could only conclude
that the offer was in some manner inconvenient for
the British government, which had motives for join-
ing France in acting at Washington.   From Russell's
misstatement of the interview of May 18, it appeared
that he wished to conceal, or not to avow, the motives
of his action or the action itself.   From the delays
interposed by Russell, Adams must conclude that the
British cabinet was trying one device after another
to evade the proposition; and finally, from the
written declaration of August 19 he could draw no
other inference than that Russell had resorted to the
only defensive weapon left him, in order to avoid the
avowal of his true motives and policy.

Just or not, these were necessary conclusions for
any minister of the United States in 1861, who had
to shape a course of conduct in the face of universal
ill-will.   In such a situation the business of a diplomatist was to account in some way for the mysterious
acts of his enemies in order not to be taken by surprise when the blow should come.   A little study of
the history of the Declaration of Paris suggested motives which might offer a clew not only to Russell's
strange conduct in May and July, but to the danger
it threatened to the United States.

The Declaration of Paris while purporting to add
four principles to international law, did in fact offer
only two.   The principle that neutral goods were not
liable to condemnation under enemy's flag, and the

18

other that blockades to be binding must be effective, were then and had always been acknowledged maxims of law, as well established as any of the common rules of a little respected code had usually been. Only two of the principles involved new points. One was that privateering should be abolished; the other was that the neutral flag covered enemy's goods.

Of the two new principles the first was indisputably advantageous to Great Britain, and never met with opposition from her. Earl Russell could have no objection to the abandonment of privateering by the United States. The secret of his evident unwillingness to the adherence of the United States on any terms to the Declaration of Paris could not be found in the Article on privateering; but if it was not there in Article 1, or in Articles 3 and 4, it must be sought in Article 2, that the neutral flag covered enemy's goods.

Considering that England was about to become a neutral, the idea of her hostility to a provision so favorable to neutrals was apparently unreasonable; but in April and May, 1861, the American Union was supposed likely to fall apart without serious trouble, and the permanent interests of Great Britain as a belligerent still outweighed her momentary interests as a neutral. The principle that the neutral flag covered enemy's goods was a neutral and American interest against which Great Britain had fought with something like desperation.

This second Article of the Treaty of Paris was

always regarded as hostile to British power, and was accepted by England only as a sacrifice under motives sufficiently strong to justify it. Russell himself objected to it and opposed it, and the whole conservative spirit of the kingdom uniformly maintained that Great Britain had " a great and preponderating interest in maintaining the legitimate rights of belligerents, and cannot afford to sacrifice such legitimate exercise of belligerent power as is justified by the law of nations."

The Ministry of 1854 decided to concede the sanctity of the neutral flag for reasons well understood. One of these reasons was that by this concession England obtained the abandonment of the practice of privateering. The other reason was given by Lord Palmerston officially from his place on the Treasury Bench in the House of Commons on the night of March 18, 1862. He said that had the Government not taken the course it did take in 1854; had it insisted on maintaining the right of search and seizure of enemy's goods in neutral ships, — such persistence would within six months have added a war with the United States to the war they were then waging with Russia. According to Palmerston, the British government was forced by the great and growing power of the United States into an unwilling assent to principles which it held to be dangerous to the maritime power of England.

The continuance of the later policy was naturally dependent on the continuance of the motives that led the British government to adopt it. If fear of the power of the American Union produced the leniency toward neutrals, the removal of this fear would remove the motive to persevere in the leniency. The same men and the same ideas ruled England in 1861 as in 1856; and both Palmerston and Russell were statesmen of the old school, whose views of the United States had not essentially changed since the War of 1812.

The dissolution of the American Union was foreseen from the moment of Abraham Lincoln's election as President in November, 1860. After five months of doubt and preparation, the civil war broke out beyond restraint, April 12, 1861, and the news reached England, April 20. Three agents of the insurgent government were already on the spot, — Yancey, Rost, and Mann, — and Lord John Russell admitted them to an interview, May 4, in which they urged at great length the cause of their new republic. Only two days afterward, May 6, Russell wrote to Cowley at Paris, directing him to invite the French government to join in an effort to obtain from the two contending parties in America their adherence to the second, third, and fourth Articles of the Declaration of Paris. Only two days after the British government had reason to know officially the rupture of the American Union, it began to disregard its pledge given five years before in the Treaty of Paris, under the avowed idea that the power of the United States was too dangerous to be thwarted. The plan of Lord John Russell was merely to provide a temporary arrangement protecting British neutral rights while saving British belligerent practices. He proposed " to invite the two contending parties to act upon the principles laid down in the second and third Articles of the Declaration of Paris." He did not propose to enter into any arrangement for adopting principles, or for acting on them beyond the time of hostilities. At the close of hostilities the proposed arrangement was to terminate, and the British rights of belligerency were to remain at all times intact.

The United States were required to promise only that belligerent rights should not, during the coming hostilities, be used against British commerce; while Russell and Palmerston retained the right to revive at any future time the exercise of those belligerent rights against the enfeebled and divided States which they expected to survive the civil war. Had the United States been permitted to accede to the Declaration of Paris pure and simple, Great Britain would have lost her belligerent rights beyond recall, the more effectually because the United States were obliged by their Constitution to record their accession in the form of a treaty, whereas Great Britain had entered with other Powers into a mere agreement, which was binding, as Lord Malmesbury declared, only so long as it was convenient to respect it.

The British government had no reason to suppose that the United States would lay aside their objections to the Declaration of Paris, and Seward's offer to do so disconcerted Russell. In his second despatch to Lyons, of May 18, he made no suggestion of adhesion pure and simple, but he said that he could not accept the renunciation of privateering on the part of the United States, " if coupled with the condition that her Majesty's government should enforce its renunciation on the Confederate States ; " yet when the United States offered to renounce privateering without coupling to it any condition whatever, Russell introduced conditions on his part which he knew would prevent President Lincoln from carrying out his purpose.

Whether these were the motives of Russell or not, they were the motives that the American Legation in London was irresistibly obliged to impute to him. After the manner in which Russell received the advances of President Lincoln, no American minister in London could safely act on any other assumption than that the British government meant, at the first convenient opportunity, to revive the belligerent pretences dormant since the War of 1812.

THE LEGAL–TENDER ACT.[1]

During the Rebellion the United States armies suffered many disasters in the field, which for the moment were felt as personal misfortunes by every loyal citizen. So strong was the public feeling of anger and astonishment, that Congress appointed committees of investigation to examine into the causes of these military failures, and subjected the conduct of the war to a searching and sometimes a severe criticism. In finance the nation suffered only one great disaster, but its effects have extended far beyond the period of the war, and are likely to be felt for an indefinite time to come. The causes of this catastrophe have not been investigated by Congress; but as the day may probably arrive when the national government will admit that the act of national bankruptcy was a calamity involving the credit of every man in whose charge the people then placed the common interests, it may be useful to point out the path which any future Congressional committee on the Conduct of the Finances will be obliged to follow in investigating the causes which led to that mis-

[1] An article by Francis A. Walker and Henry Adams, in the "North American Review" for April, 1870.

carriage, the results of which have exceeded in importance any defeat of the national armies or the failure of any campaign.

The timid and hesitating criticism with which the subject has been commonly treated speaks ill for the sound sense of the community. The public has adopted the idea that it is itself the responsible governing power, and its representatives only delegates to enroll its orders, until the healthy process of criticising a policy once adopted seems to it almost an attack on its own authority. The confusion involved in this assumption of responsibility is peculiarly unfortunate. The task of citizens who are selected to govern is one thing. They bear the burden of leaders, and they enjoy the honor; they are at liberty to excuse or palliate their mistakes, their ignorance, or their crimes by whatever arguments they can make to answer their purpose. The task of the public is wholly different. It is that of insisting, without favor or prejudice, on the observance of truth in legislation and in the execution of the laws. To apply the principles of truth is the first duty of every writer for the press and every speaker on the hustings. Whatever seems harsh in criticism or vehement in temper may be excused in the citizen who clings to the logic of fundamenta' principles, and leaves to those whose public conduct fails to reach his standard the labor of justifying themselves in the best way they can.

Critics of American finance commonly begin with the assumption that the Legal-Tender Act was necessary and inevitable. As a matter of criticism, nothing can be less sensible than such a beginning; and as a matter of intelligence, nothing can be feebler. Congress and the country permitted no such assumption to be made in excuse for the beaten, generals at Fredericksburg and Chancellorsville. No satisfactory conclusion can be reached from such a premise. No sound result can be obtained except by assuming at the outset that the Legal-Tender Act was not necessary; that the public was not responsible for it; that the men who made it law were answerable to the people for their act, and are bound to show that so extraordinary and so grave a misfortune could by no means have been avoided. If they fail to prove their case, they are condemned.

The law of legal tender, passed by Congress in February, 1862, cannot be assumed to have been necessary, and its supporters are bound to prove that they had no alternative. To this task Mr. Spaulding, the principal author of the measure, has applied himself; while, on the other hand, Mr. Chase, without whose assent the law could not have passed, has assumed the contrary ground.[1]   At the outset, a

[1] History of the Legal-Tender Paper Money issued during the Great Rebellion, being a Loan without Interest, and National Currency. Prepared by Hon. E. G. SPAULD.NG, Chairman of the Sub-Committee of Ways and Means at the time the Act was passed. Buffalo. 1869.

Opinion delivered in the Supreme Court of the United States by CHIEF-JUSTICE CHASE, on the 7th of February, 1870, in Regard to the Construction of the Legal-Tender Act.

strong presumption against the law is raised by the unquestionable fact that the men who in 1862 were charged with the conduct of the finances, and were responsible for this law in particular, had no claim to confidence on the ground of their financial knowledge or experience. Something better might have been expected among a people devoted to commerce and habituated to self-government. Military disasters were to be looked for, seeing that the nation had no training or taste for war; but though war or art or philosophy or abstract knowledge were beyond the range of public or popular interest, an experience of two hundred years ought to have insured the country against mistakes in practical politics. Such was far from the truth. Among the leading statesmen then charged with responsibility, not one was by training well fitted to perform the duties of finance minister, or to guide the financial opinions of Congress.

The Secretary of the Treasury, certainly the most capable of the men then connected with finance, suffered under the disadvantage of inexperience. In the Senate, finance, like every other subject, was treated rather as though it were a branch of the common or constitutional law, than as though it were a system with established principles and processes of its own; but in the House of Representatives the want of education was most apparent and most mischievous, while by a significant coincidence the law of legal tender, more than almost any other great financial measure of the Rebellion, was peculiarly

the work of this House. Of the members who originated and whose activity carried through all opposition the Act of February, 1862, it is difficult to speak
in language which will not seem unduly and un-
reasonably severe. Yet it may honestly be doubted
whether since Kleon, the leather-seller, was sent by
the people of Athens to command its armies at
Sphacteria and Amphipolis, and since Aristophanes
on the public stage covered the powerful popular
leader with an immortal ridicule which surely re-
flected most severely on the Athenian people itself, —
it may honestly be doubted whether history records
an occasion when the interests of a great country
in an extreme emergency have been committed to
hands more eminently disqualified for the trust.

In February, 1862, Thaddeus Stevens was chairman
of the Committee of Ways and Means, from which
emanates the ordinary financial legislation of Congress.   That Mr. Stevens was as little suited to
direct the economical policy of the country at a critical moment as a naked Indian from the plains to
plan the architecture of St. Peter's or to direct the
construction of the Capitol, expresses in no extreme
language the degree of his unfitness. That Stevens
was grossly ignorant upon all economical subjects
and principles was the least of his deficiencies. A
dogmatic mind, a high temper, and an overbearing
will are three serious disqualifications for financial
success, especially when combined with contempt
for financial knowledge.   It is no exaggeration to say

that every quality of his nature and every incident of his life which gave Stevens power in the House, where he was almost omnipotent in the legislation which belonged to the war and to reconstruction, conspired to unfit him for the deliberate and difficult discussions of finance. Yet the principal burden of blame or praise for the financial legislation of that momentous year is not to be awarded to Stevens. In the press of business upon the committee, when in the brief space of a few months the whole system of loans, of taxation, and of currency demanded by a war of tremendous proportions had to be created, so to speak, out of nothing, two sub-committees were formed to divide the duties which fell upon the committee. One of these, under the lead of Morrill of Vermont, undertook to enlarge and adjust the scheme of taxation to the new necessities of the government. The other, under the chairmanship of the Hon. Elbridge G. Spaulding of New York, assumed the care of the national currency, the raising of loans, and the issue of Treasury notes or bonds. Stevens remained chairman of the whole committee, charging himself particularly with the matter of appropriations, and lending his powerful voice to both sections below him, as either by turn encountered opposition in carrying its measures through the House.

The intellect of a Congressman, gifted with no more than the ordinary abilities of his class, is scarcely an interesting or instructive subject of study; nor are the discussions that arise among such men likely to be rich in stores of knowledge or experience; but when an accidental representative carries " over the Administration and through Congress," [1] as Spaulding is claimed to have done, and he clearly did, a measure of such far-reaching consequences as the Legal-Tender Act of 1862, the character of that person's mind and the facts of his life cease to be matters of insignificance. One may well inquire who it was that could lead a nation so far astray, and what the condition of things that made it possible for him to effect results of such magnitude. Financiers who make an addition of hundreds of millions of dollars to the debts of their countries, representing not a penny of value enjoyed, are entitled to a place in history whether they boast the intellectual capacity of Pitt or of Spaulding.

Unlike Stevens, Spaulding had the advantage or disadvantage of a certain sort of financial experience. He had been for a time treasurer of the State of New York. By profession he was, in 1862, president of a joint-stock bank at Buffalo, and on this circumstance he based his chief claim to speak as an expert in finance. At the conference on the 11th of January, 1862, at the Treasury, between the Secretary, the committees of Congress, and the representatives of the principal Northern banks, — a conference

[1] Spaulding's share in the passage of the Act is described in these words by his colleague, Hon. T. M. Pomeroy, in a speech delivered in the House of Representatives Feb. 19, 1862, reprinted in Spaulding's book, p. 132.

whose momentous importance will require close attention, — Spaulding expressed his convictions both " as a banker and legislator." The association of functions was not unimportant, and Spaulding was right in laying stress upon it. Had he not been a banker as well as a legislator, the Legal-Tender Act might never have been enacted. Being a provincial banker, and at the same time chairman of a subcommittee dealing with the nominally financial but really universal interests of thirty millions or more of citizens, and dealing too with the whole future of a nation whose development no bounds seem to limit, Spaulding naturally applied to the situation the principles of finance he had learned in shaving notes at a country bank.

The situation was unquestionably serious; but few persons now retain any distinct recollection of its actual shape. To the minds of men living in 1870 the events of 1862 appear bound in close connection with the long series of events that have intervened. The necessity of the Legal-Tender Act is now assumed, not on account of what had happened before the law was passed, or on account of anything that was foreseen by its authors, but because of what afterward occurred, — the exigencies of a situation far more difficult and alarming than existed at that earlier time. Against such a confusion of ideas every candid man should be on his guard. The vague notion that sooner or later legal-tender paper was inevitable, is part of the loose and slovenly popular criticism with which the subject has been habitually treated, and is scarcely worth comment; but the actual circumstances under which Congress declared the measure to be necessary are a matter of fact, and with these law, history, and political science have first to deal.

Congress met Dec. 2, 1861, and Secretary Chase immediately set before it an account of the financial situation, and his own scheme for supplying the wants of the Treasury. He required about $200,000,000, in addition to resources already provided, in order to meet the demands of the next half-year. His immediate necessity was for $100,000,000 within three months. He estimated that the debt would reach $517,000,000 on the 1st of July, 1862, and that a year later it would probably become $900,000,000. In fact it rose to $1,100,000,000. A part of the heavy government expenses was to be met by taxation; a part by the sale of bonds; and for the rest Secretary Chase proposed the assumption by the government of the bank circulation, amounting to some $200,000,000, with a view not only of obtaining the money, but of providing a sound currency on which to conduct the war. The secretary did not, in this connection, overlook the possibility of resorting to a forced paper circulation, but " the immeasurable evils of dishonored public faith and national bankruptcy " deterred him from recommending the measure, or rather obliged him to reject it as dangerous and unnecessary.

Thus, on the 1st of December, 1861, according to the Secretary of the Treasury, no occasion existed for resorting to the moderate measure of issuing government paper, except so far as concerned a possible guaranty to a new bank circulation. The idea of legal tender was expressly rejected. The government believed itself able to meet its demands on the basis of the bank circulation, provided Congress would place the bank circulation on an available footing. Nothing was done by Congress toward supplying the wants of the Treasury until, toward the end of December, Spaulding began to draft a bill for establishing a national banking currency. While preparing this draft, Spaulding, " upon mature reflection, came to the conclusion that the bill could not be passed and made available quick enough to meet the crisis then pressing upon the government for money to sustain the army and navy. He therefore drafted a legal-tender Treasury-note section." This was done about December 30 ; and this was the origin of the measure destined to have a vast influence on the American people. The " mature reflection " of Mr. Spaulding could discover no other or better method of supplying a temporary want of $100,000,000 than a resort to the last expedient known to finance, — what he himself calls a forced loan, made in the first year of the war by means equivalent to a debasement of the standard of value and a bankruptcy of the government. Any reader in the least familiar with financial history must appreciate the extravagance of Spaulding's assumption. That he acted with honesty and good intention no one will think it worth while to dispute; but that he had a conception of the consequences of what he was doing, or that he grasped in any degree the principles of statesmanship, no unprejudiced or cool observer could imagine. Like all ignorant men impatient of resistance or restraint, the moment he saw an obstacle he knew but one resource, — an appeal to force.

Spaulding then, "upon more mature consideration," converted this section into a separate bill, and laid it before his committee. The committee was by no means unanimous in accepting Spaulding's views of necessity. It is true that the only doubt entertained by Thaddeus Stevens regarded the constitutionality of the law; and one is at loss whether most to wonder at the ignorance thus betrayed or at the Constitutional scruples which suggested themselves to this veteran expunger of Constitutions. Stevens and one half the committee approved the bill, but the other half stood out firmly against it, and only as a matter of courtesy allowed it to be reported to the House.

The bill, reported Jan. 7, 1862, authorized the issue of $100,000,000 in Treasury notes, to be a legal tender, and exchangeable on demand for six per cent bonds. Public opinion at once became sharply divided on the merits of the measure. Delegates from the Boards of Trade and banks of the principal Northern cities appeared in Washington to oppose the bill; and on the 11th of January these gentlemen met the

Secretary of the Treasury and 'the finance committees of the Senate and House, at Secretary Chase's office in the Department. There the whole financial policy of the government was made ,a subject of discussion, and the two paths between which the country was still at liberty to choose were marked out with precision. Spaulding, on the one hand, insisted not only that his measure was the best, but that it was the only means of raising the money required, and he demanded to know what alternative could be suggested. On the part of the bank committees, James Gallatin of New York submitted a complete financial scheme, and replied to Spaulding's inquiry by the simple remark that the government should sell its bonds in the open market for what they would bring, without limitation of price. To this suggestion Spaulding made the following response : —

"The Sub-Committee of Ways and Means, through Mr. Spaulding, objected to any and every form of ' shinning ' by government through Wall or State streets to begin with ; objected to the knocking down of government stocks to seventy-five or sixty cents on the dollar, the inevitable result of throwing a new and large loan on the market without limitation as to price ; claimed for Treasury notes as much virtue of par value as the notes of banks which have suspended specie payments, but which yet circulate in the trade of the North ; *and finished with firmly refusing to assent to any scheme which should permit a speculation by brokers, bankers, and others in the government securities, and particularly any scheme which should double the public debt of the country,*

*and double the expenses of the war, by damaging the credit
of the government* to the extent of sending it to ' shin'
through the shaving shops of New York, Boston, and
Philadelphia. He affirmed his conviction as a banker
and legislator, that it was the lawful policy as well as
the manifest duty of the government, in the present exigency, to legalize as tender its fifty millions issue of
demand Treasury notes, authorized at the extra session in
July last, and to add to this stock of legal tender, immediately, one hundred millions more. *He thought that this
financial measure would carry the country through the war,
and save its credit and dignity.* At the same time we
should insist upon taxation abundantly ample to pay the
expenses of the government on a peace footing, and interest of every dollar of the public obligation, and to give
this generation a clear show of a speedy liquidation of
the public debt."

Before further comment on this speech, the fact
must be noticed that throughout the legal-tender contest in 1862 no question was involved but one of
resource. The sum of one hundred million dollars
was wanted to carry on the government, and Spaulding closed every mouth by asking how else the money
could be raised, since the banks could provide no
more coin, and their paper would not properly answer the purpose. At that time no one thought of
any ulterior process of " floating the bonds," which
became the ultimate function of the legal-tender
paper ; and indeed this argument, which implied an
intentional depreciation of the paper, would in 1862
have scarcely worked in favor of the bill. How little

weight was put on the idea of " making money easy "
is evident from the whole debate ; but as far as Spaulding is concerned, the following letter, written Jan. 8,
1862, is sufficient : —

DEAR SIR, — In reply to yours of the 4th instant, I
would say that the Treasury Note Bill for $100,000,000
agreed upon in committee yesterday is a measure of *necessity* and not one of *choice*. You criticise matters very
freely, and very likely you may be right in what you
say. We will be out of means to pay the daily expenses
in *about thirty days*, and the committee do not see any
other way to get along till we can get the tax-bills ready,
except to issue temporarily Treasury notes. Perhaps you
can suggest some other mode of carrying on the government for the next one hundred days. . . . It is much
easier to *find fault* than it is to suggest *practicable means
or measures*. We must have at least $100,000,000 of
paying means during the next three months, or the government must stop payment. . . . I will thank you to
suggest a better *practicable* mode of getting $100,000,000
of paying means during the next three months. I would
be glad to adopt it, and the committee would be glad to
adopt it. Let us have *your specific plan* for this purpose, one that will produce the money, and we will be
very much obliged to you.

This curious letter, which Spaulding has published,
italics and all, as a valuable document, tells the story
of the legal tender in its origin. As a specimen of
American finance and Congressional ability it will
live in history. It presents the view on which, then
as now, the adherents of this measure have always

wished to place it before the public, — as the only alternative to the immediate stoppage of government. Not as a means of supplying currency, or of easing the money market, or of "floating" bonds, was the legal-tender paper first created, but solely to supply a temporary want of $100,000,000, without which the Treasury must stop payments. Spaulding flung into the face of every doubter his contemptuous request to suggest some better mode of raising the money, or in future to keep silence.

Three days after this letter was written, James Gallatin, on the part of the New York banks, replied to Spaulding's entreaties by the remark of a man who knew what he was talking about, that Secretary Chase need only sell his bonds at their market value, and obtain what money he wanted. To this suggestion Spaulding was called upon for a rejoinder. Obviously he was bound to show that Gallatin was mistaken; that no such alternative existed; and that, for some reason or other, government bonds could not be sold in the way proposed. In the speech just quoted Spaulding did undertake to answer Gallatin, but he took no such ground as this; he did not deny the efficacy of the proposed measure. He did not even question that the resource suggested was simple and easy. He appealed to the dignity of the government.

It appears, therefore, that there was an alternative to legal tender, in spite of Spaulding's assertions that there was none. The existence of this alternative was acknowledged by the supporters of the bill almost in the same breath with which they declared legal tender to be a necessity. In his speech of January 28, on introducing the bill in the House of Representatives, Spaulding said : —

"The bill before us is a war measure, — a measure of *necessity*, and not of choice. . . . *We have the alternative* either to go into the market and sell our bonds for what they will command, or to pass this bill. . . . If you offer to the people and put upon the market $300,000,000 to the highest bidder in the present state of affairs, they would not be taken except at ruinous rates of discount. . . . I fear the twenty years six per cent bonds would under the pressure fall to 75, 70, 60, and even 50 cents. . . . Why, then, go into the streets at all to borrow money? I prefer to assert the power and dignity of the government by the issue of its own notes."

Samuel Hooper, who was second on Mr. Spaulding's committee, said : —

"The propositions of committees from Boards of Trade and banks, which recently visited Washington, differed from the theory of this bill so far as to require that . . . the government bonds must first be disposed of, and the money received for them paid to the contractors. . . . The obvious effect of such an arrangement would be to put the reins of our national finances in the hands of the banks. . . . *To render the government financially more independent*, it is necessary to make the United States notes a legal tender. *It is possible that they would become a practical tender without providing for them to be a legal tender.*"

The alternative, therefore, as seen by Hooper, was not between legal tender and a stoppage of payments, but between legal tender and dependence on the banks. John A. Bingham's idea of necessity was only a little more ridiculous.

"Great names," said Bingham, "have been invoked [against legal tender] in this debate. For what purpose? For the purpose of laying at the feet and at the mercy of brokers and hawkers on 'Change the power of the people over their monetary interests in this hour of their national exigency."

Thaddeus Stevens, again, had views of his own in regard to the meaning of the word "necessity."

"This bill," said he, "is a measure of necessity, not of choice. . . . *Here, then, in a few words lies your* CHOICE. Throw bonds at six or seven per cent on the market between this and December enough to raise at least $600,000,000, or issue United States notes. . . . I maintain that the highest sum you could sell your bonds at would be seventy-five per cent, payable in currency itself at a discount. That would produce a loss which no nation or individual doing a large business could stand a year."

John Sherman also used the word "necessity" in a sense which would have been ludicrous if the subject had concerned the metaphysical doctrine of fate and free-will: "We must no longer hesitate as to the necessity of this measure. That necessity does exist, and now presses upon us. I rest my vote upon the proposition that this is a necessary and proper measure *to furnish a currency.*" A better example of anti-climax is seldom seen in rhetoric.

It would be pleasant to linger over this subject, and enjoy among these apparently tedious speeches the touches of involuntary humor which a critic finds so difficult to resist, but evidence is not needed on a point that is self-evident; and unquestionably even the strongest supporters of the bill did not in any true and absolute sense maintain that legal tender was necessary, but only that it was preferable to the process of selling bonds at a discount and retaining the old bank currency.

Finance is a subject which the liveliest writer may despair of making popular, since the sight or suspicion of it is alone enough to cause every reader, except the dullest, to close the most promising volume. A writer can have no hope of gaining a general hearing on such a topic. Rarely can he expect sympathy even among business men, unless he adopts the views they hold. Yet notwithstanding this, it is and will remain true, and not only true but interesting, that in the large experience of modern nations some· solid principles in finance have been established too firmly to be shaken; and whether or no busy politicians or local bankers choose to believe them, and whether or no the ordinary reader choose to listen to them, the principles are sound, and will hold.

Hitherto in human history the mind of man has succeeded in conceiving of but two means by which governments can obtain money. One of these is, to take. The other is, to borrow. The hybrid and self-contradictory notion of a forced loan resolves ultimately into one or the other of these conceptions, and as a permanent policy is impossible. In practice, where a government does not take, it must borrow.

Almost all modern nations are, to a greater or less extent, habitual borrowers so far as their governments are concerned, and during two hundred years of experience the principles which regulate loans have been studied with some care, and simplified in some degree into a science. After innumerable costly experiments and elaborate study of the interests and motives of lenders and borrowers, the effect of complicated financial schemes and special pledges and conditions, it seems to be now acknowledged by the shrewdest governments that the simplest bargain is the best for the public, and that all financial tricks and devices, all attempts to coax or deceive capitalists into better conditions than they are ready to offer, in the end injure only the government and the people. Simplicity has of late years been carried by the great borrowing nations to a degree of perfection beyond which there seems to be no possibility of passing. According to this principle, governments sell their own credit without stipulation, reserve, or condition. They sell, for example, their promise to pay a thousand dollars a year so long as it is demanded. To this promise no condition, expressed or implied, is attached, except that the payment of a nominal principal may at any time discharge the debt. For this promise they obtain whatever they can ; and experience has proved that in the competition of the world the bargain thus struck is for both parties the fairest.

Another simple law has also been established : and this is that lenders will always prefer, and pay most for, a security on which there is a certainty of permanence or a chance of profit, other things being equal : that is to say, that a security is relatively less valuable as it approaches its par and its redemption than it should be, judging from the price paid for an exactly similar security which has a better chance of permanence or a wider limit of possible profit. The English 3 per cents at eighty would commonly have a marked advantage in the markets over $3\frac{1}{2}$ per cents, — in the first place, because the margin of possible profit would be greater ; and in the second place, because there would be no prospect of disturbance in the one case, while in the other redemption would be near at hand. Experience shows that governments as a rule obtain relatively a low price for a security which they insist upon selling at par.

Most governments adapt their offer to the market in such a way as to combine these inducements. If the market rate of interest is at 4 per cent, they commonly offer $3\frac{1}{2}$ or 3 per cent, and thus dispose of their credit at a discount on better terms than if they attempted to outbid the market rate. The American government has commonly pursued a different course. While insisting that it will borrow only at the market rate, that is, at par, it has found itself compelled to concede something in order to borrow at all.   In the first place it has conceded a high rate of interest ; but this is not enough.   Lenders require permanence.   It accepts, therefore, the condition that it shall not attempt to redeem its bonds until after the lapse of a term of years, — five or ten, or whatever may be agreed upon.   The expedient is clumsy ; but the prejudice against usury compels its adoption, although, like all such devices, it works in practice only against the public interest and in favor of the capitalist.

Every established principle of finance indicated that government credit could be sold to more advantage at a certain nominal discount than if a higher interest or any equivalent condition were insisted upon in order to " float " it at par.   If the government had chosen to authorize the sale of six per cent bonds at their market price, as it did in the War of 1812, omitting from the contract all restriction on its own free control over them, it would have done what all established financial rules enjoin ; and for such bonds it would have obtained the best terms then to be had, while at the present day the nation would have owed a homogeneous debt, with which it would have been free to deal as it chose.   Congress declined to do this.   Spaulding apparently wished to discover some principle in finance by which the government might raise money through a process which should be neither taxation nor loan.   Before three years had passed, the government was selling its six per cent bonds at a rate equivalent to very nearly thirty-five cents on

the dollar ; but in 1861 the idea of its credit selling
at a discount of twenty or thirty or forty per cent
was so revolting as not to be entertained. Gallatin
talked in vain. Nor were members of Congress alone
extravagant on this theme. At least one gentleman
who should have known better, — Moses H. Grinnell,
of New York, — encouraged the same delusion. "As
for G [allatin] and a few egotistical gentlemen that act
with him, they should be driven out of Washington,
as they only embarrass the government. There are
not eight bank presidents that side with G [allatin].
He is an odd fish, — has very little influence here."
These were the terms used by Grinnell in a letter
dated Jan. 30, 1862 ; and it was a curious sign of
the times that the son of Albert Gallatin — the only
man who seems to have had a knowledge of what
the occasion required — should have been " an odd
fish."

The idea about " shinning " through Wall Street was
absurd, seeing that every government always does and
always must borrow on the best terms it can get, or
not borrow at all, in which case it can have no resource but to tax. The event soon showed that the
men who treated so contemptuously the idea of the
nation's credit being sold at a discount were the first
to convert their legal-tender paper into the instrument by which the government was to " shin," not
only through Wall Street during the short emergency
of the war, but through every lane and alley of the
land during a period that now seems interminable.

Congress and the Government followed Spaulding's doctrine, that the nation's credit must not be sold at a discount; and as the laws of society are inflexible, while the laws of Congress are not omnipotent, a period of " shinning " ensued which has seldom had a parallel. The dollar which Congress set up was " shaved " through Wall Street at twenty, thirty, forty, fifty, and sixty cents discount. Europe bought United States six per cents at about thirty-five cents on the dollar, notwithstanding Stevens's asseverations that no nation could afford to borrow at seventy without being ruined in a year. If Spaulding and his friends could have foreseen not only that the government would be compelled to perform this process of " shinning" during four long years, but that, thanks to them and to them alone, the government credit and its broken promises-to-pay would for years longer be hawked about Wall Street at whatever price they could command, and would become the support by which Jay Gould and James Fisk, Jr., and their like, would succeed in bolstering up their scandalous schemes against the pressure of sound economical laws, — the statesmen of 1862 might perhaps have gained more sensible ideas in regard to the treatment of government credit.

In justice to the Secretary of the Treasury it must be said that on the day of the conference he showed no symptom of yielding to Spaulding's influence. He remained then as before hostile to the principle of legal tender, and before the bank delegates left Wash-

ington he succeeded in agreeing with them upon a
new financial arrangement which rejected the resort
to legal tender, and adopted his own policy in regard
to the bank currency. Spaulding and his committee
deemed the scheme inadequate, and withheld their
assent ; but a different reason caused the compromise
between Chase and the banks to fail. The gentleman who represented the Boston banks on that occasion found on his return to Massachusetts that the
arrangement he had made was not satisfactory to
them, and at once telegraphed this information to
the secretary. Then for the first time Chase yielded
his better judgment, and relying on his own power
and will to control the issues, accepted the policy of
legal tender, for which Boston influence thus became
immediately answerable. Having once made his determination to adopt the policy, the secretary was not
a man to hesitate in carrying it out. He had been
drawn into it against his most deeply rooted convictions and his better judgment ; but no sooner was
the decision made, than he threw his whole weight
in favor of the bill.

Thus, in spite of the Treasury and the banks and
the active remonstrances of a great part of the community, the bill came before the House of Representatives as a government measure. Two months of
delay and confusion had seriously complicated the
difficulties of the case, but even yet no necessity existed which could in any just sense be considered to
require the adoption of legal tender. The cry of

necessity was indeed raised, and prolonged without a pause, but it was raised merely because no solid argument could be found. The ablest members of Congress denied the necessity without qualification, and, as has already been shown, the ideas of necessity held by the different supporters of the bill were almost as various as the speeches.

The debate began January 28 by a speech from Spaulding, in which he explained at considerable length his reasons for forcing on the country a measure so generally obnoxious. Spaulding was at that moment in a position of vast responsibility. His activity and persistence had carried the bill " over the Administration," and were to carry it through the House. However open to criticism his opinions may have been, Spaulding has a right to claim that they were little if at all inferior in merit to those expressed by the other friends of the bill. The good sense and high moral standard of a few men served only to make more conspicuous the cloud of ignorance against which their efforts were thrown away. This language is strong, but it is true. With difficulty could any human being compress within the same limited space a greater number of mistaken ideas than are contained in the following extract from Spaulding's speech of January 28 : —

" The bill before us is a war measure, — a measure of necessity, not of choice. . . . Congress may judge of the necessity in the present exigency. It may decide whether it will authorize the Secretary of the Treasury to issue

demand Treasury notes, and make them a legal tender in
payment of debts ; or whether it will put its six or seven
per cent bonds on the market, at ruinous rates of discount,
and raise the money at any sacrifice the money-lenders
may require, to meet the pressing demands upon the
Treasury.   In the one case the government will be able
to pay its debts at fair rates of interest; in the other, it
must go into the streets *shinning* for the means, like an
individual in failing circumstances, and sure of being
used up in the end by the avarice of those who may exact unreasonable terms.   But, sir, knowing the power of
money, and the disposition there is among men to use it
for the acquisition of greater gain, I am unwilling that
this government, with all its immense power and resources, should be left in the hands of any class of men,
bankers or money-lenders, however respectable or patriotic they may be.   The government is much stronger
than any of them.   Its capital is much greater.   It has
control of all the bankers' money and all the brokers'
money, and all the property of the thirty millions of people under its jurisdiction.   Why then should it go into
Wall Street, State Street, Chestnut Street, or any other
street, begging for money?   Their money is not as secure
as government money.   All the gold they possess would
not carry on the government for ninety days.   They issue
only promises to pay, which, if Congress does its duty,
are not half so secure as United States Treasury notes
based on adequate taxation of all the property of the
country.   *Why, then, go into the streets at all to borrow
money?*   I am opposed in our present extremities to
all shifts of this kind.   I prefer to assert the power
and dignity of the government by the issue of its own
notes."

He would be a bold man who should undertake to say that these remarks can be made intelligible, but the conclusion is clear enough, and is worth attention. Had Mr. Spaulding's studies ever led him to read Goethe's Faust, he might at this point have recalled the scene where Mephistopheles, in the character of court-jester, invents for the empire a legal-tender currency based on the firm foundation of old treasures which in past ages might have been hidden underground, and applauds his own creation as better than coin, because if the bankers refused to give coin for it, the holder would at worst have only the trouble of digging. The great satirist with all his genius was not so great a satirist as Mr. Spaulding. He never thought of carrying his sarcasm so far as to invoke the *dignity* of the empire as the chief glory of paper money, and yet Mephistopheles closed the scene with the exulting exclamation, —

" Wer zweifelt noch an unsers Narren Witz ! "

Yet one thing remains to be said before quitting Spaulding. If he sincerely believed that the government need not go into the streets to borrow money, and that a simple assertion of its own dignity would place it in command of indefinite resources, — in other words, if he thought that the dignity of the government forbade its borrowing except on its own terms, and that there was no necessity for it to borrow at all, he was bound to explain his consent that the government should pay six per cent or even one

20

per cent for money, or should promise to repay any money whatever.

The argument of Samuel Hooper was less extrava-gant. He avoided committing himself beyond a cautious opinion that the paper issue would make the government financially more independent, and that if Secretary Chase were discreet, the quality of legal tender would help him to keep the notes at par. The latter opinion might perhaps be questioned, and indeed the chief-justice has himself questioned it in his late judgment; but at least it was not absurd.

Bingham rivalled Spaulding, though in a different way. His speech was necessarily made without reference to financial principles, since Bingham made no pretence to acquaintance with that subject. He assumed at the outset that the bill was necessary, because it was said to be necessary, and then burst into a denunciation of all persons who refused to believe in the necessity. Roscoe Conkling was the victim first immolated.

" Sir," said Bingham, " as a representative of the people I cannot keep silent when I see efforts made upon this side of the House and upon that, to lay the power of the American people to control the currency at the feet of brokers and of city bankers, who have not a tittle of authority, save by the assent or forbearance of the people, to deal in their paper issued as money. I am here to-day to assert the rightful authority of the American people as a nationality, sovereignty, under and by virtue of their Constitution."

Such legal finance would not call for notice except that it came from a leader in Congress, who in order to protect the sovereignty of the American people from bankers and brokers insisted upon creating a legal-tender paper currency, which has always been and always will be the most efficient instrument ever discovered for the purposes of this very class of men. Bingham denounced his opponents for acting with the purpose of sacrificing the public interest to the interest of bankers and brokers. It was mortifying to observe the ignorance and vulgar prejudice with which the bankers and brokers of the country were always mentioned in these debates. Perhaps no other single characteristic offered so much instruction in regard to the temper and the range of thought exhibited in this momentous discussion. Stevens, with his usual discrimination, characterized the dealers in money as " sharks and brokers," to which he afterward added " harpies." Shellabarger of Ohio, after appropriating bodily and almost literally several pages of Macaulay's most luminous and most familiar writing, in the effort to maintain himself on Macaulay's level without Macaulay's aid could discover no more original idea for his peroration than to denounce the outside opposition to this bill as coming from interested persons, in the expectation " that out of the blood of their sinking country they may be enabled to coin the gains of their infamy." Even Henry Wilson announced that the practical question lay between " brokers and jobbers and moneychangers on the one side, and the people of the United States on the other."

Invective like this properly belonged only to a debating-club of boys; but if invective were to be used, and if these bankers had been represented in Congress by any person capable of using it, he might have retaliated in a manner which would have left little opportunity for an effective rejoinder. He might have replied that men who claimed to be trusted in regard to a financial exigency; who asserted in one breath that a necessity existed which in the next breath they acknowledged did not exist; who presumed on this unwarrantable plea of necessity to exculpate themselves from what, without exculpation, was the wickedest vote the representatives of the people could ever give, — a vote which delivered labor to the mercy of capital; a vote which forced upon the people that as money which in no just sense was money; a vote which established as law one of the most abominable frauds which law could be prostituted to enforce, — that such persons were not qualified to judge of other men's patriotism, honesty, or good sense.

A very large part of the debate turned on the technical construction of the Constitution; and many members of the Legislature who hesitated about nothing else found an insurmountable obstacle there. The Constitutional argument, whatever its weight may be, is one on which only lawyers will be likely to insist. Whether under a strict interpretation of Constitutional powers the law of legal tender is justified or not, can make but little difference to persons who look for their principles of action beneath the letter of the Constitution, — to the principles upon which all government and all society must ultimately rest. The law of legal tender was an attempt by artificial legislation to make something true which was false. This is the sum-total of the argument against legal tender; and this argument rests on the maxim that the foundation of law is truth. If the rhetoric of Congressional orators or the ingenuity of professional lawyers can reduce the principle involved to simpler elements than this, at all events neither the debates at the Capitol nor the arguments at the bar, however brilliant or elaborate they may have been, have as yet shown any probability of success.

It would be pleasant to extract from the speeches delivered in favor of this bill such portions as show depths of knowledge, elevation of morals, or breadth of mind. Nothing of the sort exists. Almost all the soundest minds in the House declared themselves against legal tender and denied its necessity. Judge Thomas of Massachusetts and Roscoe Conkling of New York, Morrill of Vermont, from the Committee of Ways and Means, Horton of Ohio, also of the Ways and Means, all the Democratic members, and others who contented themselves with a silent vote, opposed the legal-tender clause. The speech of Owen Lovejoy of Illinois was in its short space as clear, as vigorous, and from a rhetorical point of view as perfect, as the oldest statesman or the most exacting critic or the deepest student of finance could have hoped or wished to make. The opponents of the measure were far superior in intellect to its supporters; their arguments were essentially sound, and under ordinary circumstances would probably have proved successful; but they could not deal with the authority of the Executive, which Chase used with all his energy in favor of the bill. On the 6th of February Spaulding pressed his measure to a vote, and it passed the House by a majority of ninety-three to fifty-nine.

One can scarcely resist the conclusion that had the bill originated in the Senate, and been discussed without the prejudice arising from the responsibility of rejecting what was approved by the House and urged by the Executive, and had it been acted upon before so much valuable time was lost, the country would probably for the time have been spared the great misfortune of its adoption. This opinion is rendered probable by the higher and more statesmanlike spirit in which the Senate discussed the proposed measure. If a word of unqualified admiration could please the ear or help to soothe the rest of a statesman whose loss the nation has regretted but has never fairly appreciated, one would take a personal pleasure in repeating the language of William Pitt Fessenden of Maine, who reported this bill to the Senate : —

" The question after all returns, Is this measure absolutely indispensable to procure means? If so, as I said before, necessity knows no law. What are the objections to it? I will state them as briefly as I can. The first is a negative objection. A measure of this kind certainly cannot increase confidence in the ability or integrity of the country. . . .

" Next, in my judgment, it is a confession of bankruptcy. . . .

" Again, say what you will, nobody. can deny that it is bad faith, . . . and encourages bad morality both in public and private. . . .

" Again, it encourages bad morals, because if the currency falls (*as it is supposed it must, else why defend it by a legal enactment*), what is the result? It is that every man who desires to pay off his debts at a discount, no matter what the circumstances are, is able to avail himself of it against the will of his neighbor who honestly contracted to receive something better.

" Again, sir, necessarily as a result, in my judgment, it must inflict a stain upon the national honor. . . .

" Again, sir, it necessarily changes the value of all property. . . .

" Again, sir, a stronger objection than all that I have to this proposition is that the loss must fall most heavily upon the poor by reason of the inflation."

Fessenden concluded by declaring that in his opinion the legal-tender clause was not necessary, and he reported several amendments. One of these, the second, he described in these terms : " The committee . . . give to the secretary the power to sell the bonds of the government at any time that it may be necessary, at the market price, in order to raise coin. *That can always be done.*" This amendment was ultimately adopted and became part of the bill; but the secretary preferred reaching the same result by a different policy, and the old system was therefore retained.

Collamer of Vermont took yet stronger and more uncompromising ground. " Even if it was. a *necessity*," said he, " I would not vote for this measure." Fidelity to a trust is not so universal but that one might sympathize with a man who when placed between the alternative of destruction on the one hand and what he thinks a breach of trust on the other, in spite of necessity still maintains the standard of honor; but there was in reality no such bravado in this declaration of Judge Collamer. No mere impracticability prompted his resistance, but a superior discernment that the evidence of necessity which imposes on a legislative body in times of panic is not to be trusted. Even on a calculation of chances, it is always more likely that other resources are available than that so desperate an expedient should offer the only hope of salvation. Collamer's speech was an energetic expression of his resolution, not that he would refuse to obey necessity, but that he would refuse to believe it.

The position taken by Charles Sumner wanted only the same defiant confidence in the laws of truth to make it more impressive than any of the others. Unhappily, by the side of Fessenden and Collamer, his conclusions seemed tinged with irresolution : —

" And now, as I close, I will not cease to be frank. Is it necessary to incur all the unquestionable evils of inconvertible paper, forced into circulation by act of Congress ; to suffer the stain upon our national faith ; to bear the stigma of a seeming repudiation ; to lose for the present that credit which in itself is a treasury ; and to teach debtors everywhere that contracts may be varied at the will of the stronger? Surely, there is much in these inquiries which may make us pause. . . . It is hard, very hard, to think that such a country, so powerful, so rich, and so beloved, should be compelled to adopt a policy of even questionable propriety. . . . Surely we must all be against paper money, — we must all insist on maintaining the integrity of the government ; and we must all set our faces against any proposition like the present, except as a temporary expedient rendered imperative by the exigency of the hour. . . . Others may doubt if the exigency is sufficiently imperative, *but the Secretary of the Treasury does not doubt.* . . . Reluctantly, painfully, I consent that the process should issue."

The authority of the Secretary of the Treasury overruled the scruples of the Senate, and the bill passed by a majority of five votes on the legal-tender clause. It is scarcely worth while to carry the scene back to the House, in order to ascertain the fate of the Senate amendments, or to cull from the second debate new subjects for quotation. Spaulding at least did strongly and invariably insist upon the difference between legal-tender notes that were fundable and the later issue of greenbacks which were not so. In point of fact the difference was slight. There was nothing in the condition of fundability which made legal tender anything but legal tender; nor would the principle of legal tender have been any sounder, even though attached to the bonds themselves. As the later issues of legal tender were made, and the depreciation became excessive, Spaulding by similar steps became virtuous, until at last his virtue grew intense. He attributed the failure of his favorite financial scheme to the mistakes of others, and he proposed as an infallible cure a restoration of his funding proviso. He never succeeded in gaining a higher stand-point than this, or looking over a wider horizon where he could measure the uncontrollable power of the elements which he, like the unlucky companions of Ulysses, ignorantly set free.

Such was the history of the Legal-Tender Bill. So far as any evidence of its necessity can be drawn from the action of the Executive at the time, the late decision of Chief-Justice Chase has left no doubt as to the facts. That Chase should as Secretary of the Treasury have adopted the course he did was doubly unfortunate, — in the first place, because he created legal tender; and in the second place, because when the delusion was over, and his mind reverted to its first sound principles, the action he had taken as Secretary of the Treasury remained in the public memory to reduce the authority of the opinions he was bound to express as chief-justice. Into the legal correctness or political propriety of these opinions it is no purpose of this essay to enter. No one who holds strong convictions against legal tender as a measure of finance is likely to trouble his mind with the question whether such a power has or has not been conferred by the Constitution upon Congress. Though it were conferred in the most explicit terms language is capable of supplying, there could be no excuse on that account for changing an opinion as to its financial merits; and its financial merits are not a subject for lawyers, or even for judges, as such, to decide. These happily rest on principles deeper than statute or than Constitutional law. They appeal to no written code; and whenever the public attempts to overrule them, the public does so at its own peril.

One more point remains. The common impression is that even though there were no actual necessity for a law of legal tender so early as February, 1862, yet at some subsequent time the enactment of such a law would have proved inevitable. This opinion should properly form the subject of a separate paper. If it be acknowledged that the law of February, 1862, was unnecessary and passed by a practical deception, the condition of the argument is changed. Whenever the public has reached this point, it can enter upon the wider field of discussion into which so vague and general a proposition must lead. Without venturing at present on a denial of the theory, since this would require much explanation and reasoning, it is fair to say that although the subject is scarcely capable of

positive demonstration, absolutely no evidence proves
that the government might not have carried the war
to a successful conclusion without the issue of legal-
tender paper. Such appears to be the opinion of the
chief-justice, as it is undoubtedly the inference from
economical principles.

After the first issues of the paper money, its original purpose and importance as a resource against a
temporary exigency — that purpose which had been
used in forcing the bill through Congress — was lost
from sight, and the paper assumed new functions as
a financial instrument.

The government, adhering to the policy of selling
its bonds only at par, was obliged to consider its paper
as the par standard, and to issue enough paper to
"float" the successive loans. This was equivalent
to selling its credit at the market price, with the
addition of voluntarily degrading its own standard
of value. In order to protect the nation's credit
from degradation in the hands of bankers and brokers, the government dishonored it of its own free
will. As a financial policy, this tortuous and disreputable expedient will not bear examination; but one
incidental function of the paper, closely connected
with this, claims more attention. The issue of paper
money in large quantities does produce a temporary
and feverish excitement, which during a certain
length of time may facilitate borrowing, though at
a frightful ultimate cost. If the object of legal tender were to cause this temporary stimulus, and if this

stimulus can be proved to have been essential to financial success, the management of the nation's financial affairs during the war may admit of excuse if not of praise. Neither of these conditions can be established.

THE NEW YORK GOLD CONSPIRACY.[1]

THE Civil War in America, with its enormous issues
of depreciating currency and its reckless waste of
money and credit by the government, created a speculative mania such as the United States, with all its
experience in this respect, had never before known.
Not only in Broad Street, the centre of New York
speculation, but far and wide throughout the Northern States, almost every man who had money employed a part of his capital in the purchase of stocks
or of gold, of copper, of petroleum, or of domestic
produce, in the hope of a rise in prices, or staked
money on the expectation of a fall. To use the jar-
gon of the street, every farmer and every shop-keeper
in the country seemed to be engaged in " carrying "
some favorite security " on a margin." Whoever
could obtain a hundred dollars sent it to a broker
with orders to buy whatever amount of stocks the
broker would consent to purchase. If the stock rose,
the speculator prospered; if it fell until the deposit or
margin was lost, the broker demanded a new deposit,
or sold the stock to protect himself. By means of

[1] From the Westminster Review, for October, 1870.

this simple and smooth machinery, which differs in no essential respect from the processes of *roulette* or *rouge-et-noir*, the nation flung itself into the Stock Exchange, until the " outsiders," as they were called, in opposition to the regular brokers of Broad Street, represented the entire population of the American Republic. Every one speculated, and for a time successfully.

The inevitable reaction began when the government, about a year after the close of the war, stopped its issues and ceased borrowing. The greenback currency had for a moment sunk to a value of only 37 cents to the dollar. On the worst day of all, the 11th of July, 1864, one sale of $100,000 in gold was actually made at 310, equivalent to about 33 cents in the dollar.[1] At that point the depreciation stopped, and the paper which had come so near falling into entire discredit steadily rose in value, first to 50 cents, then to 60 and 70, until in the summer of 1869 it stood at about $73\frac{1}{2}$ cents.

So soon as the industrious part of the public felt the touch of solid values, the fabric of fictitious wealth began to melt away under their eyes. Before long the so-called " outsiders," the men who speculated on their own account, and could not act in agreement or combination, began to suffer. One by one, or in masses, they were made the prey of larger operators ; their last margins were consumed, and

[1] See Men and Mysteries of Wall Street, by James K. Medbery, pp. 250, 251.

they dropped to the solid level of slow, productive industry. Some lost everything, many lost still more than they had; and few families of ordinary connection and standing in the United States cannot tell, if they choose, some story of embezzlement or breach of trust committed in those days. Some men who had courage and a sense of honor, found life too heavy for them; others went mad. The greater part turned in silence to their regular pursuits, and accepted their losses as they could. Almost every rich American could produce from some pigeon-hole a bundle of worthless securities, and could show checkbooks representing the only remaining trace of margin after margin consumed in attempts to satisfy the insatiable broker. A year or two of incessant losses swept the weaker gamblers from the street.

Even those who continued to speculate found it necessary to change their mode of operations. Chance no longer ruled over the Stock Exchange and the gold market. The fate of a battle, the capture of a city, or the murder of a President had hitherto broken the plans of the strongest combinations, and put all speculators, whether great or small, on fairly even ground; but as the period of sudden and uncontrollable disturbing elements passed away, the market fell more and more completely into the hands of cliques which found a point of adhesion in some great mass of incorporated capital. Three distinct railways, with their enormous resources, became the property of Cornelius Vanderbilt, who by means of their credit and capital again and again swept millions of dollars into his pocket by a process curiously similar to gambling with loaded dice.   Vanderbilt was one of the most respectable of these great operators.   The Erie Railway was controlled by Daniel Drew, and while Vanderbilt at least acted in the interests of his corporations, Drew cheated equally his corporation and the public. Between these two men and the immense incorporated power they swayed, smaller operators one after another were crushed, until the survivors learned to seek shelter within some clique sufficiently strong to afford protection.   Speculation in this manner began to consume itself, and the largest combination of capital was destined to swallow every weaker combination which ventured to appear in the market.

Between the inevitable effect of a healthy currency and the omnipotence of capital in the stock market, a sounder state of society began.   The public, which had been robbed with cynical indifference by Drew and Vanderbilt, could feel no sincere regret when they saw these two cormorants reduced to tearing each other.   In the year 1867 Vanderbilt undertook to gain possession of the Erie Road, as he had already obtained possession of the New York Central, the second trunk-line between New York and the West.   Vanderbilt was supposed to own property to the value of some $50,000,000, which might all be made directly available for stock operations.   He bought the greater part of the Erie stock.   Drew sold him all he could take, and then issued as much more

21

as was required to defeat Vanderbilt's purpose. **After** a violent struggle, which overthrew the guaranties of social order, Drew triumphed, and Vanderbilt abandoned the contest. The Erie corporation paid him a large sum to reimburse his alleged losses. At the same time it agreed that Drew's accounts should be passed, and he obtained a release in full, and retired from the direction. The Erie Road, almost exhausted by such systematic plundering, was left in the undisturbed, if not peaceful, control of Mr. Jay Gould and Mr. James Fisk, Jr., whose reign began in the month of July, 1868.

Jay Gould was a partner in the firm of Smith, Gould, & Martin, brokers in Wall Street. He had been before engaged in railway enterprises, and his operations had not been of a nature likely to encourage public confidence in his ideas of fiduciary relations. He was a broker, and a broker is almost by nature a gambler, — perhaps the last profession suitable for a railway manager. In character he was marked by a disposition for silent intrigue. He preferred to operate on his own account, without admitting other persons into his confidence. His nature suggested survival from the family of spiders : he spun webs, in corners and in the dark. His disposition to subtlety and elaboration of intrigue was irresistible. He had not a conception of a moral principle. The class of men to whom he belonged understood no distinction between right and wrong in matters of speculation, so long as the daily settlements were punctually effected. In this respect Gould was probably as honest as the mass of his fellows, according to the moral standard of the street; but he was an uncommonly fine and unscrupulous intriguer, skilled in the processes of stockgambling, and passably indifferent to the praise or censure of society.

James Fisk, Jr., was still more original in character. He was not yet forty years of age, and had the instincts of fourteen. He came originally from Vermont, probably the most respectable and correct State in the Union, and his father had been a pedler who sold goods from town to town in his native valley of the Connecticut. The son followed his father's calling with boldness and success. He drove his huge wagon, made resplendent with paint and varnish, with four or six horses, through the towns of Vermont and Western Massachusetts; and when his father remonstrated at his reckless management, the young man, with his usual bravado, took his father into his service at a fixed salary, with the warning that he was not to put on airs on the strength of his new dignity. A large Boston firm which had supplied young Fisk with goods on credit, attracted by his energy, took him into the house. The war broke out; his influence drew the firm into some bold speculations which were successful. In a few years he retired with some $100,000, which he subsequently lost. He formed a connection with Daniel Drew in New York, and a new sign, ominous of future trouble, was raised in Wall Street, bearing the names of Fisk & Belden, brokers.

Personally Fisk was coarse, noisy, boastful, ignorant, the type of a young butcher in appearance and mind. Nothing could be more striking than the contrast between him and his future associate Gould. One was small and slight in person, dark, sallow, reticent, and stealthy, with a trace of Jewish origin; the other was large, florid, gross, talkative, and obstreperous. Fisk's redeeming point was his humor, which had a flavor of American nationality. His mind was extraordinarily fertile in ideas and expedients, while his conversation was filled with unusual images and strange forms of speech, quickly caught up and made popular by the New York press. In respect to honesty as between Gould and Fisk, the latter was perhaps, if possible, less deserving of trust than the former. A story not without a stroke of satirical wit was told by him to illustrate his estimate of abstract truth. An old woman who had bought of the elder Fisk a handkerchief which cost ninepence in the New England currency, where six shillings are reckoned to the dollar, complained to Mr. Fisk, Jr., that his father had cheated her. Mr. Fisk considered the case maturely, and gave a decision based on *a priori* principles. " No ! " said he, " the old man wouldn't have told a lie for ninepence ; " and then, as if this assertion needed some reasonable qualification, he added, " though he would have told eight of them for a dollar ! " The distinction as regarded the father may have been just, since the father held old-fashioned ideas as to wholesale and retail trade; but in regard to the son this relative degree of truth cannot be predicated with confidence, since, if the investigating committee of Congress and its evidence are to be believed, Mr. Fisk seldom or never speaks truth at all.[1]

An intrigue equally successful and disreputable brought these two men into the Erie board of directors, whence they speedily drove their more timid predecessor Drew. In July, 1868, Gould made himself president and treasurer of the corporation. Fisk became comptroller. A young lawyer named Lane became counsel. These three directors made a majority of the executive committee, and were masters of Erie. The board of directors held no meetings. The executive committee was never called together, and the three men — Fisk, Gould, and Lane — became from that time the absolute, irresponsible owners of the Erie Railway, not less than if it had been their personal property and plaything.

This property was in effect, like all the great railway corporations, an empire within a republic. It

---

[1] House of Representatives. Report, No. 31. Forty-first Congress, Second Session. Report of the Committee on Banking and Currency, in response to a Resolution of the House of Representatives, passed Dec. 13, 1869, directing the Committee "to investigate the causes that led to the unusual and extraordinary fluctuations of Gold in the City of New York, from the 21st to the 27th of September, 1869;" accompanied by the testimony collected by the Committee.

consisted of a trunk-line of road four hundred and fifty-nine miles in length, with branches three hundred and fourteen miles in extent, or seven hundred and seventy-three miles of road in all. Its capital stock amounted to about $35,000,000. Its gross receipts exceeded $15,000,000 per annum. It employed not less than fifteen thousand men, and supported their families. Over this wealth and influence, — greater than that directly swayed by any private citizen, greater than is absolutely and personally controlled by most kings, and far too great for public safety either in a democracy or in any other form of society, — the vicissitudes of a troubled time placed two men in irresponsible authority; and both these men belonged to a low moral and social type. Such an elevation has been rarely seen in modern history. The most dramatic of modern authors, Balzac himself, who loved to deal with similar violent alternations of fortune, or Alexandre Dumas, with all his extravagance of imagination, never reached a conception bolder or more melodramatic than this, or conceived a plot so enormous, or a catastrophe so original, as was to be developed.

One of the earliest acts of the new rulers was such as Balzac or Dumas might have predicted and delighted in. They established themselves in a palace. The old offices of the Erie Railway were in the lower part of the city, among the wharves and warehouses, — a situation no doubt convenient for business, but not agreeable as a residence; and the new proprietors naturally wished to reside on their property. Mr. Fisk and Mr. Gould accordingly bought a building of white marble, not unlike a European palace, situated about two miles from the business quarter, and containing a large theatre, or opera-house. They also purchased several smaller houses adjoining it. The opera-house cost about $700,000, and a large part of the building was at once leased by the two purchasers to themselves as the Erie corporation, to serve as offices. This suite of apartments was then furnished by themselves, as representing the corporation, at an expense of some $300,000, and in a style which, though called vulgar, was not more vulgar than that of almost any palace in Europe. The adjoining houses were connected with the main building; and in one of these Mr. Fisk had his private apartments, with a private passage to his opera-box. He also assumed direction of the theatre, of which he became manager-in-chief. To these royal arrangements he brought tastes commonly charged as the worst results of royal license. The atmosphere of the Erie offices was not disturbed with moral prejudices ; and as the opera supplied Mr. Fisk's mind with amusement, so the opera *troupe* supplied him with a permanent harem. Whatever Mr. Fisk did was done on an extraordinary scale.

These arrangements regarded only the pleasures of the American Aladdin. In the conduct of their interests, the new directors showed a capacity for large conceptions and a vigor in the execution of their schemes that alarmed the entire community. At the annual election in 1868, when Gould, Fisk, and Lane, having borrowed or bought proxies for the greater part of the stock, caused themselves to be elected for the ensuing year, the respectable portion of the public throughout the country was astonished and shocked to learn that the new board of directors contained two names peculiarly notorious and obnoxious to honest men, — William M. Tweed and Peter B. Sweeney. To every honest American they conveyed a peculiar sense of terror and disgust. The State of New York in its politics was much influenced, if not controlled, by the city of New York. The city politics were so entirely in the hands of the Democratic party as to preclude even the existence of a strong minority. The party organization centred in a political club, held together by its patronage and by a system of jobbery unequalled elsewhere in the world. The Tammany Club, thus swaying the power of a small nation of several million souls, was itself ruled by William M. Tweed and Peter B. Sweeney, absolute masters of this system of theft and fraud, and to American eyes the incarnation of political immorality.

The effect of this alliance was felt in the ensuing winter in the passage of a bill through the State legislature, and its signature by the governor, abolishing the former system of annual elections of the entire board of Erie directors, and authorizing the board to classify itself in such a manner that only a portion should be changed each year. The principle of the bill was correct; but its practical effect enabled Gould and Fisk to make themselves directors for five years in spite of any attempt on the part of the stockholders to remove them. The formality of annual re-election was spared them; and so far as the stockholders were concerned, there was no great injustice in the act. The Erie Road was in the peculiar position of being without an owner. There was no *cestui que trust*, unless the English stockholders could be called such. In America the stock was almost exclusively held for speculation, not for investment; and in the morals of Wall Street, speculation had almost come to mean disregard of intrinsic value. In this case society at large was the injured party, and society knew its risk.

This step was only a beginning. The Tammany ring exercised a power beyond politics. Under the existing Constitution of the State, the judges of the State courts are elected by the people. Thirty-three such judges formed the State judiciary, and each of the thirty-three was clothed with equity powers running through the whole State. Of these judges Tammany Hall elected several, and the Erie Railway controlled others in country districts. Each of these judges might forbid proceedings before any and all the other judges, or stay proceedings in suits already commenced. Thus the lives and the property of the public were in the power of the new combination; and two of the city judges, Barnard and Cardozo, had already acquired a peculiarly infamous reputation as so-called "slaves to the ring," which left no question as to the depths to which their prostitution of justice would descend.

The alliance between Tammany and Erie was thus equivalent to investing Gould and Fisk with the attributes of sovereignty ; but in order to avail themselves to the utmost of their judicial powers, they also required the ablest legal assistance. The degradation of the bench had been rapidly followed by the degradation of the bar. Prominent and learned lawyers were already accustomed to avail themselves of social or business relations with judges to forward private purposes. One whose partner might be elevated to the bench was certain to be generally retained in cases brought before this special judge ; and litigants were taught by experience that a retainer in such cases was profitably bestowed. Others found a similar advantage resulting from known social relations with the court. The debasement of tone was not confined to the lower ranks of advocates ; and probably this steady demoralization of the bar made it possible for the Erie ring to obtain the services of Mr. David Dudley Field as its legal adviser. Mr. Field, a gentleman of European reputation, in regard to which he was understood to be peculiarly solicitous, was an eminent law reformer, author of the New York Code, delegate of the American Social Science Association to the European International Congress, and asserted by his partner, Mr. Shearman, in evidence before a committee of the New York legislature, to be a man of quixotic sense of honor. Mr. Shearman himself, a gentleman of English parentage, had earned public gratitude by arraigning and deploring with unsurpassed courage and point the condition of the New York judiciary, in an admirable essay in the " North American Review " for July, 1867. The value of Mr. Field's services to Messrs. Fisk and Gould was not to be measured even by the enormous fees their generosity paid him. His power over certain judges became so absolute as to impress the popular imagination ; and the gossip of Wall Street insisted that he had a silken halter round the neck of Judge Barnard and a hempen one round that of Cardozo. He who had a year before threatened Barnard on his own bench with impeachment next appeared in the character of Barnard's master, and issued as a matter of course the edicts of his court.

One other combination was made by the Erie managers to extend their power. They bought a joint-stock bank in New York city, with a capital of $1,000,000. The assistance thus gained was purchased at a moderate price, since it was by no means represented by the capital. The great cliques and so-called "operators" of Wall Street and Broad Street carry on their transactions by a system of credits and clearing-houses with little use of money. The banks certify their checks, and the certified checks settle balances. Nominally and by law the banks only certified to the extent of *bona fide* deposits, but in reality the custom of disregarding the strict letter of the law was not unknown; and in case of the bank in question, the Comptroller of the Currency, an officer of the national Treasury, testified that on an examination of its affairs in April, 1869, out of fifteen checks deposited in its hands as security for certifications made by it, selected at hazard for inquiry, and representing a nominal value of $1,500,000, three only were good. The rest represented accommodation extended to brokers and speculators without security. This bank on Thursday, Sept. 24, 1869, certified checks to the amount of nearly $7,500,000 for Gould alone. What sound security Gould deposited against this mass of credit may be left to the imagination. His operations were not confined to this bank alone, although this was the only one owned by the ring.

Thus Gould and Fisk created a combination more powerful than any that has been controlled by mere private citizens in America or in Europe since society for self-protection established the supreme authority of the judicial name. They exercised the legislative and the judicial powers of the State; they possessed almost unlimited credit, and society was at their mercy. One authority alone stood above them, beyond their control; and this was the distant but threatening figure of the national government.

Powerful as they were, the Erie managers were

seldom in funds. The marble palace in which they
lived, the theatre they supported, the bribery and pro-
fusion of management by which they could alone
maintain their defiance of public opinion, the enormous schemes for extending their operations into
which they rushed, all required greater resources
than could be furnished even by the wholesale plun-
der of the Erie Road. They were obliged from time
to time to issue from their castle, and harry the industrious public or their brother freebooters. The
process was different from that known to the dark
ages, but the objects and the results were the same.
At one time Fisk is said to have ordered heavy speculative sales of stock in an express company which
held a contract with the Erie Railway. The sales
being effected, the contract was declared annulled.
The stock naturally fell, and Fisk realized the difference. He then ordered heavy purchases, and having
renewed the contract the stock rose again, and Fisk
a second time swept the street.[1] In the summer and
autumn of 1869 the two managers issued and sold
two hundred and thirty-five thousand new shares of
Erie stock, or nearly as much as its entire capital
when they assumed power in July, 1868. With the
aid of the money thus obtained, they succeeded in
withdrawing about $12,500,000 in currency from cir-
culation at the very moment of the year when currency was most in demand in order to harvest the
crops. For weeks the nation writhed and quivered

[1] Men and Mysteries of Wall Street, p. 168.

under the torture of this modern rack, until the national government itself was obliged to interfere and threaten a sudden opening of the Treasury. Whether the Erie speculators operated for a rise or for a fall, whether they bought or sold, and whether they were engaged in manipulating stocks or locking up currency or cornering gold, they were always a nuisance and scandal.

In order to understand a so-called corner in gold, readers must bear in mind that the supply of gold immediately available for transfers was limited within distinct bounds. New York and the country behind it contained an amount usually estimated at about $20,000,000. The national government commonly held from $75,000,000 to $100,000,000, which might be thrown bodily on the market if the President ordered it. To obtain gold from Europe or other sources required time.

In the second place, gold was a commodity bought and sold like stocks, in a special market or goldroom situated next the Stock Exchange in Broad Street and practically a part of it. In gold as in stocks, the transactions were both real and speculative. The real transactions were mostly purchases or loans made by importers who required coin to pay customs-duties on their imports. This legitimate business was supposed to require from $5,000,000 to $7,500,000 per day. The speculative transactions were wagers on the rise or fall of price, and neither required any transfer of gold nor implied its existence, although in times of excitement hundreds of millions were nominally bought, sold, and loaned.

Under the late Administration, Mr. McCulloch, then Secretary of the Treasury, had thought it his duty to guarantee a stable currency, although Congress forbade him to restore the gold standard. During four years gold had fluctuated little, and principally from natural causes, and the danger of attempting to create an artificial scarcity had prevented the operators from trying an experiment sure to irritate the government. The financial policy of the new Administration was not so definitely fixed, and the success of a speculation would depend on the action of Mr. Boutwell, the new secretary, whose direction was understood to have begun by a marked censure on the course pursued by his predecessor.

Of all financial operations, cornering gold is the most brilliant and the most dangerous, and possibly the hazard and splendor of the attempt were the reasons of its fascination to Jay Gould's fancy. He dwelt upon it for months, and played with it like a pet toy. His fertile mind discovered that it would prove a blessing to the community; and on this theory, half honest and half fraudulent, he stretched the widely extended fabric of the web in which mankind was to be caught. The theory was partially sound. Starting from the principle that the price of grain in New York was regulated by the price in London, and was not affected by currency fluctuations,

Gould argued that if the premium on gold could be raised from thirty to forty cents at harvest-time, the farmers' grain would be worth $1.40 instead of $1.30; and as a consequence the farmer would hasten to send his crop to New York over the Erie Railway, which was sorely in need of freights. With the assistance of another gentleman, Gould calculated the exact premium at which the Western farmer would consent to dispose of his grain, and thus distance the three hundred sail then hastening from the Danube to supply the English market. Gold, which was then heavy at 134, must be raised to 145.

This clever idea, like the other ideas of the gentlemen of Erie, had the single fault of requiring that some one somewhere should be swindled. The scheme was probably feasible; but sooner or later the reaction from such an artificial stimulant must have come, and whenever it came some one must suffer. Nevertheless, Gould probably argued that so long as the farmer got his money, the Erie Railway its freights, and he his small profits on the gold he bought, he need not ask who else might be injured; and indeed by the time the reaction came and gold was ready to fall as he expected, Gould would probably have been ready to assist the process by speculative sales in order to enable the Western farmer to buy his spring goods cheap as he had sold his autumn crops dear. Gould was equally ready to buy gold cheap and sell it dear on his private account;

and as he proposed to bleed New York merchants for the benefit of the Western farmer, so he was willing to bleed Broad Street for his own. The patriotic object was the one which for obvious reasons Gould preferred to put forward, and on which he hoped to rest his ambitious structure.

The operation of raising the price of gold from 133 to 145 offered no great difficulty to men who controlled the resources of the Erie Railway. Credit alone was needed, and of credit Gould had an unlimited supply. The only serious danger lay in the possible action of the national government, which had not taken the philanthropic view of the public good peculiar to the managers of Erie. Secretary Boutwell, who should have assisted Gould in " bulling " gold, was gravely suspected of being a bear, and of wishing to depress the premium to nothing. If the Secretary of the Treasury were determined to stand in Gould's path, even the combined forces of Erie and Tammany dared not jostle against him ; and therefore Gould must control the government, whether by fair means or foul, by persuasion or by purchase. He undertook the task ; and after his proceedings in both directions have been thoroughly drawn into light, the public can see how dramatic and artistic a conspiracy in real life may be when slowly elaborated from the subtle mind of a clever intriguer, and carried into execution by a band of unshrinking scoundrels.

The first requisite for Gould's purpose was a chan-

22

nel of direct communication with the President ; and
here he was peculiarly favored by chance. Mr. Abel
Rathbone Corbin, formerly lawyer, editor, speculator,
lobby-agent, familiar, as he claims, with everything,
had succeeded during his varied career in accumu-
lating from one or another of his hazardous pursuits
a comfortable fortune, and had crowned his success,
at the age of sixty-seven or thereabout, by contracting a marriage with General Grant's sister at the
moment when General Grant was on the point of
reaching the highest eminence possible to an American citizen. To say that Corbin's moral dignity had
passed absolutely pure through the somewhat tainted
atmosphere in which his life had been spent would
be flattering him too highly ; but at least he was no
longer engaged in active occupation, and he lived
quietly in New York watching the course of public affairs, and remarkable for respectability becoming to a President's brother-in-law. Gould enjoyed
a slight acquaintance with Corbin, and proceeded to
improve it. He assumed and asserts that he felt a
respect for Corbin's shrewdness and sagacity. Corbin claims to have first impressed the crop theory
on Gould's mind ; while Gould testifies that he in-
doctrinated Corbin with this idèa, which became a
sort of monomania with the President's brother-in-
law, who soon began to preach it to the President
himself. On the 15th of June, 1869, the President
came to New York, and was there the guest of Corbin, who urged Gould to call and pay his respects to

the Chief Magistrate. Gould had probably aimed at this result. He called; and the President of the United States not only listened to the president of Erie, but accepted an invitation to Fisk's theatre, sat in Fisk's private box, and the next evening became the guest of these two gentlemen on their Newport steamer, — while Fisk, arrayed, as the newspapers reported, " in a blue uniform, with a broad gilt cap-band, three silver stars on his coat-sleeve, lavender gloves, and a diamond breast-pin as large as a cherry, stood at the gangway, surrounded by his aids, be-starred and bestriped like himself," and welcomed his distinguished friend.

The Erie managers had already arranged that the President should on this occasion be sounded in re-gard to his financial policy; and when the selected guests — among whom were Gould, Fisk, and others — sat down at nine o'clock to supper, the conversa-tion was directed to the subject of finance. " Some one," says Gould, " asked the President what his view was." The " some one " in question was of course Fisk, who alone had the impudence to put such an inquiry. The President bluntly replied that there was a certain amount of fictitiousness about the pros-perity of the country, and that the bubble might as well be tapped in one way as another. The remark was fatal to Gould's plans, and he felt it, in his own words, as " a wet blanket."

Meanwhile the post of assistant-treasurer at New York had become vacant, and it was a matter of interest to Gould that some person friendly to himself should occupy this position, which in its relations to the public is second in importance only to the Secretaryship of the Treasury itself. Gould consulted Corbin, and Corbin suggested the name of General Butterfield, — a former officer in the volunteer army. The appointment was not a wise one; nor does it appear in evidence by what means Corbin succeeded in bringing it about. He was supposed to have used A. T. Stewart, the wealthy importer, as his instrument for the purpose; but whatever the influence may have been, Corbin appears to have set it in action, and General Butterfield entered upon his duties toward the 1st of July.

The preparations thus made show that some large scheme was never absent from Gould's mind, although between the months of May and August he made no attempt to act upon the markets. Between August 20 and September 1, in company with Messrs. Woodward and Kimber, two large speculators, he made what is known as a pool or combination to raise the premium on gold, and some ten or fifteen millions were bought, but with very little effect on the price. The tendency of the market was downward, and was not easily counteracted. Perhaps under ordinary circumstances he might have abandoned his project; but an incident suddenly occurred which drew him headlong into the operation.

Whether the appointment of General Butterfield strengthened Gould's faith in Corbin's secret powers does not appear in evidence, though it may readily be assumed as probable ; but the next event seemed to authorize an unlimited faith in Corbin, as well as to justify the implicit belief of an Erie treasurer in the corruptibility of all mankind. The unsuspicious President again passed through New York, and came to breakfast at Corbin's house on the 2d of September. He saw no one but Corbin while there, and the same evening at ten o'clock departed for Saratoga. Gould was immediately informed by Corbin that the President, in discussing the financial situation, had shown himself a convert to the Erie theory about marketing the crops, and had " stopped in the middle of a conversation in which he had expressed his views and written a letter " to Secretary Boutwell. This letter was not produced before the investigating committee ; but Secretary Boutwell testified as follows in regard to it : —

" I think on the evening of the 4th of September I received a letter from the President dated at New York, as I recollect it ; I am not sure where it is dated. I have not seen the letter since the night I received it. I think it is now in my residence in Groton. In that letter he expressed an opinion that it was undesirable to force down the price of gold. He spoke of the importance to the West of being able to move their crops. His idea was that if gold should fall, the West would suffer and the movement of the crops would be retarded. The impression made on my mind by the letter was that he had rather a strong opinion to that effect. . . . Upon the receipt of the President's letter on the evening of the 4th of September, I telegraphed to Judge Richardson [Assistant Secretary at Washington] this despatch : ' Send no order to Butterfield as to sales of gold until you hear from me.' "

Gould had succeeded in reversing the policy of the national government ; but this was not all. He knew what the government would do before any officer of the government knew it. Gould was at Corbin's house on the 2d of September ; and although the evidence of both these gentlemen was very confused on the point, the inference is inevitable that Gould saw Corbin privately within an hour or two after the letter to Boutwell was written ; and that at this interview, while the President was still in the house, Corbin gave information to Gould about the President's letter, — perhaps showed him the letter itself. Then followed a transaction worthy of the French stage. Corbin's evidence gives his own account of it : —

" On the 2d of September (referring to memoranda) Mr. Gould offered to let me have some of the gold he then possessed. . . . He spoke to me, as he had repeatedly done before, about taking a certain amount of gold owned by him. I finally told Mr. Gould that for the sake of a lady, my wife, I would accept $500,000 of gold for her benefit, as I shared his confidence that gold would rise. . . . He afterward insisted that I should take a million more, and I did so on the same condition for my wife. He then sent me this paper."

The paper in question was as follows : —

SMITH, GOULD, MARTIN, & CO., Bankers.

11 BROAD STREET, NEW YORK, Sept. 2, 1869.

Mr. ——

DEAR SIR, — We have bought for your account and risk, —

500,000, gold, 132, R.

1,000,000, gold, 133⅝, R.

which we will carry on demand with the right to use.

SMITH, GOULD, MARTIN, & CO.

The memorandum meant that for every rise of one per cent in the price of gold Corbin was to receive $15,000, and his name nowhere to appear. If Gould saw Corbin in the morning and learned from him what the President had written, he must have made his bargain on the spot, and then going directly to the city he must in one breath have ordered this memorandum to be made out and large quantities of gold to be purchased before the President's letter left Corbin's house.

No time was lost. The same afternoon Gould's brokers bought large amounts in gold. One testifies to buying $1,315,000 at 134⅛. September 3 the premium was forced up to 36 ; September 4, when Boutwell received his letter, it had risen to 37. There Gould met a check, as he described his position in nervous Americanisms : —

" I did not want to buy so much gold. In the spring I put gold up from 32 to 38 and 40, with only about seven millions. But all these fellows went in and sold short, so that in order to keep it up I had to buy or else to back down and show the white feather. They would sell it to you all the time. I never intended to buy more than four or five millions of gold, but these fellows kept purchasing it on, and I made up my mind that I would put it up to 40 at one time. . . . We went into it as a commercial transaction, and did not intend to buy such an amount of gold. I was forced into it by the bears selling out. They were bound to put it down. I got into the contest. All these other fellows deserted me like rats from a ship. Kimber sold out and got short. . . . He sold out at 37. He got short of it, and went up " (or, in English, he failed).

The bears would not consent to lie still and be flayed. They had the great operators for once at a disadvantage, and were bent on revenge. Gould's position was hazardous. When Kimber sold out at 37, which was probably on the 7th of September, the market broke; and on the 8th the price fell back to 35. At the same moment, when the " pool " was ended by Kimber's desertion, Corbin, with his eminent shrewdness and respectability, told Gould " that gold had gone up to 37," and that he " should like to have this matter realized," — which was equivalent to saying that he wished to be paid something on account. This was said September 6 ; and Gould was obliged the same day to bring him a check for $25,000, drawn to the order of Jay Gould, and indorsed in blank by him with a proper regard for Corbin's modest desire not to have his name appear. The transaction did credit to Corbin's sagacity, and showed at least that he was acquainted with the

men he dealt with. Undoubtedly it placed Gould in
a difficult position; but as Gould already held some
fifteen millions of gold and needed Corbin's support,
he preferred to pay $25,000 outright rather than al-
low Corbin to throw his gold on the market. Yet the
fabric of Gould's web had been so seriously injured
that for a week — from the 8th to the 15th of September — he was unable to advance and equally unable to retreat without severe losses. He sat at his
desk in the opera-house, silent as usual, tearing little
slips of paper which he threw on the floor in his
abstraction, while he revolved new combinations in
his mind.

Down to this moment James Fisk, Jr., had not
appeared in the affair. Gould had not taken him
into his confidence; and not until after September
10 did Gould decide that nothing else could be done.
Fisk was not a safe ally in so delicate an affair;
but apparently no other aid offered itself. Gould
approached him; and as usual Gould's touch was
like magic. Fisk's evidence begins here, and may
be believed when very strongly corroborated: —

" Gold having settled down to 35, and I not having
cared to touch it, he was a little sensitive on the subject, feeling as if he would rather take his losses without
saying anything about it. . . . One day he said to me,
' Don't you think gold has got to the bottom?' I replied that I did not see the profit in buying gold unless
you have got into a position where you can command
the market. He then said he had bought quite a large

amount of gold, and I judged from his conversation that he wanted me to go into 'the movement and help strengthen the market. Upon that I went into the market and bought. I should say that was about the 15th or 16th of September. I bought at that time about seven or eight millions, I think."

The market responded slowly to these enormous purchases ; and on the 16th the clique was still struggling to recover its lost ground.

Meanwhile Gould placed a million and a half of gold to the account of General Butterfield, as he had done to the account of Corbin, and notified him of the purchase ; so Gould swears, in spite of General Butterfield's denial. The date of this purchase is not fixed. Through Corbin a notice was also sent by Gould about the middle of September to the President's private secretary, General Porter, informing him that half a million was placed to his credit. Porter repudiated the purchase, but Butterfield took no apparent notice of Gould's transaction on his account. On the 10th of September the President again came to New York, where he remained his brother-in-law's guest till the 13th ; and during this visit Gould again saw him, although Corbin avers that the President then intimated his wish to the servant that this should be the last time Gould obtained admission. " Gould was always trying to get something out of him," he said ; and if he had known how much Gould had succeeded in getting out of him, he would have admired the man's genius, even while shutting the door in his face.

On the morning of September 13 the President set out on a journey to the little town of Washington, situated among the mountains of western Pennsylvania, where he was to remain a few days. Gould, who consulted Corbin regularly every morning and evening, was still extremely nervous in regard to the President's policy; and as the crisis approached, his nervousness led him into the blunder of doing too much. Probably the bribe offered to Porter was a mistake, but a greater mistake was made by pressing Corbin's influence too far. Gould induced Corbin to write an official article for the New York press on the financial policy of the government, — an article afterward inserted in the "New York Times" through the kind offices of Mr. James McHenry; and he also persuaded or encouraged Corbin to write a letter directly to the President. This letter, written September 17 under the influence of Gould's anxiety, was instantly sent by a special messenger of Fisk to reach the President before he returned to the capital. The messenger carried also a letter of introduction to General Porter, the private secretary, in order to secure the personal delivery of this important despatch.

On Monday, September 20, gold again rose. Throughout Tuesday and Wednesday Fisk continued to purchase without limit, and forced the price up to 40. At that time Gould's firm of Smith, Gould, & Martin, through which the operation was conducted, had purchased some $50,000,000; yet the bears went on selling, although they could continue the contest only by borrowing Gould's own gold. Gould, on the other hand, could no longer sell and clear himself, for the reason that the sale of $50,000,000 would have broken the market. The struggle became intense. The whole country watched with astonishment the battle between the bulls and the bears. Business was deranged, and values were unsettled. There were indications of a panic in the stock market; and the bears in their emergency vehemently pressed the government to intervene. Gould wrote to Boutwell a letter so impudent as to indicate desperation and loss of his ordinary coolness. He began: —

SIR, — There is a panic in Wall Street, engineered by a bear combination. They have withdrawn currency to such an extent that it is impossible to do ordinary business. The Erie Company requires eight hundred thousand dollars to disburse, — . . . much of it in Ohio, where an exciting political contest is going on, and where we have about ten thousand employed; and the trouble is charged on the Administration. . . . Cannot you, consistently, increase your line of currency?"

From a friend such a letter would have been an outrage; but from a member of the Tammany ring, the principal object of detestation to the government, such a threat or bribe — whichever it may be called — was incredible. Gould was, in fact, at his wits' end.

He dreaded a panic, and he felt that it could no longer be avoided.

The scene next shifts for a moment to the distant town of Washington, among the hills of western Pennsylvania. On the morning of September 19, President Grant and his private secretary General Porter were playing croquet on the lawn, when Fisk's messenger, after twenty-four hours of travel by rail and carriage, arrived at the house, and sent in to ask for General Porter. When the President's game was ended, Porter came, received his own letter from Corbin, and called the President, who entered the room and took his brother-in-law's despatch. He then left the room, and after some ten or fifteen minutes' absence returned. The messenger, tired of waiting, then asked, " Is it all right ? " " All right," replied the President ; and the messenger hastened to the nearest telegraph station, and sent word to Fisk, " Delivered ; all right."

The messenger was altogether mistaken. Not only was all not right, but all was going hopelessly wrong. The President had at the outset supposed the man to be an ordinary post-office agent, and the letter an ordinary letter which had arrived through the post-office. Not until Porter asked some curious question as to the man, did the President learn that he had been sent by Corbin merely to carry this apparently unimportant letter of advice. The President's suspicions were excited ; and the same evening, at his request, Mrs. Grant wrote a hurried note to Mrs. Corbin, telling her how greatly the President was distressed at the rumor that Mr. Corbin was speculating in Wall Street, and how much he hoped that Mr. Corbin would " instantly disconnect himself with anything of that sort."

This letter, subsequently destroyed — or said to have been destroyed — by Mrs. Corbin, arrived in New York on the morning of Wednesday, September 22, the day when Gould and his enemies the bears were making simultaneous appeals to Secretary Boutwell. Mrs. Corbin was greatly excited and distressed by her sister-in-law's language. She carried the letter to her husband, and insisted that he should instantly abandon his interest in the gold speculation. Corbin, although considering the scruples of his wife and her family highly absurd, assented to her wish ; and when Gould came that evening as usual, with $50,000,000 of gold on his hands and extreme anxiety on his mind, Corbin read to him two letters, — the first, written by Mrs. Grant to Mrs. Corbin; the second, written by Mr. Corbin to President Grant, assuring him that he had not a dollar of interest in gold. The assurance of this second letter was, at any sacrifice, to be made good.

Corbin proposed that Gould should give him a check for $100,000, and take his $1,500,000 off his hands. A proposition more impudent than this could scarcely be imagined. Gould had already paid Corbin $25,000, and Corbin asked for $100,000 more at the moment when it was clear that the $25,000 he had

received had been given him under a misunderstanding of his services. He even represented himself as
doing Gould a favor by letting him have a million
and a half more gold at the highest market price, at
a time when Gould had fifty millions which he must
sell or be ruined. What Gould might under ordinary circumstances have replied, may be imagined;
but for the moment he could say nothing. Corbin
had but to show this note to a single broker in
Wall Street, and the fabric of Gould's speculation
would fall to pieces. Gould asked for time, and
went away. He consulted no one; he gave Fisk
no hint of what had happened. The next morning
he returned to Corbin, and made him the following
offer : —

   " ' Mr. Corbin, I cannot give you anything if you will
go out. If you will remain in, and take the chances of
the market, I will give you my check [for $100,000].'
' And then,' says Corbin, ' I did what I think it would have
troubled almost any other business man to consent to
do, — refuse one hundred thousand dollars on a rising
market. If I had not been an old man married to a
middle-aged woman, I should have done it (of course
with her consent) just as sure as the offer was made.
I said, " Mr. Gould, my wife says *no!* Ulysses thinks
it wrong, and that it ought to end." So I gave it
up. . . . He looked at me with an air of severe distrust, as if he was afraid of treachery in the camp. He
remarked, " Mr. Corbin, I am undone if that letter gets
out." . . . He stood there for a little while looking very
thoughtful, exceedingly thoughtful. He then left and

went into Wall Street; . . . and my impression is that he it was, and not the government, that broke that market.' "

Corbin was right; throughout all these transactions his insight into Gould's character was marvellous.

It was the morning of Thursday, September 23. Gould and Fisk went to Broad Street together; but as usual Gould was silent and secret, while Fisk was noisy and communicative. Their movements were completely separate. Gould acted through his own firm of Smith, Gould, & Martin, while Fisk operated principally through his old partner, Belden. One of Smith's principal brokers testifies : —

" ' Fisk never could do business with Smith, Gould, & Martin very comfortably. They would not do business for him. It was a very uncertain thing of course where Fisk might be. He is an erratic sort of genius. I don't think anybody would want to follow him very long. I am satisfied that Smith, Gould, & Martin controlled their own gold, and were ready to do as they pleased with it without consulting Fisk. I do not think there was any general agreement. . . . None of us who knew him cared to do business with him. I would not have taken an order from him nor had anything to do with him.' " Belden was considered a very low fellow. " ' I never had anything to do with him or his party,' said one broker employed by Gould. ' They were men I had a perfect detestation of ; they were no company for me. I should not have spoken to them at all under any ordinary circumstances.' " Another says, " ' Belden is a man in whom I never had any confidence in any way. For months before that, I would not have taken him for a gold transaction.'"

Yet Belden bought millions upon millions of gold. He himself swore that he had bought twenty millions by Thursday evening, without capital or credit except that of his brokers. Meanwhile Gould, on reaching the city, had at once given secret orders to sell. From the moment he left Corbin he had but one idea, which was to get rid of his gold as quietly as possible. "I purchased merely enough to make believe I was a bull," says Gould. This double process continued all that afternoon. Fisk's wild purchases carried the price to 144, and the panic in the street became more and more serious as the bears realized the extremity of their danger. No one can tell how much gold which did not exist they had contracted to deliver or pay the difference in price. One of the clique brokers swears that by Thursday evening the street had sold the clique one hundred and eighteen millions of gold; and every rise of one per cent of this sum implied a loss of more than $1,000,000 to the bears. Naturally the terror was extreme, for half Broad Street and thousands of speculators would have been ruined if compelled to settle gold at 150 which they had sold at 140. By that time nothing more was heard in regard to philanthropic theories of benefit to the Western farmer.

Gould's feelings may easily be imagined. He knew

that Fisk's reckless management would bring the government upon his shoulders, and he knew that unless he could sell his gold before the order came from Washington he would be a ruined man. He knew, too, that Fisk's contracts must inevitably be repudiated. This Thursday evening he sat at his desk in the Erie offices at the opera-house, while Fisk and Fisk's brokers chattered about him.

"I was transacting my railway business. I had my own views about the market, and my own fish to fry. I was all alone, so to speak, in what I did, and I did not let any of those people know exactly how I stood. I got no ideas from anything that was said there. I had been selling gold from 35 up all the time, and I did not know till the next morning that there would probably come an order about twelve o'clock to sell gold."

Gould had not told Fisk of Corbin's retreat, or of his own orders to sell.

Friday morning Gould and Fisk went together to Broad Street and took possession of the private back-office of a principal broker, "without asking the privilege of doing so," as the broker observes in his evidence. The first news brought to Gould was a disaster. The government had sent three men from Washington to examine the bank which Gould owned; and the bank sent word to Gould that it feared to certify for him as usual, and was itself in danger of a panic, caused by the presence of officers, which created distrust of the bank. It barely managed to save itself. Gould took the information silently, and his firm redoubled sales of gold. His partner, Smith, gave the orders to one broker after another, — " Sell ten millions ! "   " The order was given as quick as a flash, and away he went," says one of these men. " I sold only eight millions." " Sell, sell, sell ! do nothing but sell ! only don't sell to Fisk's brokers," were the orders which Smith himself acknowledges. In the gold-room Fisk's brokers were shouting their rising bids, and the packed crowd grew frantic with terror and rage as each successive rise showed their increasing losses. The wide streets outside were thronged with excited people ; the telegraph offices were overwhelmed with messages ordering sales or purchases of gold or stocks ; and the whole nation was watching eagerly to see what the result of this convulsion was to be. Trade was stopped, and even the President felt that it was time to raise his hand. No one who has not seen the New York gold-room can understand the spectacle it presented, — now a pandemonium, now silent as the grave. Fisk, in his dark back-office across the street, with his coat off, swaggered up and down, " a big cane in his hand," and called himself the Napoleon of Wall Street. He believed that he directed the movement, and while the street outside imagined that he and Gould were one family, and that his purchases were made for the clique, Gould was silently flinging away his gold at any price he could get for it.

Whether Fisk expected to carry out his contract and force the bears to settle, or not, is doubtful ; but the evidence seems to show that he was in earnest, and felt sure of success. His orders were unlimited. " Put it up to 150 ! " was one which he sent to the gold-room. Gold rose to 150. At length the bid was made, " 160 for any part of five millions ! " and no one any longer dared take it. " 161 for five millions ! " " 162 for five millions ! " No answer was made, and the offer was repeated, " 162 for any part of five millions ! " A voice replied, " Sold one million at 62 ! " The bubble suddenly burst; and within fifteen minutes, amid an excitement without parallel even in the wildest excitements of the war, the clique brokers were literally swept away and left struggling by themselves, bidding still 160 for gold in millions which no one would any longer take their word for, while the premium sank rapidly to 135. A moment later the telegraph brought from Washington the government order to sell, and the result was no longer possible to dispute. Fisk had gone too far, while Gould had secretly weakened the ground under his feet.

Gould was saved. His fifty millions were sold; and although no one knows what his gains or losses may have been, his firm was able to meet its contracts and protect its brokers. Fisk was in a very different situation. So soon as it became evident that his brokers would be unable to carry out their contracts, every one who had sold gold to them turned in wrath to Fisk's office. Fortunately for him it was protected by armed men whom he had brought with him from

his castle of Erie; but the excitement was so great
that both Fisk and Gould thought best to retire as
rapidly as possible by a back entrance leading into
another street, and to seek the protection of the
opera-house. There nothing but an army could dis-
turb them; no civil mandate was likely to be served
without their permission within those walls, and few
men cared to face Fisk's ruffians in order to force an
entrance.

The winding up of this famous conspiracy may be
told in few words; but no account could be complete which failed to reproduce in full the story of
Fisk's last interview with Corbin, as told by Fisk
himself : —

" I went down to the neighborhood of Wall Street Friday morning, and the history of that morning you know.
When I got back to our office, you can imagine I was in
no enviable state of mind, and the moment I got up street
that afternoon I started right round to old Corbin's to
rake him out. I went into the room, and sent word that
Mr. Fisk wanted to see him in the dining-room. I was
too mad to say anything civil, and when he came into the
room, said I, ' You damned old scoundrel, do you know
what you have done here, you and your people?' He
began to wring his hands, and, ' Oh,' he says, ' this is
a horrible position! Are you ruined?' I said I didn't
know whether I was or not; and I asked him again if he
knew what had happened. He had been crying, and said
he had just heard; that he had been sure everything was
all right; but that something had occurred entirely different from what he had anticipated. Said I, ' That don't

amount to anything ; we know that gold ought not to be at 31, and that it would not be but for such performances as you have had this last week ; you know damned well it would not if you had not failed.' I knew that somebody had run a saw right into us, and said I, ' This whole damned thing has turned out just as I told you it would.' I considered the whole party a pack of cowards, and I expected that when we came to clear our hands they would sock it right into us. I said to him, ' I don't know whether you have lied or not, and I don't know what ought to be done with you.' He was on the other side of the table, weeping and wailing, and I was gnashing my teeth. ' Now,' he says, ' you must quiet yourself.' I told him I did n't want to be quiet. I had no desire to ever be quiet again, and probably never should be quiet again. He says, ' But, my dear sir, you will lose your reason.' Says I, ' Speyers [a broker employed by him that day] has already lost his reason ; reason has gone out of everybody but me.' I continued, ' Now, what are you going to do ? You have got us into this thing, and what are you going to do to get us out of it ? ' He says, ' I don't know. I will go and get my wife.' I said, ' Get her down here ! ' The soft talk was all over. He went upstairs, and they returned tottling into the room, looking older than Stephen Hopkins. His wife and he both looked like death. He was tottling just like that. [Illustrated by a trembling movement of his body.] I have never seen him from that day to this."

This is sworn evidence before a committee of Congress ; and its humor is the more conspicuous, because the story probably contained from beginning to end not a word of truth. No such interview ever

occurred, except in the unconfined apartments of
Fisk's imagination. His own previous statements
make it certain that he was not at Corbin's house
at all that day, and that Corbin did come to the
Erie offices that evening, and again the next morning.
Corbin denies the truth of the account without limitation; and adds that when he entered the Erie offices
the next morning, Fisk was there. "I asked him how
Mr. Gould felt after the great calamity of the day
before." He remarked, "Oh, he has no courage at all.
He has sunk right down. There is nothing left of
him but a heap of clothes and a pair of eyes." The
internal evidence of truth in this anecdote would support Mr. Corbin against the world.[1]

[1] Mr. Fisk to the Editor of the Sun:—

ERIE RAILWAY COMPANY, COMPTROLLER'S OFFICE,
NEW YORK, Oct. 4, 1869.
To the Editor of the Sun.

DEAR SIR, — . . . Mr. Corbin has constantly associated with me;
. . . *he spent more than an hour with me in the Erie Railway Office
on the afternoon of Saturday, September 25, the day after the gold
panic.* . . . I enclose you a few affidavits which will give you further
information concerning this matter.

I remain your obedient servant,

JAMES FISK, JR.

Affidavit of Charles W. Pollard.

State of New York, City and County of New York, ss.

C. W. Pollard being duly sworn, says: "I have frequently been
the bearer of messages between Mr. James Fisk, Jr., and Mr. Abel R.
Corbin, brother-in-law of President Grant. . . . Mr. Corbin called on
me at the Erie building on Thursday, 23d September, 1869, telling me
he came to see how Messrs. Fisk and Gould were getting along. . . .
He called again on Friday, the following day, at about noon; appeared

In regard to Gould, Fisk's graphic description was probably again inaccurate. Undoubtedly the noise and scandal of the moment were extremely unpleasant to this silent and impenetrable intriguer. The city was in a ferment, and the whole country pointing at him with wrath. The machinery of the gold exchange had broken down, and he alone could extricate the business community from the pressing danger of a general panic. He had saved himself, but in a manner that could not have been to his taste. Yet his course from this point must have been almost self-evident to his mind, and there is no reason to suppose that he hesitated.

Gould's contracts were all fulfilled. Fisk's contracts, all except one, in respect to which the broker was able to compel a settlement, were repudiated. Gould probably suggested to Fisk that it was better to let Belden fail, and to settle a handsome for-

to be greatly excited, and said he feared *we* should lose a great deal of money. The following morning, Saturday, September 25, Mr. Fisk told me to take his carriage and call upon Mr. Corbin and say to him that he and Mr. Gould would like to see him (Corbin) at their office. I called and saw Mr. Corbin. He remarked upon greeting me: 'How does Mr. Fisk bear his losses?' and added, '*It is terrible for us.*' He then asked me to bring Mr. Fisk up to his house immediately, as he was indisposed, and did not feel able to go down to his (Fisk's) office. I went after Mr. Fisk, who returned immediately with me to Mr. Corbin's residence, but shortly after came out with Mr. Corbin, who accompanied him to Mr. Fisk's office, where he was closeted with him and Mr. Gould for about two hours. . . . "

There are obvious inconsistencies among these different accounts, which it is useless to attempt to explain. The fact of Saturday's interview appears to be beyond dispute.

tune on him, than to sacrifice something more than
$5,000,000 in sustaining him. Fisk therefore threw
Belden over, and swore that he had acted only under
Belden's order; in support of which statement he
produced a paper to the following effect: —

September 24.

DEAR SIR, — I hereby authorize you to order the purchase and sale of gold on my account during this day to
the extent you may deem advisable, and to report the
same to me as early as possible. It is to be understood
that the profits of such order are to belong entirely to me,
and I will, of course, bear any losses resulting.

Yours,

WILLIAM BELDEN.

JAMES FISK, JR.

This document was not produced in the original,
and certainly never existed. Belden himself could
not be induced to acknowledge the order; and no one
would have believed him had he done so. Meanwhile
the matter is before the national courts, and Fisk may
probably be held to his contracts; but it will be difficult to execute judgment upon him, or to discover
his assets.

One of the first acts of the Erie gentlemen after
the crisis was to summon their lawyers and set in
action their judicial powers. The object was to prevent the panic-stricken brokers from using legal
process to force settlements, and so render the entan-
glement inextricable. Messrs. Field and Shearman
came, and instantly prepared a considerable number
of injunctions, which were sent to their judges, signed

at once, and immediately served. Gould then was able to dictate the terms of settlement; and after a week of paralysis, Broad Street began to show signs of returning life. As a legal curiosity, one of these documents issued three months after the crisis may be reproduced in order to show the powers wielded by the Erie managers : —

SUPREME COURT.

| H. N. SMITH, JAY GOULD, H. H. MARTIN, and J. B. BACH, Plaintiffs,
against
JOHN BONNER and ARTHUR L. SEWELL, Defendants. | Injunction by order. |

It appearing satisfactorily to me by the complaint duly verified by the plaintiffs that sufficient grounds for an order of injunction exist, I do hereby order and enjoin . . . that the defendants, John Bonner and Arthur L. Sewell, their agents, attorneys, and servants, refrain from pressing their pretended claims against the plaintiffs, or either of them, before the Arbitration Committee of the New York Stock Exchange, or from taking any proceedings thereon, or in relation thereto, except in this action.

GEORGE G. BARNARD, J. S. C.

NEW YORK, Dec. 29, 1869.

Bonner had practically been robbed with violence by Gould, and instead of his being able to bring the robber into court as the criminal, the robber brought him into court as criminal, and the judge forbade him to appear in any other character. Of all Mr. Field's distinguished legal reforms and philanthropic projects, this injunction is beyond a doubt the most brilliant and the most successful.[1]

[1] These remarks on Mr. Field's professional conduct as counsel of the Erie Railway excited a somewhat intemperate controversy, and Mr. Field's partisans in the press made against the authors of the "Chapters of Erie" a charge that these writers "indelicately interfered in a matter alien to them in every way," — the administration of justice in New York being, in this point of view, a matter in which Mr. Field and the Erie Railway were alone concerned.   Mr. Field himself published a letter in the "Westminster Review" for April, 1871, in which, after the general assertion that the passages in the "New York Gold Conspiracy" which related to him " cover about as much untruth as could be crowded into so many lines," he made the following corrections :

First, he denied, what was never suggested, that he was in any way a party to the origin or progress of the Gold Conspiracy, until (secondly) he was consulted on the 28th of September, when (thirdly) he gave an opinion as to the powers of the members of the Gold and Stock Exchanges.   Fourthly, he denied that he had relations of any sort with any judge in New York, or any power over these judges, other than such as English counsel have in respect to English judges.   Fifthly, he asserted that among twenty-eight injunctions growing out of the gold transactions his partners obtained only ten, and only one of these ten, the one quoted above, from Justice Barnard.   Sixthly, that this injunction was proper to be sought and granted.   Seventhly, that Mr. Bonner was not himself the person who had been " robbed with violence," but the assignee of the parties.

On the other hand, Mr. Field did not deny that the injunction as quoted was genuine, or that he was responsible for it, or that it did, as asserted, shut the defendants out of the courts as well as out of the Gold Exchange Arbitration Committee, or that it compelled them to appear only as defendants in a case where they were the injured parties.

In regard to the power which Mr. Field, whether as a pri-

The fate of the conspirators was not severe. Corbin went to Washington, where he was snubbed by the President, and disappeared from public view, only coming to light again before the Congressional committee. General Butterfield, whose share in the transaction is least understood, was permitted to resign his office without an investigation. Speculation for the next six months was at an end. Every person involved in the affair seemed to have lost money, and dozens of brokers were swept from the street. But Jay Gould and James Fisk, Jr., continued to reign over Erie, and no one can say that their power or their credit was sensibly diminished by a shock which for the time prostrated the interests of the country.

Nevertheless, sooner or later the last traces of the disturbing influence of war and paper money will disappear in America, as they have sooner or later disappeared in every other country which has passed through the same evils. The result of this convulsion itself has been in the main good. It indicates the

vate individual or as Erie counsel, exercised over the New York bench, his correction affected the story but little. In regard to Mr. Bonner, the fact of his being principal or representative scarcely altered the character of Mr. Field's injunction. Finally, so far as the text is concerned, after allowing full weight to all Mr. Field's corrections, the public can decide for itself how many untruths it contained. The subject ceased to be one of consequence even to Mr. Field after the subsequent violent controversy which arose in March, 1871, in regard to other points of Mr. Field's professional conduct.

approaching end of a troubled time. Messrs. Gould
and Fisk will at last be obliged to yield to the force
of moral and economical laws. The Erie Railway will
be rescued, and its history will perhaps rival that of
the great speculative manias of the last century. The
United States will restore a sound basis to its currency, and will learn to deal with the political reforms it requires. Yet though the regular process of
development may be depended upon, in its ordinary
and established course, to purge American society of
the worst agents of an exceptionally corrupt time,
the history of the Erie corporation offers one point
in regard to which modern society everywhere is directly interested. For the first time since the creation of these enormous corporate bodies, one of them
has shown its power for mischief, and has proved
itself able to override and trample on law, custom,
decency, and every restraint known to society, without scruple, and as yet without check. The belief is
common in America that the day is at hand when
corporations far greater than the Erie — swaying
power such as has never in the world's history been
trusted in the hands of private citizens, controlled by
single men like Vanderbilt, or by combinations of
men like Fisk, Gould, and Lane, after having created
a system of quiet but irresistible corruption — will
ultimately succeed in directing government itself.
Under the American form of society no authority
exists capable of effective resistance. The national
government, in order to deal with the corporations,

must assume powers refused to it by its fundamental law, — and even then is exposed to the chance of forming an absolute central government which sooner or later is likely to fall into the hands it is struggling to escape, and thus destroy the limits of its power only in order to make corruption omnipotent. Nor is this danger confined to America alone. The corporation is in its nature a threat against the popular institutions spreading so rapidly over the whole world. Wherever a popular and limited government exists this difficulty will be found in its path ; and unless some satisfactory solution of the problem can be reached, popular institutions may yet find their existence endangered.

THE SESSION. 1869–1870.[1]

THAT the government of the United States is passing through a period of transition is one of the common-places of politics. This transition, which few persons deny, illustrates in a scientific point of view the manner in which principles are established. The generation that framed the American form of government meant it to be, not only in mechanism but in theory, a contradiction to opinions commonly accepted in Europe. The men who made the Constitution intended to make by its means an issue with antiquity; and they had a clear conception of the issue itself, and of their own purposes in raising it. These purposes were perhaps chimerical; the hopes then felt were almost certainly delusive. Yet persons who grant the probable failure of the scheme, and expect the recurrence of the great problems in government which were then thought to be solved, cannot but look with satisfaction at the history of the Federal Constitution as the most convincing and the most interesting experiment ever made in the laboratory of political science, even if it demonstrates the impossibility of success through its means.

[1] From the North American Review for July, 1870.

The great object of terror and suspicion to the people of the thirteen provinces was *power ;* not merely power in the hands of a president or a prince, of one assembly or of several, of many citizens or of few, but power in the abstract, wherever it existed and under whatever name it was known. "There is and must be," said Blackstone, "in all forms of government, however they began or by what right soever they exist, a supreme, irresistible, absolute, uncontrolled authority, in which the *jura summi imperii,* or the rights of sovereignty, reside ;" and Parliament is the place "where that absolute despotic power which must in all governments reside somewhere is intrusted by the Constitution of the British kingdoms." Supreme, irresistible authority must exist somewhere in every government — was the European political belief; and England solved her problem by intrusting it to a representative assembly to be used according to the best judgment of the nation. America, on the other hand, asserted that the principle was not true; that no such supreme power need exist in a government; that in the American government none such should be allowed to exist, because absolute power in any form was inconsistent with freedom ; and that the new government should start from the idea that the public liberties depended upon denying uncontrolled authority to the political system in its parts or in its whole.

Every one knows with what logic this theory was worked out in the mechanism of the new republic. Not only were rights reserved to the people never to be parted with, but rights of great extent were reserved to the States as a sacred deposit to be jealously guarded. Even in the central government, the three great depositories of power were made independent of each other, checks on each other's assumption of authority, separately responsible to the people, that each might be a protection and not a danger to the public liberties. The framers of the Constitution did not indeed presume to prescribe or limit the powers a nation might exercise if its existence were at stake. They knew that under such an emergency paper limitations must yield; but they still hoped that the lesson they had taught would sink so deep into the popular mind as to cause a re-establishment of the system after the emergency had passed. The hope was scarcely supported by the experience of history, but, like M. Necker in France, they were obliged to trust somewhat to the " virtues of the human heart."

The two theories of government stood face to face during three quarters of a century. Europe still maintained that supreme power must be trusted to every government, democratic or not; and America still maintained that such a principle was inconsistent with freedom. The civil war broke out in the United States, and of course for the time obliterated the Constitution. Peace came, and with it came the moment for the settlement of this long scientific dispute. If the Constitutional system restored itself, America was right, and the oldest problem in political science was successfully solved.

Every one knows the concurrence of accidents, if anything in social sequence can be called accident, which seemed to prevent a fair working of the tendency to restoration during the four years that followed the close of actual war. With the year 1869 a new and peculiarly favorable change took place. Many good and true Americans then believed that the time had come, and that the old foundation on which American liberties had been planted would be fully and firmly restored. A brilliant opportunity occurred for the new Administration, not perhaps to change the ultimate result, but to delay some decades yet the demonstration of failure. The new President had unbounded popular confidence. He was tied to no party. He was under no pledges. He had the inestimable advantage of a military training, which, unlike a political training, was calculated to encourage the moral distinction between right and wrong.

No one could fail to see the mingled feelings of alarm and defiance with which senators and politicians waited President Grant's first move. Not they alone, but almost the entire public, expected to see him at once grasp with a firm hand the helm of government, and give the vessel of state a steady and determined course. The example of President Washington offered an obvious standard for the ambition of Grant. It was long before the conservative class of citizens, who had no partisan prejudices, could convince themselves that in this respect they had not perhaps overrated so much as misconceived the character of Grant, and that they must learn to look at him in a light unlike any they had been hitherto accustomed to associate with him. This misconception or misunderstanding was 'not matter for surprise, since even to the President's oldest and most intimate associates his character is still in some respects a riddle, and the secret of his uniform and extraordinary success a matter of dispute. Indeed, if he ever fell into the mischievous habit of analyzing his own mind, he could answer his own questions in no manner that would satisfy curiosity. Nothing could be more interesting to any person who has been perplexed with the doubts which President Grant's character never fails to raise in every one who approaches him, than to have these doubts met and explained by some competent authority, — by some old associate like General Sherman, with an active mind ever eager to grapple with puzzles ; by some civil subordinate such as a civil subordinate ought to be, quick at measuring influences and at unravelling the tangled skein of ideas which runs through the brains of an Administration. Yet as a rule, the reply to every inquiry comes in the form of confessed ignorance: "We do not know why Grant is successful; we only know that he succeeds."

Without attempting to explain so complicated an enigma, one might still predict General Grant's probable civil career from facts open to all the world. Grant's mind rarely acts from any habit of wide generalization. As a rule, the ideas executed with so much energy appear to come to him one by one, without close logical sequence; and as a person may see and calculate the effect of a drop of acid on an organic substance, so one may sometimes almost seem to see the mechanical process by which a new idea eats its way into Grant's unconscious mind, — where its action begins, and where its force is exhausted. Hence arise both advantages and misfortunes. This faculty for assimilation of ideas, this nature which the Germans would call objective, under ordinary circumstances and when not used by selfish men for corrupt purposes gives elasticity, freedom from inveterate prejudices, and capacity for progress. It would be likely to produce a course of action not perhaps strictly logical, or perfectly steady, or capable of standing the sharper tests of hostile criticism, but in the main practical, sensible, and in intention honest. When used by Jay Gould and Abel Rathbone Corbin with the skill of New York stock-brokers for illegitimate objects, the result is the more disastrous in proportion to the energy of execution for which the President is remarkable.

Most persons, and especially those who had formed their ideas of the President from his Vicksburg campaign, entertained a different notion of his intellectual qualities. The Vicksburg campaign puzzled equally the enemies and the friends of General Grant. General Sherman's frank expression of surprise found its way into print in the form of a sincere tribute of admiration spoken by a man conscious of having underrated his superior officer. The public, on the strength of this brilliant campaign, assumed with reason that a general capable of planning and executing a military scheme such as Napoleon might have envied, must possess an aptitude for elaboration of idea and careful adaptation of means to ends such as would in civil administration produce a large and vigorous political policy. Yet no such refinement of conception was in Grant's nature; no such ambition entered his head, — he neither encouraged it nor believed in its advantages. His own idea of his duties as President was openly and consistently expressed, and is best described as that of the commander of an army in time of peace. He was to watch over the faithful administration of the government; to see that the taxes were honestly collected, that the disbursements were honestly made, that economy was strictly enforced, that the laws were everywhere obeyed, good and bad alike; and as it was the duty of every military commander to obey the civil authority without question, so it was the duty of the President to follow without hesitation the wishes of the people as expressed by Congress.

This is not the range of duties prescribed to an American President either by the Constitution or by custom, although it may be that which Congress desires and to which the system tends. The President may indeed in one respect resemble the commander of an army in peace, but in another and more essential sense he resembles the commander of a ship at sea. He must have a helm to grasp, a course to steer, a port to seek; he must sooner or later be convinced that a perpetual calm is as little to his purpose as a perpetual hurricane, and that without headway the ship can arrive nowhere. President Grant assumed at the outset that it was not his duty to steer; that his were only duties of discipline.

Under these circumstances, with a President who while disbelieving in the propriety of having a general policy must yet inevitably assume responsibility, — with one too whose mind, if not imaginative or highly cultivated, was still sensitive to surrounding influences, — the necessity was all the greater that the gentlemen on whose advice and assistance he would be compelled to lean should be calculated to supplement his natural gifts. From him the public had not required high civil education. Rulers have always the right to command and appropriate the education and the intelligence of their people. Knowledge somewhere, either in himself or in his servants, is essential even to an American President, — perhaps to him most of all rulers; and thus, though it was a matter of comparatively little importance that the President's personal notions of civil government were crude, and his ideas of political economy those of a feudal monarch a thousand years ago, it was of the highest consequence that his advisers should supply the knowledge that he could not have been expected to possess, and should develop the ideas which his growing experience would give him. Questions of finance having assumed overruling importance, a responsibility of the most serious character would evidently rest on the Secretary of the Treasury.

The official importance of the Secretary of the Treasury can hardly be over-estimated. Not only is his political power in the exercise of patronage greater than that of any other Cabinet officer, but in matters of policy almost every proposition of foreign or domestic interest sooner or later involves financial considerations and requires an opinion from a financial stand-point. Hence in the English system the head of administration commonly occupies the post of premier lord of the Treasury. In the American form of government the head of the Treasury is also the post of real authority, rivalling that of the President, and almost too powerful for harmony or subordination. The secretary's voice ought to have more weight with the President than that of any other adviser. The secretary's financial policy ought to be the point on which each member of the Administration is united with every other. At a time like the summer of 1869, when old issues were passing away and a new condition of things was at hand, when the public was waiting to be led or kneeling to take up its master, it was more than ever important that the President should have in the Treasury a man who could command and compel respect.

Secretary Boutwell was not a person to make good the needs of the President. General Grant wanted civil education, but in return was open to new ideas, and had the capacity to learn from any one who had the faculty to teach. Mr. Boutwell had no faculty for teaching, and little respect for knowledge that was not practical. He believed in knowledge so far as was convenient to justify his theory that knowledge was a deception. He believed in common schools, and not in political science; in ledgers and cash-books, but not in Adam Smith or J. S. Mill, — as one might believe in the multiplication-table, but not in Laplace or Newton. By a natural logic he made of his disbelief in the higher branches of political science a basis for his political practice; and thus grounding action on ignorance, he carried out his principle to its conclusions. He too, like the President, announced that he had no policy; and even more persistently than the President he attempted to govern on the theory that government was no concern of his. Other persons in a similar position would commonly have leaned either to the theorists on one side, or to so-called practical men on the other; but Mr. Boutwell treated both with the same indifference. He had all the theorists in Europe and America to choose from, but he did not listen to their teachings; he had all the practical men in the country at his service, but he did not follow their advice; he had all the best members of the Legislature to depend upon, but he did not desire their assistance; he had a costly and elaborate machinery maintained by the country to furnish him with any information he might require, but Mr. Boutwell never required information. Nay, sitting twice a week in consultation with his colleagues in the Cabinet, Mr. Boutwell cannot have controlled their measures or even discussed his own. The President himself at the time of his Message could hardly have been consulted by the secretary.

To analyze a policy which does not exist, to trace the adaptation of means to ends where no adaptation was intended, is a waste of time and ingenuity. Yet no man can succeed in obliterating all ideas from his mind, or can prevent his acts from showing traces of intelligence. This relation between ideas and acts, commonly known as a policy, was visible in Mr. Boutwell's course, although it was visible only within a narrow range. Of most political leaders it might have been foretold with certainty that they would expend their energy on a restoration of the currency, or on a reduction of the taxes, confident that if these were once settled the financial situation would be secure. Mr. Boutwell's passion was different. He had only one object of great ambition, but this was to redeem the national debt. To do this from day to day; to collect more and more millions from the people; to cut down the expenses to their lowest point; to accumulate the surplus in the Treasury; to buy with it, month by month, more and more of the government's own debts, and thus to see the huge mass of indebtedness slowly dwindle and diminish in his hands, — this was a tangible, self-evident proof of success, which appealed directly to the lowest order of intelligence, and struck with the greatest possible force the mind of the voting public. To this idea Mr. Boutwell sacrificed currency reform, revenue reform, and every hope of relief from taxation; and to this idea he subordinated even his own next ambition, that of lowering the rate of interest on the debt. Beyond this he abnegated ideas. He did nothing, said nothing, heard nothing, except when necessity compelled.

Although the policy thus embraced by Mr. Boutwell was neither broad nor deep, and certainly not that of a great statesman, yet in pursuing this easy and simple course Mr. Boutwell may have taken the most direct path to an apparently brilliant success, — a success far better calculated for his purposes than though he had strayed aside into the vast and comprehensive reforms which would have dazzled the imaginations of Turgot, of Pitt, or of Hamilton. But the success which is gained by so meagre and sterile a conception is of little permanent value, even when compared with a bold and generous failure. If a critic were called upon to name the most unfortunate of all the financiers who have ever controlled the resources of France, he might, from Mr. Boutwell's point of view, find difficulty in discovering a more conspicuous failure than the administration of Turgot. If he applied the same process to British finance, he might probably be compelled at last to fix upon no less illustrious a career than that of William Pitt. But if he were to test his theory by the opposite experiment of selecting from English history the nearest approach to Mr. Boutwell's ideal of financial success, he would certainly be compelled to pass in silence over the names of Montagu and of Walpole, of Pitt, of Peel, and of Gladstone, in order to draw from its almost forgotten resting-place the memory of some third-rate Chancellor of the Exchequer, some Nicholas Vansittart, whose very name is a blank even to the students of biographical cyclopædias. Vansittart, indeed, would in most respects, except for his curious financial knowledge and his reverence for the financial teachings of his great master Pitt, serve well as the ideal of Mr. Boutwell. A Chancellor of the Exchequer who coming into office in 1812, at almost the darkest moment of England's struggle with the world, remained at the head of the finances through the war ; met and triumphantly stood the shock of the return from Elba, and of Waterloo ; carried England back to specie payments after twenty years of paper money ; at a single operation reduced the interest on a capital of nearly $800,000,000, at that time the largest sum ever dealt with in a mass ; and who, to crown all, arrived at the height of his ambition in 1823 by raising the surplus, applicable to the reduction of debt, to the unprecedented point of $25,000,000 in spite of the opposition of the whole body of liberal and educated politicians, — a Chancellor of the Exchequer with twelve years of such triumphs as these could scarcely be denied the credit of supreme and unrivalled success. Yet such is the perverseness of history, and so unreasonable is human prejudice, that not only the contemporaries of Mr. Vansittart, although attached to him by his genial and good-natured manners, but also posterity, to which his name is so little familiar, have combined in agreeing that as a financial minister he was a conspicuous example of incompetence, who for years hung like a clog on the progress of England.

So far as finance was concerned, Mr. Boutwell's policy might have been poorer even than it was, and yet the vigor of the country would have made it a success. The greatest responsibilities of a Secretary of the Treasury are not financial, and an administration framed upon the narrow basis of mere departmental activity must be always, except under the strongest of Presidents, an invitation to failure. The stormiest of Cabinets, the most venturesome of advisers, the boldest of political rivals for power, are likely to produce in combination a better result than that unorganized and disjointed harmony, that dead unanimity, which springs from divided responsibility. Mr. Boutwell had neither the wish nor the scope to assume the functions or to wield the power of his office; and instead of stamping upon the President and his administration the impress of a controlling mind, he drew himself back into a corner of his own, and encouraged and set the example of isolation at a time when concentrated action was essential to the Executive.

Even in the quietest of times and under the most

despotic chief such a departmental government is a doubtful experiment, but in the summer and autumn of 1869 it was peculiarly ill-timed. Every politician felt that the first year of the new Administration would probably fix the future character of the government. The steady process by which power was tending to centralization in defiance of the theory of the political system; the equally steady tendency of this power to accumulate in the hands of the Legislature at the expense of the Executive and the Judiciary; the ever-increasing encroachments of the Senate, the ever-diminishing efficiency of the House; all the different parts and processes of the general movement which indicated a certain abandonment of the original theory of the American system, and a no less certain substitution of a method of government that promised to be both corrupt and inefficient, — all these were either to be fixed upon the country beyond recall, or were to be met by a prompt and energetic resistance. To evade the contest was to accept the revolution. To resist with success, the President must have built up his authority upon every side until the vigor of his Administration overawed the Senate, and carried away the House by the sheer strength of popular applause. That such a result was possible no one can doubt who had occasion to see how much it was dreaded by the Washington politicians of the winter and spring of 1869, and how rapidly they resumed confidence on discovering that the President had no such schemes.

By the time Congress came together, in December, 1869, the warm hopes which illumined the election of November, 1868, had faded from the public mind. Clearly, the Administration was marked by no distinctive character. No purpose of peculiar elevation, no broad policy, no commanding dignity indicated the beginning of a new era. The old type of politician was no less powerful than under other Presidents. The old type of idea was not improved by the personal changes between 1861 and 1870. The Administration was not prepared for a contest with Congress, and at the last moment it was still without a purpose, without followers, and without a head.

Under these circumstances the President's Message was sent to the Capitol. It was studied with the more curiosity because it was supposed to reflect the internal condition of the government. Nothing could have presented a less reassuring prospect. The want of plan and unity of idea was so obvious that no one needed to be assured of the harmony of the Administration. An Administration that did not care enough for its own opinions to quarrel about them was naturally harmonious. The President and the Secretary of the Treasury were discovered expressing opinions and offering recommendations diametrically opposed to each other, apparently unconscious that under ordinary theories of government a head is required. Nor was this all. The absence of a strong mind in the Treasury was as conspicuous in what was omitted as in what was said. Not only was the political economy, both of the Message and of Mr. Boutwell's Report, a subject into which the ridicule of the press cut with easy facility, to the mortification of every friend of the Government, but even where simpler declarations, not requiring previous knowledge of principles, would have satisfied every purpose, their absence was almost as marked as was the presence of Mr. Boutwell's famous barrels of flour. In regard to the currency alone was the President in advance of public opinion, and in regard to the currency his secretary offered him no active support. Other reforms shared a worse fate. The reduction of taxes was discouraged, the civil service was not noticed, and tariff reform was distinctly opposed. Had it not been for the good sense of the remarks on reconstruction and foreign affairs, the President's first appearance before Congress would have hazarded the reproach of absurdity.

The result, already a foregone conclusion, became apparent when Congress took up its work. So far as initiative was concerned, the President and his Cabinet might equally well have departed separately or together to distant lands. Their recommendations were uniformly disregarded. Mr. Sumner, at the head of the Senate, rode rough-shod over their reconstruction policy, and utterly overthrew it in spite of the feeble resistance of the House. Senator Conkling then ousted Sumner from his saddle, and headed the Senate in an attack upon the Executive as represented by Judge Hoar, the avowed *casus belli* being that the attorney-general's manners were unsatisfactory to the Senate. Then Conkling attacked the Census Bill, where he had a three-fold victory; and it would be hard to say which of the three afforded him the keenest gratification. Single-handed he assailed Sumner, the House, and the Executive, and routed them all in disastrous confusion. Never was factiousness more alluring or more successful than under Conkling's lead. Then again Sumner came to the front, and obtained a splendid triumph over the President in the struggle over San Domingo. Senator Sherman was less vigorous and less fortunate in regard to the currency and funding measures, but Boutwell asked so little it was difficult for Sherman to do more than ignore him; and even in the House, Mr. Dawes, the official spokesman of the Government, if the Government has an official spokesman, startled the country by a sudden and dashing volunteer attack on the only point of General Grant's lines on the security of which he had prided himself, — his economy; and to this day no man understands how Dawes's foray was neutralized or evaded, or whether he was right or wrong.

The principal subjects of the session within the scope of the present review have been Reconstruction, Finance, and Foreign Affairs.

On the subject of Reconstruction little need be said. The merits or demerits of the system adopted

are no longer a subject worth discussion. The resistance to these measures rested primarily on their
violation of the letter and spirit of the Constitution
as regarded the rights of States, and the justification
rested not on a denial of the violation, but in overruling necessity. The measures were adopted with
reluctance by a majority of Congressmen, they were
approved with equal reluctance by a majority of the
people ; but they have become law, and whatever
harm may ultimately come from them is beyond recall and must be left for the coming generation, to
which the subject henceforth belongs, to regulate according to its circumstances and judgment. The
present generation must rest content with knowing
that so far as legal principles are involved, the process of reconstruction has reached its limits in the
legislation of 1869. The powers originally reserved
by the Constitution to the States are in future to
be held by them only on good behavior and at the
sufferance of Congress ; they may be suspended or
assumed by Congress ; their original basis and sanction no longer exist; and if they ever offered any
real protection against the assumption of supreme
and uncontrolled power by the central government,
that protection is at an end. How far Congress will
at any future day care to press its authority, or how
far the States themselves may succeed in resisting
the power of Congress, are questions which must be
answered by a reference to the general course of
events. Something may be judged of the rate of

25

progress from the theory so energetically pressed during the past season by Senator Sumner, that the New England system of common schools is a part of the republican form of government as understood by the framers of the Constitution, — an idea that would have seemed to the last generation as strange as though it had been announced that the electric telegraph was an essential article of faith in the early Christian Church. Something also may be judged from the condition of New York city and the evident failure of the system of self-government in great municipalities. Something more may be guessed from the rapid progress of corruption in shaking public confidence in State legislatures. Finally, something may be inferred from the enormous development of corporate power, requiring still greater political power to control it. Under any circumstances the first decisive, irrevocable step toward substituting a new form of government in the place of that on which American liberties have heretofore rested has been taken, and by it the American people must stand.

Finance, if not so important as Reconstruction, had at least the advantage of novelty. Reduction of taxation was the popular cry. Reform of taxation was equally essential. Secretary Boutwell, and with him though less positively the President, resisted at the outset either reduction or reform. The process of bond-buying supplied in Boutwell's mind the want of any more difficult conception, while in regard to free-trade ideas the secretary, like all political New England, sympathized with the President in cold indifference. The revenue reformers had not expected such a result; they were not prepared for the hostility they met from the Administration, and were thus placed in a position of great difficulty.

Whatever was the reason that the President leaned to high protectionist ideas, no one was more surprised or less gratified than many of his warmest friends when they found the fact announced in his Message. Undoubtedly the reformers had hoped and expected to have his sympathy in their efforts for revenue reform, as they had hoped it in regard to civil-service reform, and as they received it in the case of the currency; nor was there reason to suppose that the President, even on this important subject, acted from firm conviction, or considered the matter in reference to any general class of political ideas. The responsibility for the President's course could not be thrown upon his Secretary of the Treasury, since Secretary Boutwell on this subject as on all others, except one, abnegated influence. The difficulty was that the Administration without active hostility blocked the path of the reformers. It would consent to no absolute war upon them, but its practical influence was more mischievous than the bitterest warfare. To break down the monopolies which the central government had created and was engaged in supporting, and whose corrupt influence was felt at every step, seemed the first and most pressing necessity to those who be-

lieved that a purer political and moral atmosphere
was only to be found by freeing the country from
them; but to do this by disjointed, unorganized effort, without support from the Administration and
in face of a large party majority, against the sneers
and contempt of every Republican Congressman from
New England, without a voice of open or secret encouragement and at the same time to meet and
overcome Pennsylvania and her organized body of
allies, — to do it all by means of the Republican party
when the Republican party in Congress dreaded nothing so much as the necessity of meeting this issue,
seemed a project of hopeless temerity.

The small body of men in and out of Congress who
were determined to force the issue of reform began
the winter under every influence of discouragement.
Not only had the President abandoned them, but
Congress was in the hands of their opponents; and
the Committee of Ways and Means, controlled by
protectionist influence, prepared an ingenious bill,
calculated to reduce taxation and to check popular
complaint, but still more carefully constructed to
maintain and increase the protecting duties wherever
special interests asked it. The Forty-first Congress
was considered as more thoroughly devoted to protectionist ideas than any of its predecessors, and
about fifty Democratic votes were all that could be
classed as determined for free-trade, with the exception of three or four Western Republicans. Tariff
reform, as advocated by David A. Wells, commanded

a certain amount of sympathy; but its friends in the House were few and timid, while the charge of free-trade sounded to their ears as terrible as that of having worn a rebel uniform or having been out with the Ku-klux Klan. To convert such a body of men by such small means as the reformers could command was a desperate undertaking. The friends of reform in 1869, quitting in despair the President and his Cabinet with their inertia and cold neutrality, and Congress with its bristling hostility, turned to ask counsel of the popular masses. They worked throughout the summer and autumn with all the energy they possessed, and they continued to work throughout the winter, not in the lobbies of the Capitol or in the ante-chambers of the departments, but directly and earnestly upon popular opinion. As spring approached they began to resume confidence. Their leaders in Washington, whose interest was sharpened by the anxiety to maintain control of their constituencies, received from every quarter beyond the Alleghanies, with few exceptions, assurances of popular support, so vigorous and so universal that their tone began to change from depression to boldness, and they felt themselves strong enough to do without the Administration if the Administration could do without them. From every great organ of public opinion in the Western country they poured out a volume of argument and appeal that no popular influence could resist. Party lines were broken under their incessant attrition. Members of Congress began to hesitate, to consult, and to seek information. The formal opening debate upon the new tariff developed the existence of a feeling such as no one had expected ; and when the bill went into committee to be taken up in detail, it is hard to say who were more astonished, protectionists or reformers, to learn that in the first division the reformers carried the reduction on sugar by a majority of two.

Then ensued a struggle which dumfounded the friends of the tariff, who at first refused to credit their defeat, and insisted on considering it an accident due to the absence of their allies. When the same result occurred again and again, while the resistance to the bill became more and more general instead of diminishing, they began to comprehend their danger. General Schenck, who made every effort to force his measures through the House, with more success than any other member could have obtained, soon lost his temper, having at best no very considerable supply of temper to lose, and described his difficulties in graphic language.

" There is nobody in this House," said he, " upon either side, there is nobody anywhere that has watched the progress of the Tariff Bill through the Committee of the Whole, who does not know that peculiarly, and beyond perhaps the manifestation of hostility and attack upon any other measure in this or almost any former Congress, it has been fought inch by inch, step by step, line by line, persistently, with heavy attacks and with light attacks, — and most frequently light. I defy a denial of that."

The fact was not one which the reformers proposed to deny. Not only did they intend to resist all increase of protective duties, but they meant to lower the duties wherever they could. They urged their amendments to every line and word with a persistency which astonished themselves; and, what was still more surprising, the House in Committee of the Whole supported their efforts, and drove the Committee of Ways and Means to amend its own bill. Nor did their success end there. The whole subject was forced before the public attention, and the political issue for the coming elections was marked out beyond evasion.

Meanwhile Secretary Boutwell yielded so far to the popular outcry that he unwillingly accepted the necessity of reducing, if not of reforming, taxation, and the President showed signs of yielding to both demands. Their acceptance of the principle of reform, though too late to give aid to reformers, might perhaps have served to save a few Republican Congressmen from defeat in the autumn elections; but it was a sign of weakness rather than of strength, and indicated a want of stability which had scarcely been expected. As for Secretary Boutwell's persistent efforts to obtain authority to fund a portion of the debt, the subject is somewhat too technical for ordinary readers, and is fortunately subordinate in importance. Whatever respect Boutwell's policy deserved, it received extremely little, and may be dismissed without further comment. In regard to the currency, where reform ought properly to have begun, no approach to agreement could be made. The subject was amply discussed, both formally and informally. Every method of contraction, both direct and indirect ; every process of acting on the national greenback circulation through the national banking currency, or on the banking currency through the greenback circulation, on either separately or on both at once ; every theory, no matter how new or how old ; every objection, no matter how frivolous, — all in turn were argued and laid aside, because public opinion was not yet ripe for action. As usual, nothing could be done by the government, which invariably failed to govern.

In the midst of this universal dead-lock on every issue except reconstruction, the Supreme Court on the 7th of February pronounced its decision that the Legal-Tender Act, so far as it applied to debts contracted before its passage, exceeded the authority of Congress, and assumed powers forbidden by the Constitution.

To any one on the stand-point assumed at the outset of these remarks, the decision of the Supreme Court must obviously have appeared not only sound in itself, but the single step which had been taken by any department of the government since the close of the war toward the restoration either of a solid basis to the currency or of a solid foundation to the republic. It was a moderate and cautious reassertion of the fundamental principle on which the private liberties of the American citizen had been originally based. It was the only indication yet seen that Hamilton and Madison might have been right in hoping that their system of checks and balances would operate to restore an equilibrium once disturbed by the exigencies of a troubled time. As such it received popular acquiescence. Hardly a murmur was raised against it by the press. Only in Congress, where opposition might naturally have been expected, was hostility shown to a movement threatening the usurped power of Congress alone; and only in the Senate, which has always been, as it always must be, the furnace of intrigue and aggression, was actual attack upon the Court expected.

The public naturally assumed that the Administration would be glad to accept and support this decision, not only because the interests of the Executive and the Supreme Court are identical, or because this special decision tended to check the arrogant and domineering Congressional power, which had been felt in a manner humiliating to the Cabinet, but because the decision strengthened the declared policy of the President in regard to the currency, and partially withdrew the government from the false position into which it had confessedly been forced by the exigencies of war. Hence, although senators instantly declared that the decision should be reversed, and that no candidate favorable to the decision should be confirmed to either of the seats on the Supreme bench then vacated by the deaths of Justices Grier

and Stanton, a strong feeling of surprise and astonishment was perceptible when gentlemen supposed to be thoroughly well informed asserted that
the President, the Secretary of the Treasury, and
Attorney-General E. R. Hoar were agreed in considering the decision as an attack upon the policy
of the war, a denial of necessary powers to Congress,
and a Democratic electioneering trick. The incre-
dulity was great when authority above ordinary doubt
further asserted, on direct information from the
White House, that neither Judge Bradley nor Judge
Strong would have been nominated to the bench,
had it been supposed that either of them favored the
legal-tender decision. These nominations, whether
influenced by such a consideration or not, removed
all doubt from senators' minds in regard to this particular difficulty; while at the same time little doubt
could remain in the public mind that a reversal obtained by introducing on the bench two gentlemen
occupying the position of Messrs. Strong and Bradley
would establish beyond dispute a precedent for pack-
ing the Court whenever it suited Congress to do so,
and destroying the independence of the Judiciary as
a co-ordinate branch of the American government.

Judge Strong took his seat on the 14th of March.
Judge Bradley was confirmed by the Senate a week
later, and summoned by telegraph to Washington.
He took his seat on the 23d of March. Two days
later, at the earliest possible moment, the attorney-
general surprised the Court by moving to take up

and argue two cases formerly passed over, which involved the principle of the legal-tender decision.

In the course of the attorney-general's remarks he said : —

" This Court, at a time when by law it consisted of nine judges, did by a majority of four to three enter its judgment, with two vacancies upon the bench ; and it stands therefore, reducing it to its essence, that upon the judicial opinion of a single man, whose voice turned the majority, that great question is adjudicated. And if (which is a supposable case) it turned out that it was an opinion about which even the deciding judge of the Court had entertained a different opinion at some other time, it would come down to the point that on the differing opinions at different times of his life of a single man, the whole Constitutional power of Congress . . . was to be subverted."

What answer this personal attack on the chief-justice would have received had it been made by an attorney-general of Massachusetts before the Supreme Bench of that State, with Hoar, C. J., presiding, must be matter of opinion, only to be decided by an appeal to that tribunal under these conditions. He would have been a rash attorney-general who attempted to browbeat a court so constituted. Whether the opinions of the Secretary of the Treasury in 1861 were the same as those of the chief-justice in 1870, was a question not worth discussing unless the attorney-general meant to impute dishonest and culpable motives as the cause of change ; and if this was in fact the intention, the chief-justice might probably have been satisfied with pointing out, not to the attorney-general but to the Court, the passage in the secretary's official Report of 1862, the next expression of opinion made by him to Congress after the adoption of legal tender, where he took occasion to avow his opinion that " gold and silver are the only permanent basis, standard, and measure of values recognized by the Constitution."

These points were rather matters of taste than of reasoning; but in some other respects the assertions of Mr. Hoar went to the verge of fair dealing, especially from an attorney-general appealing to two new judges selected by himself, and asking them to overthrow existing law. Strictly speaking, he was correct in saying that judgment was " entered " while there were two vacancies on the bench, and by a majority of four to three. Judgment was entered on the 7th of February. Yet the attorney-general must have been aware that the decision in the case of Hepburn *vs.* Griswold was settled as long before as November 27, 1869, and that the decision itself was read and adopted by the Court on the 29th of January, by a majority of five to three, at a time when the Court by law consisted of eight judges, and no vacancy existed on the bench. If the actual entry was postponed another week, it was probably only because the minority opinion of Justice Miller was not yet fully prepared; so that the attorney-general, by using this argument, incurred danger on the one hand of subjecting Justice Miller to the suspicion of having purposely delayed the entry in order to lay the Court open to this attack, and on the other hand of subjecting himself to the charge of acting in collusion with Justice Miller.

What occurred when the Court retired for consultation might be guessed from the subsequent scene in open Court April 11 with clearness enough to leave little doubt as to the suspicions the public, with or without reason, would certainly entertain if the attorney-general carried his purpose. Chief-Justice Chase, and Justices Nelson, Grier, and Field appear to have agreed in the statement that the two cases referred to by the attorney-general had been passed over by the Court with the understanding that they should abide the result in the case of Hepburn *vs.* Griswold, and that counsel had been so ordered. No reasonable doubt of the fact existed; and both Mr. Carlisle, counsel for the appellants in these cases, and Mr. Norton, the solicitor for the Court of Claims from which the appeal had been taken, subsequently informed the Court that they had so understood, and had received the order as stated. The ground taken by Justices Miller, Swayne, and Davis is not clearly explained; but these judges must have either rested on the fact that the order was not recorded, or they must have pleaded want of memory. The new judges held power to decide the dispute, and they did accordingly decide that the order had not been given. As the public might probably put the issue, the two new judges decided that the understanding of the Court, made long before they came upon the bench, was the reverse of what it had undoubtedly been.

The Court therefore determined, by a majority of five to four, that the cases should be argued; and already, on the motion for further delay, a scene was presented to the public such as had rarely if ever before been offered by this dignified tribunal. The four dissenting judges, the late majority, felt that they were to be tried by their own colleagues at the order of the Executive and the Senate, and they made up their minds to resist the attack with all their energy. The most memorable example in American history of partisan attack on the Judiciary was the impeachment of a judge whose name and family suggested an ominous precedent for a similar proceeding at the present day.

Whether the Administration as a whole would have allowed itself to be drawn into such a struggle may be doubted; but the determined character of the attorney-general leaves no doubt that he would have begun nothing which he did not feel it his duty to press to the extremest logical conclusions, and he had for the moment the Senate behind him. The Administration might have broken to pieces, but could not have stopped a struggle once begun. Hence many persons began to watch the course of events with uneasiness; and although little was known of the personal feelings of the contending parties, yet it was obvious that the Executive was pressing with extreme severity on the Court, and the Court was already split into two hostile parties. Even among the people the struggle had begun to rouse deep interest. Perhaps the only point on which all men and all parties agreed was that the independence of the Judiciary ought to be preserved, and the dominant political party was on the point of giving this cry to its antagonist.

Fortunately for the Court, for the Administration, and for the country, the danger, which for a moment seemed inevitable, was evaded. On the morning of April 20, the day fixed for the hearing, the judges and the counsel went to the Capitol ready to face the issue. It was an occasion of extraordinary interest, a struggle between the dignity of the Court and the power of Congress, — an unequal match, in which public sympathy could not but cluster about the four arraigned judges. Ordinary observers could think only with terror of the irreparable harm that would result if these four judges, dragged into a political contest, should be held up by popular enthusiasm as the noble objects of a miserable persecution, while the two new justices became the mark of popular hatred, and the Court itself, torn by party passions, became the centre of political strife. At that moment such a result was almost reached. There seemed to be no hesitation on any side, either among the three dissenting judges, or the two new judges, or the four judges of the old ma-

jority, and least of all in the attorney-general, whose
mind appeared to be bent with the peculiar intensity
which is the historical or traditional ideal of New
England character, on converting, as he would say —
or as others might think, on crushing — the obnoxious
Court.

All these separate actors, their internal anxieties
or passions concealed as well as might be under the
calm exterior belonging to the presence of justice,
arrived at the Capitol only to be confronted by what
had the appearance of a practical joke.   The appellants had that morning withdrawn their appeal,
and the cases were no longer before the Court.
Probably every man of the party breathed freer after
his first moment of surprise, yet the effect of the
sudden change was to cover the proceeding with
ridicule.   The attorney-general struggled against defeat, and pressed another motion to reopen the case
of Hepburn *vs.* Griswold ; but the point seemed to
have been reached beyond which none of the judges
were willing to go in straining the rules of the Court,
and as neither of the four who made the decision
desired it to be reopened, the attorney-general's
motion was without dissent refused.

Thus this peril was by a mere trick happily es-
caped, and the Court was saved ; but its rescue was
due to no strength of its own, to no aid from the
Executive, to no mercy from either branch of Congress.   It was a momentary relief from a pressing
danger ; but nothing indicated that the danger had

passed away, and whenever the Court should be again placed under the necessity of asserting the law as declared in the Constitution, it was little likely to be again preserved by such means.

If from the confused arena of internal politics the reader turns to the region of Foreign Affairs, he can find only a repetition of the same class of phenomena, offering little evidence of political progress, but pointing to some political change in a not distant future.

Foreign affairs, so far as they have had immediate importance during the last year, may be divided under two heads. In regard to each of these divisions the single controlling interest has been found in the extension of the national territory. No other real point was at issue in the foreign relations of the United States, and the two heads into which the general subject of territorial enlargement divides itself are distinct only so far as one embraces extension to the north ; the other, movement toward the tropics.

Of the departments of the government, that of foreign affairs has been, on the whole, most steady since the earliest days of the republic. It has acted upon a single general principle, which has slowly developed with the national progress until now it approaches its possible limits, — the absorption of neighboring territory. The policy of Secretary Seward was based upon this idea, which, under his direction, assumed a development somewhat too rapid for the

26

public ; and in consequence, although President Grant was in general sympathy with Seward, yet the new Administration came into power under influences that amounted to a reaction.

Little need be said of the questions in dispute with England, except that the only essential obstacle to a settlement is the English occupation of Canada. The effort of Seward to settle the Alabama claims by arbitration, and to leave the Canadian question to seek a settlement in the natural course of events, was rejected by the Senate mainly because the Senate meant that the first issue should be retained as an instrument to force the solution of the last. Without commenting upon the dignity or elevation of this policy, or upon the manner and spirit in which it has been carried into practice, it is enough to say that the new Administration on assuming office found the policy already determined by the Senate, and accepted it as a matter in regard to which the Executive was not consulted and had no voice. The subject may be here dismissed with the general remark, which time may be trusted to verify, that every separate item of American relations with England or her colonies, large or small, — whether it was a question of treaties, of claims, of boundaries, of neutrality, of Fenians, or of coal and lumber ; whether treated by the Executive, by the Senate, by the House, or by individual members of the government, — under every form and and every disguise, has been primarily and principally considered, subject to the rules of international custom, in its separate bearing on the subject of annexation.[1]

The Northern policy was therefore simple enough, and Secretary Fish, not responsible for its creation, carried out his share of it with a tact and good temper which gained for him and for the Administration general credit. But the issues involved on the side of the tropics were more difficult, and the variance of opinion was more strongly marked. From the outset of the new Administration the policy of interference in the Antilles was forced upon its attention in a manner leaving no chance of escape. The St. Thomas treaty, under which a popular vote had already been taken and the island formally transferred to an authorized agent of the United States government, had for some six months reposed on the table of the Senate Committee of Foreign Relations. If the government meant to pursue a policy of annexation in the Antilles, it was peculiarly bound, by every obligation of international decency and of common self-respect, to begin with the ratification of this treaty. Indeed, one may doubt whether the obligation to ratify was not absolute and irrespective of conditions; but in any case the refusal to ratify this treaty was only to be excused on the understanding that it implied a reversal of the policy of annexation. Whether this excuse was ever actually offered to the Danish government as a bar to its

[1] See Bancroft Davis's Letter to the N. Y. Herald of Jan. 4, 1878. Sumner's Memorandum of Jan. 17, 1871.

remonstrances could be ascertained only by reference
to the Danish government, nor is it a question of real
importance. The essential point was that government should act with self-respect and honest intentions. The refusal to ratify the St. Thomas treaty
was a strong measure which gravely compromised
the dignity of the government, and found its only
excuse in the conviction that annexation to the
southward of the continent was a danger and a
mistake. That on such a subject the Senate could
have one policy and the Executive another was equivalent to rendering the government ridiculous. For
the policy that prevails the whole government must
be held responsible.

If a new tendency to check the national extension was brought to light by this treatment of the St.
Thomas treaty, it was made more conspicuous by the
voluntary action of the Executive in regard to Cuba.
The President personally leaned toward interference
in Cuban affairs, and his Secretary of War, General
Rawlins, was earnest in support of the Cuban insurgents. The influence of Secretary Fish succeeded in
checking this bent of the Executive. Further, it was
understood that in order to obviate the want of a
harbor in the West Indies, the St. Thomas treaty being practically rejected, the Bay of Samana would be
permanently leased and occupied as a naval station.
These movements indicated that a new policy had
been adopted by the government, and that after mature deliberation the present Administration would

assume as its rule of action in the Antilles the principle which was soon to find utterance in the concise formula : " No annexation within the tropics."

Suddenly the San Domingo treaty made its appearance. Whence it came, why it was made, what influences supported it, were not explained. One point alone was clear, — that the San Domingo treaty stood in flat opposition to the entire policy pursued till then by the Administration toward the West Indies, and that neither Fish nor his colleagues as a body could have sympathized in the proposed annexation, which was contrary to their modes of thought and to their political education. No one would have believed them had they asserted their approval. No one did believe in Fish's earnestness, though he loyally and energetically supported the treaty. The obvious inference was one which the public had a right to draw, — that as heretofore Fish and his colleagues had succeeded in bringing the President to their point of view in regard to Cuba and St. Thomas, so the President had broken through the restraint and overruled Fish in regard to San Domingo.

A foreign policy so unsteady could scarcely command respect, although respect was what the Cabinet most needed to command. Whatever the Administration might choose to do, the Senate was unlikely to follow its changes of opinion, and for once the Senate had the strength of argument as well as of power on its side, while the Administration put itself in a position where success or failure was almost equally disastrous. Senator Sumner again stood forward to assume the control and direction of foreign affairs. He again wielded the power of the Senate and declared the policy of the government. The President and the Secretary of State struggled in vain against this omnipotent senatorial authority, although the President made the issue personal, and condescended to do the work of a lobbyist almost on the floor of the Senate chamber, using his personal influence to an extent scarcely known in American experience, and offering a curious commentary on his own theory of Executive duties. Senator Sumner flung them both aside, and issued his orders with almost the authority of a Roman triumvir.

The ultimate result of this contest, so far as regards foreign policy, is a subject which may be left for future annual Reviews to discuss, as the situation of affairs becomes more clearly determined. There is room for more than a doubt whether the growth of the country can be stopped by the adoption of any arbitrary law for the tropics; and the resistance now made to annexation of countries little fitted to enter into the duties of American States may ultimately yield to the growing public indifference to the States themselves. From another point of view the affair has still deeper significance, as showing an unsteadiness and a spasmodic irregularity of action in the Executive, which, contrasted with the opposite qualities displayed by the Senate, indicates that the regular diminution of Executive authority first clearly marked under Andrew Johnson has not been checked, but on the contrary has been aggravated by the appearance of some internal weakness never before known in the history of American administrations. The success of any Executive measure must now be bought by the use of public patronage in influencing the action of legislators. The Executive has yielded without a protest to this necessity, which it has helped to establish. Senators already claim special Executive offices as their private property, and their claim is conceded. A senator from Michigan claims a consulate in India; a senator from Maine claims a consulate in England ; a senator from Kansas claims the mission to the Hague, and as proof of his right of property nominates the clerk of his committee to the post. A senator who desires the removal of an excellent officer does not scruple to accuse a member of the Cabinet of interference with his patronage if his request is denied. Senators do not hesitate to insult the President by rejecting one nomination to the Supreme Court because the candidate as member of the Cabinet has failed to reach their own standard of polished manners, nor to intimate their intention of rejecting any required number of others unless the candidates are prepared to reverse, as judges of the Supreme Court, the established Constitutional law which limits the powers of Congress. Notwithstanding the exceptional case of San Domingo, the Executive has practically abandoned to the Senate the treaty-making power. The

Executive has joined with Congress in assuming the powers reserved to the States, and in attacking the authority of the Supreme Court, while the precedent of the legal-tender action appears to warrant the belief that Congress and the Executive have also established the principle that they hold between them the power to suspend private rights, not merely during war, but during will.

Not only has the internal fabric of the government been wrenched from its original balance until Congress has assumed authority which it was never intended to hold, but as the country grows and the pressure of business increases, the efficiency of the machine grows steadily less. New powers, new duties, new responsibilities, new burdens of every sort are incessantly crowding upon the government at the moment when it has become unequal to managing the limited powers it is accustomed to wield. Responsibility no longer exists at Washington. Every department of the Executive says with truth that it cannot deal with the questions before it because Congress neglects legislation. If members of Congress are charged with responsibility for the neglect, they reply that the fault is not theirs ; that the action of Congress is wholly in the hands of committees which constitute small, independent, executive councils ; that some of these committees are arbitrary, some timid ; some overpoweringly strong, some ridiculously weak ; some factious, some corrupt. The House has little or no control over the course of business. The rules have become so complicated as to throw independent members entirely into the background. The amount of business has become so enormous as to choke the channels provided for it. In the Senate greater power, less confusion, and more efficiency exist, but on the other hand more personal jealousy and factiousness. In both Houses all trace of responsibility is lost; and while the Executive fumes with impatience or resigns itself with the significant consolation that it is not to blame, that this is the people's government and the people may accept the responsibility, the members of the lower House are equally ready with the excuse that they are not responsible for the action of senators ; and senators, being responsible to no power under heaven except their party organizations, which they control, are able to obtain what legislation answers their personal objects or their individual conceptions of the public good.

Under the conditions of fifty years ago, when the United States was a child among nations, and before railways and telegraphs had concentrated the social and economical forces of the country into a power never imagined by past generations, a loose and separately responsible division of government suited the stage of national growth, and was sufficiently strong to answer the requirements of the public. All indications point to the conclusion that this system is outgrown. The government does not govern. Congress is inefficient, and becomes every year more and more incompetent, as at present constituted, to wield the enormous powers forced upon it ; while the Executive, in enjoyment of theoretical independence, is practically deprived of its necessary strength by the jealousy of the Legislature. Without responsibility, direct, incessant, and continuous, no government is practicable over forty millions of people and an entire continent ; but no responsibility exists at Washington. Every one in the least acquainted with the process of American government knows that the public business is not performed.

Meanwhile reformers are straining every nerve to carry such a reform in the tariff as may make the system, not indeed good, — they cannot even hope this, — but a shade less absurd, less mediæval, less dishonest than it now is. Perhaps, as the result of unremitted labor extended over a period of years, they may ultimately succeed in carrying their point. The national government may at last be obliged to drop the unhealthy children whose precocious birth and growth it has stimulated by drugs and drams, and their political influence may vanish from the Capitol. Yet while the whole reforming strength is laboriously concentrated on the people, with no further object than to obtain force to contest the possession of the national government with a single creature of the government's own creation, the government all the while continues to call into being other creatures more fatal to its integrity than those that already control it. While the reformers in

Congress rejoice at carrying a small reduction on pig-iron, or regret the omnipotence of the steel lobbyists, they turn about in their seats and create by a single stroke of special legislation a new Pacific railway, — an imperishable corporation with its own territory, an empire within a republic, more powerful than a sovereign State, and inconsistent with the purity of Republican institutions or with the safety of any government, whether democratic or autocratic. While one monopoly is attacked, two are created; while old and true believers in republican purity and simplicity are engaged in resisting a single corruption, they are with their own hands stimulating the growth of many more. The people require it, and even if the people were opposed, yet with the prodigious development of corporate and private wealth resistance must be vain.

Two points, distinct to outward appearance, but closely connected in reality, have received the whole attention of this Review. The first has consisted in general evidence that the original basis of reserved powers on which the Constitution was framed has yielded and is yielding to natural pressure, and the gradual concession of power to the central government has already gone so far as to leave little doubt that the great political problem of all ages cannot, at least in a community like that of the future America, be solved by the theory of the American Constitution. The second has depended on correlative evidence that the system of separate responsibility realized in the mechanism of the American government as a consequence of its jealous restriction of substantial powers will inevitably yield, as its foundation has yielded, to the pressure of necessity. The result is not pleasant to contemplate. It is not one which the country is prepared to accept or will be soon in a temper to discuss. It will not be announced by professional politicians, who are not fond of telling unpleasant truths. Nor is it here intended to suggest principles of reform. The discussion of so large a subject is matter for a lifetime, and will occupy generations. The American statesman or philosopher who enters upon this debate must make his appeal, not to the public opinion of a day or of a nation, however large or intelligent, but to the minds of those persons who in every age and in all countries attach their chief interest to working out the problems of human society.

INDEX.